IDLE HANDS
AND
EMPTY HEARTS

IDLE HANDS AND EMPTY HEARTS

Work and Freedom in the United States

NEALA SCHLEUNING

Bergin and Garvey
New York • Westport, Connecticut • London

Library of Congress Cataloging-in-Publication Data

Schleuning, Neala.
    Idle hands and empty hearts : work and freedom in the United
States / Neala Schleuning.
      p. cm.
    Includes bibliographical references.
    ISBN 0–89789–215–1 (lib. bdg. : alk. paper).—ISBN 0–89789–221–6
(pbk. : alk. paper)
      1. Work ethic. 2. Work ethic—United States. 3. Work.
I. Title.
HD4905.S29   1990
306.3′613′0973—dc20   90–429

British Library Cataloguing in Publication Data is available.

Library of Congress Catalog Card Number: 90–429
ISBN: 0–89789–215–1
      0–89789–221–6 (pbk.)

First published in 1990

Bergin & Garvey, One Madison Avenue, New York, NY 10010
An imprint of Greenwood Publishing Group, Inc.

Printed in the United States of America

∞™

The paper used in this book complies with the
Permanent Paper Standard issued by the National
Information Standards Organization (Z39.48–1984).

10 9 8 7 6 5 4 3 2 1

Copyright Acknowledgments

The author and publisher gratefully acknowledge permission to reprint material from the
following copyrighted sources.

Arnold Gehlen. *Man in the Age of Technology*. New York: Columbia University Press, 1980.

From ONE DIMENSIONAL MAN by Herbert Marcuse. Copyright © 1964 by Herbert Marcuse.
Reprinted by permission of Beacon Press.

Aaron Kramer, trans. *The Teardrop Millionaire and other poems* by Morris Rosenfeld. New
York, 1955. Reprinted by permission of Aaron Kramer.

"To Be of Use." Copyright © 1973 by Marge Piercy. Reprinted from CIRCLES ON THE
WATER, by Marge Piercy, by permission of Alfred A. Knopf, Inc. Reprinted by permission of
Wallace Literary Agency, Inc. Copyright © 1973, 1982 by Middlemarsh, Inc.

This book is dedicated to my husband, Michael Bonner, for his care and support throughout this project.

Contents

Preface

For the reader, the preface is a beginning—for the writer it is a time for reflection at the end of a long project. Looking over the book that follows, I discovered there were a few insights I wanted to share before you begin.

On reflection, I was struck by the presence of religious thinkers running like a strong warp throughout the whole tradition of political economy. Looking back over the past two hundred years of history, it would almost seem that at the point of the emergence of the industrial revolution the capitalists, the liberals (including the libertarians), and the utilitarians went one way, and a ragtag collection of religious thinkers, socialists, communists, artists, and anarchists went the other. Politics—at least political economy, it would seem—does indeed result in strange bedpartners.

Again, however, perhaps this alliance is not so strange. Both religion and politics deal with ethical questions; both are deeply involved in the day-to-day struggles for human survival; both create and perpetuate community. Work, of course, is interwoven with the same issues: ethics, survival, community. For both the skeptical radical and the religious idealist, I urge you to read on, because you have much to teach each other about good work, good economics, and good community.

A few comments on the mechanics of this manuscript: I have tried, wherever possible, to use inclusive language. Research in this area, particularly the historical material, is dominated by non-inclusive terminology. For some words, and in some particularly awkward phrases, I could not find inclusive terminology. I apologize for succumbing to the "cake of custom."

Acknowledgments

Thanks to Gene Zins, Don Olson, and Fred Whitehead, whose careful editing kept me from the most terrible blunders; Lyn Yount for her careful research assistance; Michelle Veland for her patient indexing; everyone who works with me at the Women's Center; Larry Anderson, Steve Hickerson, Bob Simonson, Jason Kessler, Mac Mackenzie, Fr. Joe Fogel, Fr. Ted Hottinger, Mary Dowd, Phyllis Wisen, Sharon Addams, and especially the interdisciplinary lunch gang—Phil Kendall, Harry Coonce, Richard Strachan, Bill Rucker (now deceased), and all the others who've joined us over the years—for their untiring enthusiasm and support for the life of the mind. Special thanks to Richard for dragging this Luddite into the computer age, and who always found my files whenever I erased them accidentally.

Chapter 1

Introduction

> The modern age can be understood as that of an unrelenting 500-year war waged to destroy the environmental conditions for subsistence and to replace them by commodities produced within the frame of the new nation state. ... Modern history, from the point of view of the losers in this war, still remains to be written.
>
> —Ivan Illich[1]

Work is energy. Work is force and power. The burning of calories, BTUs, ergs, muscle power. Energy expended, energy spent, energy exhausted. Manhours, manpower. The effort needed to get a job done.

Work is history. Work is art. Work is the slave moving stone to build the great pyramids. Work is Michelangelo freeing David from the stone. Work is my father keeping pace with the assembly line. Work is the labor of giving birth.

"I hate to work!" Work is slavery. "A woman's work is never done." Labor Day. The working class. "Get your work done before you go out to play!" A workout. Let's work it out.

To work is to be degraded, to be ground down, worn smooth as the stone step on an old building. The back bent and sore. Stoop labor. Human skill parodied by machines, the heart of human work stolen from the craftsman, the soul of work locked into the microcircuits of a computer. Work exploited, work denied. Work reduced to time and motion studies, and the worker reduced to mindless tasks.

Work is the dream of leisure, of rest, of someone or something else to do the work—a slave, one of the gods, a machine, a woman. Fiddler's Green. The Big Rock Candy Mountain. The garden of Eden. Nirvana.

TOWARD A NEW VISION OF WORK

Ever since our ancestors first discovered that one of the drawbacks of fire was that it demanded a constant supply of dry wood, people have entertained dreams of getting work done without effort. They dreamed, and planned, and then created tools to make our work less burdensome. When there was no tool, they forced others to slave for them. Work and exploitation have always gone hand in hand. Throughout history armies have been mobilized to enslave people to hard labor. The graceful towns of ancient Greece were built by slave labor as Plato and his followers created elegant intellectual arguments and ideal democratic societies. Rome, too, built its massive empire on the backs of slaves. Even the close of the twentieth century witnesses worldwide forced labor and the perpetuation of slavery in the market in women's bodies and Third World workers. Leisure on the part of one group has often been secured at the expense of another.

With the emergence of the modern technological era, the trafficking in human bodies declined as cultures adopted machines to accomplish the work of formerly exploited peoples. The machines promised a quicker, more predictable means of easing the burden of human labor. For the first time in human history, slavery declined as the number of "labor-saving" devices increased. As the presence and power of the machine grew in importance, human "work" and labor were further degraded.

Our euphoria over the machines was short-lived. Technology created as many problems as it solved. Slavery to the machines replaced personal slavery, and work itself became disassembled and fragmented. The revolution of the machines joined forces with capitalist economics to solidify the total exploitation of workers and destroy all vestiges of creativity and pleasure in work. Something went tragically wrong. Work was different now—less onerous, but empty and unfulfilling. At least slaves knew their oppressor. Under technological/industrial capitalism, the means of oppression were more subtle and impersonal, more permanent and devastating.

The economic transition to industrial capitalism was accomplished in a relatively short period of time. Cultural changes were slower, but no less relentless. Several major cultural events coincided, throwing all of Western civilization into a period of instability and change. At the beginning of the nineteenth century, Europe was swept with waves of peasant and worker rebellions. Spurred on by the new democratic thought, the enclosure of the commons, and the loss of jobs to machines, dissatisfied workers moved to action. Factory workers, quickly realizing their disestablishment, organized to salvage some control over work and the new modes of production. Joining together in labor unions and workers associations, they demanded a long list of improvements in the work world— they fought for an eight-hour day, control of the pace of work, improvement in the conditions of work—developing a new work ethic as they went. The political strategy of collective effort seemed, for a while anyway, to hold the worst abuses to a minimum, and in some cases, to make modest improvements in the lives of the workers.

One of the most important spokespersons for the worker in the nineteenth century was, of course, Karl Marx. Along with Frederick Engels, Marx documented the cultural upheaval swirling around him, and on behalf of workers everywhere, outlined a political and economic agenda that is still being carried out today. His brilliant analysis of capitalism, the alienation of labor, and the concept of class consciousness still provide one of the most complete conceptualizations of the role of work in modern culture.

Marx based his study on the true nature of human work: Work is all, work is everything, work is reality. All value resides in human labor—not in the machines, not in capital, not in things. It is easy for us today to overlook this insight—an understanding of work that preceded Marxism. Work is all, and what exists around us—things, buildings, highways or fine works of art—are the embodiments of past generations of work. Everything can be understood as work:

Along with the useful qualities of the products themselves, we put out of sight both the useful character of the various kinds of labour embodied in them, and the concrete forms of that labour; there is nothing left but what is common to them all; all are reduced to one and the same sort of labour, human labour in the abstract.[2]

At the same time as Marxism spread its revolutionary ideas throughout Europe and Michael Bakunin was deeply influencing collective development in Switzerland and the Iberian Peninsula, industrial capitalism was transforming the culture of work in the United States. Tying its fortunes to the tail of "rugged individualism"—the political/economic philosophy of industrial capitalism transformed economic life in the United States. The absence of tradition and community in the new land paved the way for the uncontrolled expansion of monopoly capitalism. Encouraged by a national policy of growth and progress, corporate abuses went unregulated as the nation spread westward.

Imagine the United States in 1788: free land for those willing to work for it, and jobs in the small towns on the frontier for any willing hand. Hard work and ingenuity guaranteed nearly instant success. Prior to industrialization, work was a cooperative effort, a way of life that assumed community and sharing. Building houses and barns, getting in the crops, hiring a small lad to work the bellows at the blacksmith shop required collaborative efforts. You couldn't afford to disagree too heartily with your neighbors—you needed them, and they needed you. You had to work at building alliances, at delicately negotiating whose hay field got cut first. You worked to the rhythms of the seasons, of the crops, and most of all, of your neighbors.

Early observers of the "American way" could not help but comment on the industriousness of the new nation. In one of the first critiques of American culture, Alexis de Tocqueville wrote in *Democracy in America* that work was "good" for a people. His brief but insightful visit to America in 1831 came at a time when Americans were truly a working people—farmers, craftspeople, seamstresses—all bespoke a culture of highly productive and creative people. People were busy—busy "making" wood (still a colloquial expression), "making hay while the sun shines," making a new nation. Work was still seen as creative, artistic—in the highly respected tradition of craftsmanship.

Americans were different, de Tocqueville believed, because we lived in a democracy. Our economic life was, of course, affected by our political organization. We were characterized, as de Tocqueville and others noted, by our national restlessness, by our passion for the pursuit of "riches," by our practical bent, and most of all by the lack of restraint in our national economic philosophy.

The greater part of the men who constitute these nations [democracies] are extremely eager in the pursuit of actual and physical gratification. As they are always dissatisfied with the position they occupy, and are always free to leave it, they think of nothing but the means of changing their fortune, or increasing it. To minds thus predisposed, every new method which leads by a shorter road to wealth, every machine which spares labor, every instrument which diminishes the cost of production, every discovery which facilitates pleasures or augments them, seems to be the grandest effort of the human intellect. It is chiefly from these motives that a democratic people addicts itself to scientific pursuits.[3]

As de Tocqueville predicted, success followed upon success as waves of immigrants worked their way westward across the continent. "Go west, young man" (and enterprising women who took up the challenge) was the watchword of a whole generation of Americans seeking the proverbial pot of gold at the end of the rainbow. With a lot of hard work and a little bit of luck, the script went, success and wealth could be found just over the horizon.

The new nation uncritically embraced the new economy of industrial capitalism, and the nature of work in the United States changed dramatically. With astonishing speed we moved from a primarily agricultural society, to a highly industrialized, urban society, and then to what Daniel Bell calls the postindustrial society—all in the past 150 years.

Today we don't ask each other what we are making, we ask each other what we "do." For many people, even the choice of doing has been taken away. Americans don't work much anymore, we don't produce much anymore, and we leave the creativity to our artists. Boarded-up buildings and unemployed workers stand idle: mute testimony to profit and progress at the expense of good work and human lives. We talk about "making it," but we don't mean creatively; rather, we mean we are surviving, staying alive. We dream empty dreams about the day when we will make it big. We have substituted lottery tickets and leveraged buyouts for faith in ourselves, for real work. As we stand on the edge of the future, our dreams fade and the frustrations with work mount. What will be the shape of work in the twenty-first century, we ask?

With the dehumanization of work, the dominant ethos that has emerged from the industrial era is a distinctly modern contempt and avoidance of work. We no longer believe that the machine will liberate us from work, and we resent subconsciously the theft of our ability to create and our growing enslavement to the machines of the technological age. In short, our work no longer has a sense of meaning, of purpose.

As our alienation from work spreads through all levels of the work world and our hostility toward the machines grows, we search for explanations for our plight. Wendell Berry suggests we begin by examining our attitudes toward work:

The growth of the exploiters' revolution on this continent has been accompanied by the growth of the idea that work is beneath human dignity, particularly any form of hand work. We have made it our overriding ambition to escape work and as a consequence have debased the products of work and have been, in turn, debased by them.[4]

Berry calls for a major revision in the ethic of work, and the reaffirmation of the centrality of work to the human experience:

But is work something that we have a right to escape? And can we escape it with impunity? We are probably the first entire people ever to think so. All the ancient wisdom that has come down to us counsels otherwise. It tells us that work is necessary to us, as much a part of our condition as mortality; that good work is our salvation and our joy; that shoddy or dishonest or self-serving work is our curse and our doom. We have tried to escape the sweat and sorrow promised in Genesis—only to find that in order to do so we must forswear love and excellence, health and joy.[5]

Despite Berry's eloquent words, we need not return to an ethic of sweat and sorrow and its attendant suffering. A two-thousand-year-old work ethic that calls for a return to hard physical labor will attract few devotees. Clearly, however, something must be done. Even though we have developed creative tools and a complex technological infrastructure to make our work easier, we find ourselves alienated from both the means and the ends of our work. The time has come for our culture to rethink the whole meaning of work: to ourselves, to one another, and to the planet we live on.

WHY I WROTE THIS BOOK

I used to be a secretary, but twenty years ago I became bored with my job and the low pay, and returned to college. Three degrees and ten years later, I found myself working as a university administrator for about the same rate of pay I had earned as a skilled secretary (adjusting for inflation during the 1970s). Today, I am again bored with my job, only now I am also underutilized. I thought that getting an education would allow me to work in more "creative" jobs. Instead, my work consists primarily of translating the "system"—the bureaucracy of the university—to others. When I'm not explaining the system, much of what I do is simply to perpetuate it—filling out and forwarding the relevant paperwork. Many of my friends and colleagues feel the same way. Whether they work behind desks in bureaucracies or on their feet in factories, very few workers feel satisfied with what they do. Generally, what work there is is underpaid and excruciatingly boring.

The end results of my work, the things I consume, are also disappointing. Americans used to be the best-fed people in the world, but my husband Mike and I do our own gardening because the food produced today for market is devoid of nutrition, bland, or inedible (especially the hard tomatoes). Increasingly we are warned that our food is dangerously polluted with pesticides and other chemicals. We avoid fruits and vegetables grown in other countries because in many cases the pesticides and herbicides banned in the United States are still legal and heavily used there. Meat is now routinely fed growth hormones, so we try to eat less meat or meat that is grown by our conscientious neighbor. The joy in the sharing of food is tempered continually by the ever-growing list of the latest foods to cause cancer.

We don't get "our money's worth" in products, either. A car is now a major investment, rivaling a home mortgage, but the product continues to decline in quality. We paid eleven thousand dollars for a Ford pickup that has a plastic grille! It is not only cars—in the short fifteen or twenty years since the early 1970s, the quality of nearly everything has declined. Planned obsolescence has been superseded by throwaway products. You can't fix a plug on a table lamp anymore.

There is no feeling of pride in the goods we produce. The glitter and clutter of our post-industrial era are spread out before us with the command to buy, buy, buy. Ads on television sell us unnecessary "gadgets" that many people, apparently, cannot live without. My favorite one is a machine that removes the little fuzzy balls that gather on synthetic fabrics: a clothes-razor of some sort. For the life of me, I can't imagine (1) why anyone would buy one; (2) how anyone could take pride in making them ("Say, I've got a great job, I make these little razors that will revolutionize your old wardrobe!"); or (3) whether it would really make a difference. Can you imagine your coworker commenting: "Boy, does that blouse look great! I remember when it was covered with all those little fuzzy balls! Whatever did you do to fix it?"

Mostly, however, I am writing this book because I can no longer make the leap of "sanity" that allows many Americans to accept the incongruities of poverty and pollution, the inane overproduction of worthless plastic junk, and the idleness and boredom of modern work.

WHAT THIS BOOK IS ABOUT

I like to work. I like to write, I like to cut wood, and I even like housework. My friends call me a workaholic behind my back. My husband Mike asked me if I could write a book on leisure, and I hesitated only a moment before I responded, "No." I don't know what "leisure" is, but I do know that I couldn't wait to get away from my official "job" to begin on this book. All I did was exchange one form of work for another. Am I masochistic? No, I am probably not. I remember the time I worked in a factory. I remember schmoozing and I remember how we all conspired to slow down the line. I remember how we could speed up the line if we wanted to, and I remember learning how to get paid for doing as little as possible. Was I, or am I lazy? Do other people feel the same way? I remember reading a study that found that workers actually worked only about 50 percent of the time for which they were paid. Is that true? Should we cut the working day to only four hours—at the same rate of pay, of course? If people really don't want to work, is that why they hate people on welfare so much—because the latter have figured out how to survive without having a boring job? Why couldn't we all have the option of being on welfare?

This book is about work—work as it used to be, as it is, and as I think it should be. It is about the philosophy of work, the art of work, the sociology of work. It is about politics and economics. It is about what is wrong with work, and it is about why we work. It is about my search for a new definition of *good work*.

This is not a book about the history of work, although it places ideas about work into their context of history and culture. It is not about management—a topic that is all the rage in the literature read by MBAs. It is not a book about the working class, or labor unions, which is what usually comes to mind when we think about work. The history of the labor union movement in America has been well documented—including the union busting of our current era. This book tries instead to get behind the outward signs of labor, to look at the idea of labor as it is manifest in the individual and in the culture.

This book will try to look at work with new eyes because many old ideas about work are in deep trouble: the idea that machines will improve the quality of life; the idea that the assembly line creates efficiency in work; the idea that unions can substantially change the way work is conducted in a capitalist society. This book will also attempt to ask better, or different, questions about work—to get to the bottom of how we work, why we work, who is working, and what is the context of work.

Work, I discovered, has to do with everything: It concerns what we make, what we do, and how we do it. Work is about energy, machines, and technology. It is also about the misuse of these things. Why do we expend 6,000 BTUs of energy on a mechanized farm to harvest only 2,000 BTUs of food energy? What will we do when we run out of oil? What does it mean that most of the seed companies in the United States are owned by the oil companies? If we are going to run out of oil, why are we increasing the use of plastic (which is made from oil, a nonrenewable resource) in everything? Paper bags can be made from trees— a renewable resource. Why are all the supermarkets switching to plastic bags, which are non-biodegradable? If we really like to make things, why is there so much ugly junk in the world? If we like to cook, why do we buy junk food?

Who makes all these crazy decisions, and why?

What does work have to do with the hole in the ozone layer?

What about work and acid rain?

What about factories and the greenhouse effect?

Why do we produce so much anyway?

This book begins with questions—questions we need to ask ourselves individually and collectively. What follows is the distillation of the central questions having to do with work in our time: Why do human beings work? What can we learn about work from history? What is the impact of technology on work? How does work affect our political lives? Do women have a different perspective on work? and finally, What is good work and how do we create a future in which good work can be realized?

All these issues are interconnected. An exploration of why we work, for example, leads to an examination of how means and ends are connected within our work. If we work for the intrinsic pleasure of making something, we won't be as pleased with a machine-made product. If we want to have greater control over our work, we need to revise the system of manufacture that is characterized by the factory and the assembly line. Everywhere we turn, work seems to lie at the heart of our very being—as individuals, as people working together, and as communities.

Sometimes we don't want to be reminded of those connections. We are happier not knowing, for example, that someone's work created Love Canal. Several years ago, I took a trip to visit an old Minnesota friend who had relocated to the hills of Virginia. One my first night there, he invited the neighbors over to meet me and share a beer or two. The discussion turned to current good news for the community: a hazardous waste dump site had just opened up and someone's brother-in-law had been hired there. "But how can you be happy about having that dump in your county?" I asked. "Well, they told us that there's natural radiation in the soil, so we needn't worry," the neighbor assured me. "But that's not true, you need to worry," I replied, "and besides, your brother-in-law might be endangered," I warned. "Look, lady," the man said quietly but firmly. "This was a chance for my brother-in-law to get a job that will support his wife and kids, and it ain't none of your business."

I knew then that it wasn't going to be easy to sort out the meaning of work as it affected individuals, communities, and the environment. Similarly, it won't be easy for us to figure out what to do about work and its consequences. Nonetheless, it seems to me that one thing is clear: we can't postpone this great debate much longer.

WHERE TO BEGIN

"Dragnet," a popular TV show during the 1950s, starred a stern, thin-lipped police detective by the name of Sergeant Friday. Each week he would grimly stare into the eyes of the general public and ask for "just the facts, Ma'am," and the crime would be solved. Facts are very important to us in today's scientifically driven reality, so if we are to establish any credibility at all, it is with cold and sobering facts that we must begin our search for good work in America.

It is nearly impossible to write a book today without making reference to at least some data. It seems that we have come to expect the need for scientific verification of our ideas, whatever they may be. In deference to individuals who are mathematically inclined, therefore, we will explore a few particularly disturbing facts about work. I think it's only fair to warn you, however, that I'm only presenting those "facts" that support my own argument. They are not objective in any sense of that term. I've chosen them because they are obvious, yet they are facts that no one wants to talk about or do anything about. I've chosen them for their shock value, too: "That *can't* be," you will say; "But it *is*," I will reply. At that point, we will sit down together and probe even more deeply into the facts and data on work and the economy that it creates. When we begin that process, we begin to change the world.

To start with, there has always been the expectation that a job should meet human survival needs. Most theories of labor assume that the worker must reproduce him- or herself at least, and not work to the point of death. Our contemporary society has established a minimum wage, for example, and the "family wage" has been a goal of working people for generations. However, the truth is that most people don't make enough money on their jobs to support their families.

In 1971, some 80 percent of service workers and workers in retail trades did not receive enough pay to support a family of four above the poverty level. The same is true of at least 75 percent of all clerical workers and laborers, both of whom are paid on about the same level, the laborers maybe a little higher than clerical workers. It is also true of close to 70 percent of all operatives and kindred workers. Only craftsworkers earn in their majority enough to lift a family of four out of the officially defined poverty category. . . . A pretty large majority of the jobs in the economy have now been transformed by the workings of the capitalist division of labor into the kinds of work one usually thinks of as second jobs—the mythical pin-money jobs which women and teenagers are supposed to be the only ones to take to supplement the major family income.[6]

Although these are startling facts, our society seems paralyzed and unable or unwilling to change this reality. To what forum do we take our complaint? Who is in charge of setting wages? What keeps us silent? Is it fear of losing jobs to the Third World?

Our work has been stolen from us. Instead of labor-saving devices, the machines have become labor-replacing devices, and we meekly step aside as more and more of us find ourselves outside the economic system—joining what Marx called the Industrial Reserve Army, waiting for the phone to ring with the offer of a job. Many of us are desperate for work, but finding it has become a major challenge. Fred Whitehead calls our curious passivity the "Mystery of Work— how we are so degraded as to actually be grateful for the 'chance' to have a job. There is something pathetic about us that we would be reduced to such a state of helplessness and powerlessness."[7] It's as if we no longer believe that we have the right even to work.

Second, few people are happy with their jobs anymore. The shift in attitudes has been fairly dramatic: Just in the last two decades, there have been major changes in both levels of job satisfaction and worker output:

There is both survey and behavioral evidence that workers are beginning to view their work as mainly instrumental, and no longer as moral, religious, patriotic, nor enriching. . . . The National Opinion Research Center reports that during the past 20 years employee satisfaction in general has been decreasing. In addition, there has been a significant drop in the satisfaction of managers, once the most satisfied of all groups. . . . Finally, there is the growing amount of loafing on the job mentioned previously, which indicates that the work ethic is more often a statement of belief than a code of behavior.[8]

Third, there are many people in our society who don't work.

This notion that "everybody" works is more a myth than a true reflection of labor statistics. Millions of people do not work. The Bureau of Census projections for 1980 broke down a population of 167,659,000 people at 16 years of age and older into 103,761,000 workers and 63,898,000 nonworkers. By these figures only 62 percent of the population was projected to be working in 1980, a rate scarcely different from 1975's count of 61 percent. The work force was expected to remain 60 percent male and 40 percent female.[9]

Some people don't work because they are retired, or too young, or handicapped. We also know that approximately 10 percent of the population is on welfare, a certain number of people are ill at any given point in time, a percentage of the population is retired, there are workers in the armed services and others in school, and about 4 to 7 percent are listed as officially unemployed.

Of course, unemployment figures only reflect those individuals who are currently actively seeking employment. When those who no longer seek work, those who are in feath- erbedding or make-work situations, drop-outs, or those in holding institutions such as reform schools and mental institutions are taken into account, real unemployment may be 20 to 25% of the potential work force.[10]

Most of these nonworking people have a means to an income, however small, and we have come to believe that a basic income is our right, our entitlement. We pay these people an income from a variety of sources: military wages, retirement pensions and social security for the elderly, welfare for young women and children, unemployment insurance, disability pay, and so forth. Aside from military pay, however, most of these "entitlements" are inadequate to meet even the most basic needs of food, fuel, and shelter.

We do pay minimal tribute to the concept of a just wage. The American people have decided that everyone (at least those people working in interstate commerce) is entitled to a minimum wage. It was determined that the minimum wage would be one-half the average wage. That fact no longer holds true. If we were to pay people a true minimum wage today in 1989, it would be $4.65 an hour. Altogether, 6.5 million Americans work for no more than the actual minimum wage of $3.35. A total of 11.5 million workers—10.5 percent of the labor force—earn $3.85 or less an hour. Over 45 percent of minimum wage jobs are held by heads of households and married women.[11]

In addition, since 1973, real wages have declined 14 percent, and while the number of jobs has increased, wages have decreased:

Since the late 1960s, roughly 67 percent of all new jobs in the United States have been in industries that paid average annual wages and salaries of less than $13,600 (in 1980 dollars). In 1969, only 45 percent of all jobs were in that category. By contrast, the industries that paid average annual wages of more than $20,250—nearly all of them in manufacturing—grew the least after 1970.[12]

We are all familiar by now with the phrase "the feminization of poverty." A recent study of incomes in the Minnesota cities of Minneapolis and St. Paul reported that 95 percent of women earned less than twenty thousand dollars a year; 87 percent earned less than fifteen thousand dollars per year, and 50 percent of women earned less than $5 per hour.[13] This is a reality that is also increasingly shared by men.

The American Standard of Living is gradually being eroded as the gap between the wealthy and the poor widens. We see the stark reality of the growing poverty nightly. We call them the homeless, and we sit transfixed over the dinner hour as the media chronicle the ongoing tragedy. There is no outrage, no editorial finger pointing; no one, in fact, seems even to be in charge of the problem. The president is let off the hook, the governor is let off the hook, the city and county, of course, can't be expected to solve the problem. The passivity on the part of Americans is ubiquitous. There is only the grim terror of knowing that we are all only one paycheck away from the streets.

As it becomes harder for households to maintain a middle-class standard of living from the earnings of a single breadwinner, those households that are unable to put together an adequate income out of the wages of several family members are ever more likely to skid into the ranks of the nation's new poor. The structural shifts in the economy fall especially hard on single-adult households, whatever the gender of that adult.[14]

It seems as though what we do (our work), when we can do it, doesn't add up to much in meeting basic human needs. The number of jobs has increased, but the number of hours worked on each job has decreased, so that more people are working part-time. The number of households has increased due to other cultural factors such as divorce, and the income per household has decreased. The middle class is gradually disappearing, as the United States moves toward a two-tier economy consisting of the very rich and the very poor.

These facts are more than dry statistics: They are an economic shorthand to describe the uncertainty and fear that hover over the working lives of most Americans. However, we should not lose sight of yet another fact: all these changes are the result of conscious decision making by someone, and as such they may be amenable to change. Our own current level of participation in decision making about the economy is nonexistent. Most of us feel pretty powerless. Decisions are made by "experts," and "Besides we've got enough to worry about"; a phrase that pretty well sums up the average person's involvement with the political life of the nation. There is a bumper sticker I see fairly often these days: it simply reads "Shit Happens," and speaks volumes about the amount of control the average person feels. One of my primary objectives in this book will be to spend a fair amount of time talking about political power, the relationship between political power and work, and how to enhance our control over our work.

Another major area of concern for the modern worker is the impact of the technological revolution on our work. The introduction of technology has had two major impacts on production: The worker has become alienated because work has become so simplified through the division of labor that it no longer holds any interest or challenge; and, as the technology becomes more automated, the actual number of jobs has decreased and the number of workers who have become "structurally unemployed" has increased. The introduction of what they used to call the machine age was heralded as the solution to human poverty. For the first time in human history, we could work less and have more, they said. We were told that technology would produce more jobs to allay the fear of displacement by machines and to overcome opposition to the mechanization of the workplace. Bitter reality has replaced this optimism: the number of poor people is expanding alarmingly, and daily more workers are threatened with the loss of meaningful work. Technology has also altered the natural world in significant, and often harmful, ways. The impact of technology on the environment will be an important sub-theme of this book.

Finally, I will make some tentative sketches toward a definition of good work; good work and its relationship to the political life of community; the aesthetic component of good work; and the importance of good work to the individual, to community, and to our natural environment. This is not the first time that our society has struggled with the nature of good work. It was important to the founding fathers and mothers who believed the nature of work to lie within a religious framework; it was important to the young men or women who discovered it in laissez faire capitalism and the crude machinations of the American entrepreneurial system. The Transcendentalists and all their ideological children found good work in a return to a simpler technology and to agrarian ideals generally.

The search for good work, history teaches us, is ultimately nurtured in community. Whether the call was "back to the land" or to join utopian alternative communities, Americans have continually struggled to define the meaning of work in the context of their lives with one another. Our task today is to recreate once again this community of good work—a purposeful democratic community where hand and heart are reintegrated in the celebration of quality work and good fellowship.

NOTES

1. Ivan Illich, *Shadow Work* (Boston and London, 1981), 139.

2. Karl Marx, *Capital: A Critical Analysis of Capitalist Production*, Vol. 1, trans. Samuel Moore and Edward Aveling, ed. Frederick Engels (Moscow, 1965), 40.

3. Alexis de Tocqueville, *Democracy in America* (New York, 1956), 167.

4. Wendell Berry, *The Unsettling of America: Culture and Agriculture* (New York, 1977), 12.

5. Ibid.

6. Harry Braverman, "The Degradation of Work in the 20th Century," *Monthly Review* 34 (May 1982): 9.

7. Fred Whitehead, personal correspondence, October 12, 1989.

8. David Macarov, "Changes in the World of Work: Some Implications for the Future," in *The World of Work*, ed. Howard F. Didsbury, Jr. (Bethesda, 1983), 18.

9. Walli F. Leff and Marilyn G. Haft, *Time without Work* (Boston, 1983), 6–7.

10. Robert M. Fulmer, "Nine Paradoxes for the 1990s," in *The World of Work*, ed. Howard F. Didsbury, Jr. (Bethesda, 1983), 45.

11. Service Employees International Union, AFL-CIO, *Americans Deserve a Living Wage: Minimum Wage* (Washington, DC, 1988), 1–2.

12. Bennett Harrison and Barry Bluestone, "Changes in the Nature of Work," *Minneapolis Star and Tribune*, July 5, 1984, 11A.

13. Data compiled by the Minnesota Women's Consortium from Minnesota Commission on the Economic Status of Women, *Women in Minnesota* (St. Paul, August 1984).

14. Harrison and Bluestone, "Changes in Work," 11A.

Chapter 2

Why Do We Work?

The Maker is the one who is part of what he makes.
　　　　　　　　　　　　　　　　　　　—Orson Scott Card

Why do human beings work? It's not often that we have occasion to ponder the meaning of an activity that occupies a third or more of our lives. For many (if not most) people in America today, work has little or no meaning. The majority of people get up every morning and reluctantly spend the greater portion of their working hours doing work that they feel is boring, degrading, and beneath their abilities. Most of us think we work in order to eat and provide a roof over our heads, but in reality, much of the value of our labor goes to pay high interest rates to bankers and to make others rich who do not work. Sometimes we work and still cannot meet basic needs—a surprising number of homeless people have full-time jobs, for example. We are driven by a sense of despair and the gnawing knowledge that we have to spend the greater part of a lifetime relentlessly pursuing survival in increasingly hollow and unfulfilling tasks.

Our future looks no brighter. As the economy gradually but relentlessly replaces craftspersons and skilled industrial workers with so-called service jobs, the intellectual content of jobs and the rate of pay decline proportionately. We are told that jobs in the service industry pay less, but we are not told why this is so. We grow increasingly more anxious as it becomes hard to find any kind of work, let alone meaningful work. As the economy becomes more automated, as production jobs are transferred to Third World markets where workers are more easily exploited, and as the trade union movement is systematically gutted, we look forward to increasing poverty and want. The very fabric of American society is unraveling as the fear of hunger and homelessness replace job security. We are increasingly obsessed with the plight of the homeless: They have become the barometer by which we, who still have homes, measure our own disenfranchisement from the economic life of America. Do we complain about work? Not in these times, when we might not have our jobs tomorrow.

It is precisely in these times, however, that we have an even greater imperative to assess the nature of work. We are, I believe, at a turning point in modern economic life. It is not only in America that the industrial world of work is increasingly coming under scrutiny. The devastation of the British economy, and the emerging economic revolutions in Eastern Europe and in the USSR all point to a profound dis-ease with the nature of work in modern society under both state socialism (Stalinism) and capitalism.

There are many reasons why people work. These reasons can be roughly divided into three areas: (1) We work because we are creators, and we create to express our individual selves or to articulate the essence of humanity. When we are working we are expressing the being of humanity in individual and/or collective terms; (2) we work because we achieve some end product/goal by working; or (3) we work because we are responsible to others.

In this chapter we will look at these and other motivations for work. We will examine as well the ways in which work can be meaningful. As human beings we need meaningful work. Work that has meaning is work that is done with a specific intent, work that is done for intrinsic as well as extrinsic reasons. It is also work that allows for a high degree of personal latitude in carrying out the work. It is the difference between work, which rewards us intellectually and psychically, and labor, which demands only physical effort.[1]

WORK AS CREATION

Work that provides an opportunity to express ourselves creatively is especially important to American workers. We pride ourselves on the importance of the individual in our society, so activities that enhance the quality of individual self-realization are highly prized. We like to have jobs that allow us to stand out from the crowd, jobs where we are rewarded for our uniqueness. To be creative means being able to "do our own thing." Few contemporary jobs allow us the opportunity to be creative, however, and even fewer provide the opportunity for true artistic creativity.

The act of creating is more often seen as a function of the artist. The severance of art from work lies at the heart of the industrial revolution and the changes it brought to our work. As work has become more and more degraded we have lost sight of a basic human axiom: To be human is to be creative, and to be creative means to realize the transformation of self through interaction with the material, physical world. As we struggle to define meaningful work, we often distinguish between work as labor and work as art. Work as art implies that there is an ingredient in work—or there should be—that satisfies a deep human impulse to create, to express the self, or to express the individual in community.

Work is an extension of our being. Implicit in this definition of work is the centrality of the human being as creator, determiner, shaper. Work is the realization of the impact of the self on reality and on the physical world, and of the way we choose to act on the world. In addition to meeting a deep human need to create, work has often been linked to the development of self-expression and the achievement of personal fulfillment. Pope John Paul II, in his *Encyclical Laborens Exercens* (On human work), links work with self-expression: It is work that ultimately makes us our most human, he argues, and for that reason alone, work is ethically good. "Work is a good thing for man—a good thing for his humanity—because through work man not only transforms nature, adapting it to his own needs, but he also achieves fulfillment as a human being and indeed in a sense becomes 'more a human being.' "[2]

According to Paul Goodman and Percival Goodman we can express ourselves not only in the doing of work but also through sharing the results of work, the products of work. We like to create things because our creation makes us feel useful to others.

Men like to make things, to handle the materials and see them take shape and come out as desired, and they are proud of the products. And men like to work and be useful, for work has a rhythm and springs from spontaneous feelings just like play, and to be useful makes people feel right. Productive work is a kind of creation, it is an extension of human personality into nature.[3]

Kenneth Maly locates the source of our self-satisfaction with work in using ourselves "efficiently." His definition of work is somewhat mechanistic: Work is doing to *be*—doing what it is that uses our energies to their fullest efficiency, doing what we need to do to be. "Work is energy. Energy is working with one's essential being . . . being what it needs to be, which means doing what it needs to do."[4]

Maly makes a distinction between work and employment. Employment is work that is not "essential to my inner being"; it is work done for something other than its own merits (for example, for money or a product); it is work that is "external to one's centeredness as a human being"; it is non-essential; and our "work capacity" is engaged in non-work.[5] Employment is non-work because it does not meet the essential inner purpose of work—work for the self, not for external goals imposed on the individual. While this is essentially a negative definition of why we work, it assumes several positive motivations for work. It should be our goal to work to create something, rather than just to work for wages. The motivation to work should arise from the quality of the work itself— we should only work if we feel it is essential to our own inner fulfillment.

Meaningful work is also work that is not mechanistic or formalistic in its expression. It is work that requires input from the worker: a physical and intellectual engagement that puts the worker "in charge" of the product and the process of work. In *Mind and Art*, Guy Sircello organizes work into a hierarchy of levels of control over the work process.[6] At the top of his hierarchy, Sircello places art and intellectual work. Art is the highest mode of human self-expression, and an important part of artistic creativity is freedom—freedom to structure the time and place of work, and freedom by the artist/worker to shape the subject of the work—in other words, the freedom to control the context in which work occurs. At the bottom of the hierarchy are those categories of work that allow the least control over structuring the experience and assign the worker the most subservient role.

Meaningful work is not only the freedom to create, but the freedom from limitations or inhibitors to self-expression: "The more limitations are placed upon the ways a kind of work can be done, the more will the self-expressive possibilities of that kind of work diminish."[7] One such issue, central to our critique of the contemporary work context, is the limitation that machines place on the expression of creativity. The more that machines do our work, the less we are able to express ourselves through work, and the more even our ability to express ourselves is limited.

Since a person's "work" fills up so much of a person's life, it is in the activities involved in that work that one would expect to find that person's "self" expressed. Conversely, if a person's work involves activities which are inherently incapable of expressing the range of traits which, we have found, might constitute a "self" of the relevant sort, that person is less likely to be able to express himself.[8]

The power to create is also the power of the *determiner*, the chooser. To the extent that we are free to make choices, so is our creativity and our total freedom enhanced. The ability to do the best kind of work is linked inexorably with the *right* to be free to create (what is called *artistic freedom*) in order to express the self. A person who creates is an empowered person. Artistic freedom means the freedom to create, to work in the way in which one chooses, and, more important, to *be* what one chooses and through work to express the self. When our work is reduced to "employment" as Maly pointed out, we have not only lost a means of self-expression, we have lost some essential ingredients of freedom as well. Alienation from our work is not only alienation from control of the product, but alienation from our sense of control over the process through which we shape our work. Therefore, the more power to create is taken from us (or we give it up), the more we lose the ability to create.

The quality of work also significantly affects the role of work in community. Meaningful work and meaningful community life are intricately woven together, and the decline of community is directly related to the impoverishment of work. Most forms of contemporary work alienate the workers physically and politically from one another. Work done in a hierarchy isolates individuals from those above and below, and as a result of the division of labor, the modern factory system breaks work down into its simplest function and the worker loses the sense of how his or her task relates to other tasks and to the whole. In the same way, workers are separated from one another. Part of this isolation is a result of technology mechanizing work, and part is a result of the division of labor.

In any case, neither the work nor the worker enters the life of the community in a meaningful way. The workers are reduced to becoming part of the machinery, to becoming anonymous, interchangeable units. This has led to an indifference to one another, to our work, and to ourselves, all of which results in a general impoverishment of community.

James Boggs, Grace Lee Boggs, Freddy Paine, and Lyman Paine were deeply concerned about this destruction of the community of work, and urged the reintegration of work into our social relations: "Just because this society defines human activity in terms of exchange value doesn't mean that you have to accept that definition. There is another attitude to work which each of us . . . can discover for our own dignity, our own selves—our own concept of self."[9] Meaningful work is work that is part of a relationship, a community: In fact, "there is no job, no activity, in which you are not relating to somebody, *if only yourself.*"[10]

Meaningful work, then, is critical to the realization of all modes of self-expression. At its best, it approaches art. At its least meaningful, it destroys community. Meaningful work brings many experiences together: a greater sense of the possibilities of the self, a product that embodies the best the worker can give, and the security of community in which work is needed and appreciated. Work as self-expression is one of the highest achievements to which the human being can aspire. Ralph Waldo Emerson was moved to attempt a definition of the deep need people have to participate in the creative process:

Art is the path of the creator to his work. The paths or methods are ideal and eternal, though few men ever see them; not the artist himself for years, or for a lifetime, unless he come into the conditions. The painter, the sculptor, the composer, the epic rhapsodist, the orator, all partake one desire, namely to express themselves symmetrically and abundantly, not dwarfishly and fragmentarily.[11]

WORK FOR AN END PRODUCT

Work is not only motivated by a need for self-expression. We can also choose to work to achieve certain ends—for a specific material or spiritual end, or even to enjoy work for its own sake. The worker can seek to create collective meaning through the making of works of art or artifacts, or work simply to experience beauty on an individual level.

Work as Intrinsically Meaningful

The notion that work can be meaningful in itself is an old one. Today, it is only in our hobbies that we approximate the feeling of doing personally enjoyable and meaningful work. The satisfaction of a job well done can be pleasure enough. According to Walli F. Leff and Marilyn G. Haft, this sense of satisfaction may have psychological roots:

[Robert W. White proposed] that there is an unlearned, independent ego-energy for exploration and manipulation—an energy that permits a person to interact effectively with the environment—that he terms "effectance." White further identified the feeling of pleasure that accompanies being active and having an influence on something as "efficacy." You can see right off that White's definition rests upon the concepts of curiosity-investigation and curiosity-manipulation which are essential for adaptation and survival. These energetic activities, performed for their own sake with no reward, have been observed in every niche of animal life.[12]

In a similar vein, Thorstein Veblen speculated on the existence of an "instinct for workmanship":

The instinct of workmanship . . . occupies the interest with practical expedients, ways and means, devices and contrivances of efficiency and economy, proficiency, creative work and technological mastery of facts. Much of the functional content of the instinct of workmanship is a proclivity for taking pains. . . . It is a disposition to do the next thing and do it as well as may be.[13]

While we need to maintain a healthy skepticism of any attribution of instincts or innate abilities to human beings, it is instructive to think that at some level— whether nature or nurture—the human being is motivated, if only in order to survive, to do work, and to do it well. Whether we have an innate need for achievement—a need that some would use to justify competitiveness and the baser qualities of capitalism—or an innate need to be effective, the enjoyment of work for its own sake is an experience to which many of us can attest.[14] Unfortunately, it is also an experience that is increasingly privatized and marginalized.

Work for Leisure

Socialist William Morris, writing about work and art in the nineteenth century, defined leisure as "the hope of pleasure in rest."[15] Work is often connected with its opposite, leisure, but the balance or tension between the two has been altered significantly in our own time. For many people, work has become so meaningless that leisure time activities must compensate by meeting the needs for self-expression or creativity.

Leisure can, in theory, be a rewarding activity. In ancient Greece, for example, leisure was a goal in and of itself. While the slaves labored, so the argument went, truly enlightened individuals could devote their time to more rewarding social activities and participation in the political life of the community. In many utopian works, this argument is used as the major rationale for the introduction of high levels of technology. Technology is good because it frees us from the drudgery of labor through the use of so-called labor-saving devices to enjoy the good life.

Today's leisure, however, has an entirely different objective. Although we have been seduced by the promises of technology, we have only produced a barren, unsatisfying leisure. Many people find themselves frantically pursuing what they call leisure time activities; activities that are merely the *consumption* of activities rather than meaningful experiences of personal or social fulfillment in and of themselves. We have lost the talent, it seems, for enjoying our leisure and also for making it meaningful. In a consumer society, where ultimately everything becomes a commodity, even leisure is trivialized.

Work to Reveal the Sacred

Throughout history, work has also been seen as a means to achieve a closer connection with the spiritual or the sacred. Work can articulate the spiritual in different ways for different people: as a relationship with a higher being or as an expression of the whole. For Eric Gill, the essence of work is a spiritual experience: "Leisure is secular, work is sacred. The object of leisure is work. The object of work is holiness."[16] Like his predecessor William Morris, Gill was a critic of the emerging industrial capitalism. He took a different tack from Morris's more traditional socialist analysis, however, calling for a "resacralisation of work" on aesthetic grounds.

My socialism was from the beginning a revolt against the intellectual degradation of the factory hands and the damned ugliness of all that capitalist-industrialism produced, and it was not primarily a revolt against the cruelty and injustice of the possessing classes or against the misery of the poor. It was not so much the working *class* that concerned me as the working *man*—not so much what he got *from* working as what he did *by* working.[17]

According to Gill, the modern philosophy of materialism and its corollary consumerism were incompatible with the individual's true ascetic spiritual nature. Gill was deeply concerned that high level imaginative skills and the development of the free will and intellectual well-being of the individual were being destroyed by degraded labor:

Not to use the imagination is to be less than human. If the images it creates do not otherwise exist, then the agent or cause of their existence is responsible for their existence. And as the activity which produces them is an intellectual activity, to deprive people of it is to reduce them to a "subhuman condition of intellectual irresponsibility." That is the condition of men in our industrialism.[18]

No amount of "fine art" in leisure time can compensate for subhuman irresponsibility in working time. If necessary work is not made holy, recreation becomes idolatry.[19]

Work as Salvation

Salvation is a different motivation from the expression of the spiritual and the sacred. The concept of work as salvation has two strong historical roots in

Western culture—in the early Christian monastic movement, and in what has been called the Protestant work ethic. Labor in the classical era was spurned as the work of slaves. Early Christian theory, based in part on Neo-Platonist thought and the heritage of the Greeks, also looked down on work—forever linking work and original sin to justify the horrors of work life in ancient societies. In the monastery movement, however, work was to take on a new meaning. The early societies of monks, seeking salvation through humility and hard labor, raised physical work to a new dignity:[20] "In it [Augustine's *Retractationes*] is the germ of the Benedictine teaching that idleness is the enemy of the soul, and there are strong words for lazy and arrogant monks who fail to set a good example for the newcomer. . . . Augustine sees a pleasure in a period of manual work."[21] According to Clarence J. Glacken, the labor of the monks was further sanctified because it was seen as an act parallel to God's creative activities in the creation: "How were the monastic ideals . . . related to the modification of the landscape? Improvements made in deserted or uninhabited lands became, to the working monks, hearths of spiritual perfection."[22]

Despite the common perception that the Protestant work ethic was self-serving, it originated as a collective work ethic. Indeed, the early American Puritans believed that the most important characteristic of a *calling* was activity in which, according to John Cotton "we may not only aim at our own, but at the public good. That is warrantable calling: 'Seek not every man his own things, but every man the good of his brother' [I Cor. 10.24]."[23] Critics of Puritanism have argued, however, that despite the theoretical strength of this collective work ethic, the equally strong strain of individualism in Puritan theology resulted in an ethic of self-aggrandizement at the expense of community.

For many Christian theorists, one of the principal reasons for work is the hope of spiritual rewards. Simone Weil explored the relationship between beauty and God—believing that through beauty, one could approach God in the most perfect way. Work then, in her formulation, was an important spiritual link: "Physical work is a specific contact with the beauty of the world, and can even be, in its best moments, a contact so full that no equivalent can be found elsewhere."[24]

E. F. Schumacher, another Christian writer, felt that one could use work to experience the godly within and to be spiritually enriched: "In the process of doing good work the ego of the worker disappears. He frees himself from his ego, so that the divine element in him can become active."[25] Through our ability to create—our work—Schumacher felt our highest self-expression was achieved.

Work as Dominion over the Earth

To work is to shape raw materials, to create products to alter the material world. Work according to some, however, implied an imperative to dominate raw materials—and the earth itself. The desire to improve the land by working with it was perverted into the compulsion to impose human power over the environment. Stewardship was abandoned, and "progress" became the new inspiration. In general, these theories celebrated the building of dams, the filling in of wetlands, and the cutting of trees as a God-given charge to remake creation in "our own image." A long-standing interpretation of the Christian creation myth focuses on the message to dominate the earth that is outlined in Genesis. This theme of domination over the earth and its beings has been linked to an imperative to work. The Catholic church, even today, reaffirms that charge: in the words of John Paul II, "Man's dominion over the earth is achieved in and by means of work. There thus emerges the meaning of work in an objective sense, which finds expression in the various epochs of culture and civilization."[26] He continues: "Understood as a process whereby man and the human race subdue the earth, work corresponds to this basic biblical concept only when throughout the process man manifests himself and confirms himself as the one who 'dominates.' "[27]

Christianity has long interpreted the fall from the Garden of Eden as a sign that humanity was cursed with having to work. This concept of original sin created by Saint Augustine linked the willful act of woman to the punishment of hard work, creating, in the Christian world, an ambiguity toward both work and women that has endured two millenia. The curse was somewhat mitigated, however, by the promise of dominion over the other beings of the earth and all the earth's resources. It is only in recent decades that this supremacy has been challenged. Contemporary ecological/environmental thought developed, in part, as a critique of this theory of domination,[28] and we will turn throughout this book, to the relationship between work and the environment in our search for a new work ethic.

WORK FOR OTHERS

Finally, work has a collective imperative. Ultimately work cannot be evaluated in isolation—to work is to be part of the human family. There is a community beyond the individual that calls forth a responsibility for care beyond the self. Work is not just for the community's use, it is central to the making of community. When we work together, we build society: "It is characteristic of work that it first and foremost unites people. In this consists its social power: the power to build a community."[29]

Many theorists see work as essential to our collective experience. Schumacher finds that one of the three purposes of human work is "to do in service to, and in cooperation with, others, so as to liberate ourselves from our inborn egocentricity."[30] Contemporary Catholic theory, too, highlights the responsibility to work for the community, even across historical time and different cultures:

Man must work out of regard for others, especially his own family, but also for the society he belongs to, the country of which he is a child and the whole human family of which he is a member, since he is the heir to the work of generations and at the same time a sharer in building the future of those who will come after him in the succession of history.[31]

The basis of human work in community is survival. While it is not the most lofty or noble reason for doing work, throughout human history there has been an imperative to work to survive. We are not free to choose survival work: it must be done. It is necessary to preserve and maintain life—the life of the individual, the family unit, the race. However, doing the necessary does not have to be an oppressive experience. Work can be fulfilling too, showing that through survival the future is once again open to possibility. When I pull the weeds in my garden, for example, I am helping the plants to survive to feed my family.

In preindustrial environments, work for self-preservation was the dominant mode of work. In our own time, work has been severed from survival, to the detriment of both work and survival. We lose our *ownership* of our work, we denigrate our contribution to work. The value in work, however, is not in the tool, we must remember, or in the machine. It is in ourselves and in the process of making and of being together.

The essence of survival work lies in the reciprocity between human beings in community, and between human beings and the natural world. Survival is accomplished through reciprocal acts of responsibility and caring. When I enter into a relationship with the natural world, I maintain the quality of my garden soil because I know I can grow more and better vegetables if I take care of the soil. When I practice restraint and set aside the seed grain, I do so because it represents the future of community. When I care for the means of agricultural production (building the soil, weeding, watering the plants) I am insuring the continuation of the ends of production—human survival.

In an earlier, simpler survival economy, barter and shared work reinforced the social nature of reciprocal economic life.

In a community where you do something for somebody, you feel that in time they will do something for you. You don't have to put an exchange value on your services or goods immediately; you don't have to turn them into commodities. . . . Questions of money and costs are shaped by the expectations of the human relationship you are going to be having with others in the community. So the social relationships determine the economic.[32]

We have lost this sense of responsibility to and connection with both the material world and a vital community of workers. Instead, survival is premised on the individual getting enough money to "spend" on food, shelter, fuel, and other needs. The concept of a minimum wage is about as close as we come in the modern era to expressing the centrality of survival as it is linked to our work.

As Pope Leo XIII has argued, however, we have not only the right but also the obligation to survive. In his "Encyclical Rerum Novarum" (The condition of labor), which Pius XI called the "Magna Charta of the social order," Leo XIII outlined the social nature of work and its relationship to survival. The obligation to survive is primary because it links the worker with others in his or her immediate community—which in Catholic thought is defined as the family.

From this obligation flows the right to a living wage, a family wage. Wages, therefore, should be enough to support the worker and his or her family at the level of self-preservation. The Catholic argument is extremely compelling:

A man's labor has two notes or characters. First of all, it is *personal*. . . . Secondly, a man's labor is *necessary*; for without the results of labor a man cannot live; and self-conservation is a law of nature, which it is wrong to disobey. Now, if we were to consider labor merely so far as it is *personal*, doubtless it would be within the workman's right to accept any rate of wages whatever. . . . But this is a mere abstract supposition; the labor of the working man is not only his personal attribute, but it is *necessary*; and this makes all the difference. . . . It follows that each one has a right to procure what is required in order to live. . . . As a rule, workman and employer should make free agreements. . . . Nevertheless, there is a dictate of nature more imperious and more ancient than any bargain between man and man, that the remuneration must be enough to support the wage earner in reasonable and frugal comfort.[33]

The primary purpose of work is to ensure the survival of the community of workers. This requires, obviously, a decent wage. However, there is more. The relationship between work and social relations in community is central to any analysis of work. In order to survive we must have community. Survival is predicated on cooperation as a natural work ethic, because survival is dependent on having a viable community—a community to which all contribute for the survival of all. Without the community, the individual cannot survive. Work then is part and parcel of the complex interactions between individuals, and intimately interconnects the political and the economic lives of a community. It is around the concept of community that future revolutionary action will come, I believe, and it will emerge from the radical restructuring of the work in those communities.

CONCLUSION: WHAT IS TO BE DONE?

These three prime motivations of work—work to create and express the self, work to achieve some particular end, and work for others—all coexist in tension with one another. As we seek to understand the nature of work, we can begin by looking around us at the place of work in our individual lives and in our neighborhoods and towns. We need to ask "What do we do for each other?" and not just "What do we do?" We need to talk about *our* work, and not just my work and your work. When we are truly invested in *our* work, we will solve the problems of who should do housework, who should care for the elderly, and how we shall create an environment for our individual creative expression. We must see the value of our work to each other, and our value in our work.

NOTES

1. This particular distinction between work and labor was first outlined by Hannah Arendt. See Hannah Arendt, *The Human Condition* (Chicago, 1958).

2. John Paul II, *Encyclical Laboren Exercens* (On human work) (Washington, DC, 1981), 20–21.

3. Paul Goodman and Percival Goodman, *Communitas: Means of Livelihood and Ways of Life* (New York, 1960), 153.

4. Kenneth Maly, "Work is Reality," *North Country Anvil*, no. 45 (1983): 12.

5. Ibid., 13.

6. Guy Sircello, *Mind and Art: An Essay on the Varieties of Expression* (Princeton, 1972).

7. Ibid., 335.

8. Ibid., 315.

9. James Boggs, Grace Lee Boggs, Freddy Paine, and Lyman Paine, *Conversations in Maine: Exploring Our Nation's Future* (Boston, 1978), 109.

10. Ibid.

11. Ralph Waldo Emerson, "The Poet," in *Selections from Ralph Waldo Emerson*, ed. Stephen Whicher (Boston, 1957), 239.

12. Walli F. Leff and Marilyn G. Haft, *Time without Work* (Boston, 1983), 41–42.

13. Thorstein Veblen, *The Portable Veblen*, ed. Max Lerner (New York, 1972), 320.

14. Leff and Haft, *Time without Work*, 41–42.

15. William Morris, *The Political Writings of William Morris*, ed. A. L. Morton (New York, 1973), 37.

16. Eric Gill, *A Holy Tradition of Working: Passages from the Writing of Eric Gill* (West Stockbridge, 1983), 45.

17. Eric Gill, *Autobiography* (London, 1940), 111.

18. Eric Gill, "The Value of the Creative Faculty in Man," in *Work and Property* (London, 1937), 79.

19. Eric Gill, "The End of the Fine Arts," in *Work and Property*, 132.

20. Clarence J. Glacken, *Traces on the Rhodian Shore: Nature and Culture in Western Thought from Ancient Times to the End of the Eighteenth Century* (Berkeley, CA, 1976), 302.

21. Ibid., 305.

22. Ibid., 308.

23. Perry Miller, ed. *The American Puritans: Their Prose and Poetry* (Garden City, NY, 1956), 174.

24. Simone Weil, *Waiting for God* (New York, 1973), 170.

25. E. F. Schumacher, *Good Work* (New York, 1979), 122.

26. John Paul II, *Encyclical Laboren Exercens*, 11.

27. Ibid., 14.

28. See especially Lynn White, Jr., "The Historical Roots of Our Ecological Crisis," *Science* 155 (10 March 1967): 1203–7.

29. John Paul II,, *Encyclical Laboren Exercens*, 46.

30. Schumacher, *Good Work*, 4.

31. John Paul II, *Encyclical Laboren Exercens*, 37.

32. Boggs, Boggs, Paine, and Paine, *Conversations in Maine*, 230.

33. Leo XIII, "Encyclical Rerum Novarum" (The condition of labor), May 1891, in *Five Great Encyclicals* (New York, 1953), 21, para. 34.

Chapter 3

The Transformation of Work

The clock in the shop, even *he* toils forever:
He points, and he ticks, and he wakes us from dreams—
A long time ago someone taught me the meaning:
His pointing his waking are more than they seem. . . .
I hear the wild yell of the boss in his ticking,
I see a dark frown in the two pointing hands;
I shudder to think it: the clock is my master!
He calls me "Machine!" "Hurry up!" he commands.
       —Morris Rosenfeld, sweatshop worker and poet, 1880[1]

What we call work today is a gross simplification of the rich and complex understanding of work that characterized medieval Europe. The medieval craftsperson has, in Western culture, been the traditional model of the ideal worker. Craftspersons were in complete control of their work: They chose the product to be made, the materials, the time to make it. The result was a handcrafted product that bore the imprint of the individual—his or her aesthetic statement. The craftsperson worked for no master. They joined together in guilds with peers, deepening the knowledge of craft through exchanges with others, and in the process of their work created a work ethic based on reciprocity.

An idea of "justice" to the community, of "right" towards both producer and consumer, which would seem so extravagant now, penetrated production and exchange [in the medieval city]. . . . It was natural and unaffected then, because the medieval artisan did not produce for an unknown buyer, or to throw his goods into an unknown market. He produced for his guild first; for a brotherhood of men who knew each other.[2]

This guild system, which was the centerpiece of medieval social, political, and economic life, was one of the first casualties of the emerging industrial capitalist system. With the death of the guilds, centralized control in all areas of work life moved forward unimpeded.

With the advent of the age of the machine, work was simplified, and we lost the diversity, health, and creativity of pre-technological work habits. Ecologically we know that to reduce diversity in the ecosystem destroys the environment as a whole. The same holds with work. We are hybrid workers now, hothouse plants, technologically altered to tolerate a highly specialized and rarefied atmosphere, but barren in ability to survive by our own wits. In the process of the transformation from a pre-technological world to the highly mechanized present, work has been so transformed that we barely recognize its outline.

Our idea and experience of work changed little up through the Middle Ages. Most work was done under conditions of extreme deprivation and near-slavery. Serfs working the land in middle Europe could be transplanted to a field in ancient Greece—where they would work hard, barely scratch a living from the earth, and die young. Life would be, echoing Hobbes, "nasty, brutish and short." If they escaped slavery, they succumbed to overwork.

In the Middle Ages, major cultural forces were set in motion that changed our attitudes toward work and the environment of work forever. Europe was emerging from feudalism, and the rising merchant class breathed life into the small city states. Important changes affecting the world of work included changes in the concept and measurement of time, the introduction of the factory system, the emergence of capitalism, the rise of the new machine technology powered by the steam engine, and the Protestant work ethic. In this chapter we will explore the implications of those changes on the nature of work.

CHANGING NOTIONS OF TIME, WORK, AND MONEY

Pre-industrial society was characterized by a strong sense of connection to cyclical time and rootedness in a communal place. Cyclical time is time measured by the cycles of the season, time that changes with the rhythms of farm work and with the rising and setting of the sun. It is *natural* time—time in which humanity and nature are in tune with one another, and motion each other to the tasks the natural rhythms call forth. It is time with the patience to wait for a flower to bloom. It is the time of births and deaths.

Everyone knew his or her place, as well. It was a matter of knowing one's place in the Great Chain of Being; of knowing one's place in the family and in the village community. People didn't move about—but there was no need to either. Place was a home, with friends and a life's work to do. Place was the whole web of relationships with family, community, earth, and cosmos.

According to Jacques LeGoff in *Time, Work and Culture in the Middle Ages*, several changes occurred toward the end of the thirteenth and into the fourteenth century that hastened the transition to the emerging technological, industrial, and scientific revolutions.[3] One of the most important shifts in cultural patterns was the harnessing of work to time by the merchant classes. In ancient societies the rhythm of work was ruled by cyclical and seasonal demands. By the fourteenth century, however, the new invention of the clock began to monitor time in a new way. Time became a quantity, something to be measured and counted. Furthermore, it could be bought and sold.

The communal clock was an instrument of economic, social, and political domination wielded by the merchants who ran the commune. They required a strict measurement of time, because in the textile business "it is fitting that most of the day workers—the proletariat of the textile trade—begin and end work at *fixed* hours." This was the beginning of the organization of work, a distant precursor of Taylorism.[4]

This new way of measuring time was quickly put to work measuring labor. Before the invention of the clock, time was marked by the ringing of church bells: bells that called worshipers to church or called the whole community to church festivals and social events of collective interest or concern. "Instead of a time linked to *events*, which made itself felt only episodically and sporadically, there arose a regular, normal time. Rather than the *uncertain* clerical hours of the church bells, there were the *certain* hours."[5] With the shift to clock time, time lost its sacred or communal meaning and took on economic importance. The community began to organize its days around the new secular time pattern imposed by the merchants. According to LeGoff, this shift was challenged by the church, but with little success:

Among the principal criticisms leveled against the merchants was the charge that their profit implied a mortgage on time, which was supposed to belong to God alone. . . . "*He would be selling time* and would be committing usury *by selling what does not belong to him*."[6]

The second cultural shift that set the stage for the industrial revolution was the systematic categorization of work and the emergence of specialists. A whole hierarchy of work was categorized according to its closeness or distance from "creative" work: a "Great Chain of Work" with God at the apex.

God's work, of course, was Creation. Any profession, therefore, which did not create was bad or inferior. It was imperative to create, as the peasant, for example, created the harvest, or at least, to transform raw material, like the artisan, into an object. If there was no creation, then there should be transformation, modification, or improvement.[7]

Initially, in the eyes of the church, the merchants did nothing creative and the activities of trade were highly suspect. Over time, however, their contributions came to be accepted by the community. Once a value had been placed on time, a new source of income emerged for the merchants—the charging of interest. The merchants legitimized their claim to interest income because their time was tied up in their business (they had to wait for a shipment, their caravan was late in returning, etc.). Once interest was no longer considered usury, the stage was set for early capitalism to expand with few moral or ethical restraints. The merchants were the last to join the Great Chain and to be "justified" in their claims to doing good work. Only physical labor was regarded with disdain.[8]

A third and final shift in the cultural attitudes toward work and labor was the growing acceptance of a money-based economy. In preindustrial Europe, work was embedded in social relationships and seldom had a cash value attached to it. The feudal economy was characterized by a complex social structure in which individuals had their economic needs met by a vast network of family support, the guilds, barter, or other acceptable means of living such as begging. The lowest and most shameful form of labor was wage labor. When you had to sell yourself for wage labor, everyone knew you had no means of support. Even begging was a more honorable livelihood, since others contributed to your upkeep.[9]

In addition, the exchange of money was looked down on: Anything "bought and paid for" was morally suspect. Morality was a matter of honor and duty, and one could be more honorable in a barter exchange because the barter implied a transaction between two individuals. Cash was outside of community, but as international trade grew, there was increased pressure to endorse cash transactions to loosen the flow of cash. The end result was a gradual shift to an abstract symbol of exchange: money.

Increasingly, work and money were seen as interchangeable. More important, for the first time money was linked to the performance of work: "For a salary to be merited, labor had to be performed. . . . The necessary and sufficient condition for legitimization of a trade and for payment of a wage was the requirement of labor."[10]

With money and time coming under the merchant's control, and with the systematic organization of the work world in a church-sanctioned hierarchy, the stage was set for the emerging merchant capital class to consolidate its cultural and economic gains. Although workers were bound to the rhythm of the clock, they still did their work in their own home environments. However, with the invention of the steam engine, the capitalist class could centralize the power to do work mechanically, and it was only a matter of time before they centralized the work itself.

THE FACTORY SYSTEM

Karl Marx called it capitalism, but to the average British worker of the eighteenth century it was not only the subtleties of concentrated capital that threatened his or her existence, but the introduction of a new cultural phenomenon—the factory. The concentration of capital was not a new phenomenon. The rich and powerful class had always existed but the factories added a new dimension to political and economic control: They introduced machines to replace workers, and they centralized the means of production.

Until the factories were built, work was still a private undertaking that one did at home or in a small shop. Craftspersons, through their guilds, controlled the process of production—and the aesthetics of the end products. Concerned as he was with the worker losing control of the means of production, Marx only paid cursory attention to the ends of production and the role of the worker in the process of creating that product. With the introduction of machines, the worker lost both economic and aesthetic control of the product.

Using the weavers as an example, two factors occurred that destroyed the domestic, or putting out system: the introduction of power looms and the building of factories to house these machines.[11] The putting out system was a simple, community-based, decentralized economy where the capitalist merchant went around the countryside from one home to another, bringing raw materials and picking up finished goods to take to the market. The factory system centralized the means of production, replacing hand looms with machines and forcing workers to leave home to earn money.

Resistance to the factory system was widespread. In the late eighteenth and early nineteenth centuries, for example, hundreds of weaving factories were destroyed and the machines smashed. The Luddites, a shadowy group of saboteurs named after Ned Ludd, one of their most famous leaders (only a few of whom were ever identified), were machine-breakers par excellence. Hundreds of mechanized looms were destroyed in nightly raids all across England. The Luddites epitomized the generalized resistance to the factories and demanded a return to a work that "gratified that innate love of independence—by leaving the workman entirely a master of his own time, and the sole guide of his actions."[12] The Luddites also smashed the power looms because the machines denied them aesthetic control over the final products. More important, however, they resisted the factory system because it took them from their homes and took control of work away from them.

Most Marxist critics of the new capitalist economy accepted as a given the need for centralization of the machines, the factory, and the resultant urbanization. Blinded by the promise of abundance the new system of manufacture seemed to imply, they basically accepted the technological transformation of work as both necessary and good. Early anarchists like Michael Bakunin, however, split with other Marxist theorists over the issue of centralization versus decentralization, and while Bakunin did not explicitly reject technology, his insistence that decentralization of political control was paramount in all human activity laid the philosophical groundwork for Peter Kropotkin's later anarchist critique of technology. By the end of the nineteenth century, the horrors of the factory system and the wage labor system were readily apparent, and Kropotkin felt that the new technologies had been instrumental in the destruction of the decentralized medieval economic order. Centralization of the means of production—which was necessitated by the introduction of machine technologies—destroyed economic autonomy, which in turn enslaved workers to both the capitalist and the machine.

Kropotkin was also one of the first individuals to call into question one of capitalism's central tenets: the economics of large-scale production. Factories did not need to be large, he countered:

Very many of our big factories are nothing else but agglomerations under a common management, of several distinct industries; while others are mere agglomerations of hundreds of copies of the very same machine; such are most of our gigantic spinning and weaving establishments. The manufacture being a strictly private enterprise, its owners find it advantageous to have all the branches of a given industry under their own management; thus they cumulate the profits of the successive transformations of the raw material. And when several thousand power-looms are combined in one factory, the owner finds his advantage in being able to hold the command of the market. But from a *technical* point of view the advantages of such an accumulation are trifling and often doubtful.[13]

Kropotkin was also one of the first anarchist thinkers to systematically question the role of technology and its effect on the political economy of a people. He based his argument on the anarchist mistrust of centralization of political power and the inherent threat to local control that the large institutions required to underwrite and maintain technological sophistication represented. He strongly believed that politics should control technological decisions rather than the other way around, and was an early critic of the nearly universal belief that the industrial revolution was driven by a desire for efficient production through technological changes. It was, he said, motivated by simple greed: "This is why the concentration so much spoken of is often nothing but an amalgamation of capitalists for the purpose of *dominating the market*, not for cheapening the technical process."[14]

Where work had previously been integrated with family life and such survival activities as gardening and the care of animals and crops, people were now forced into the rigid structure of the factory with its close supervision, its machines, and its required blocks of time away from home and community. The shift from subsistence living to wage labor was traumatic, as it tore both economic and aesthetic control from the hands of the craftspersons. This separation of labor from community resulted, according to Adam Smith, in the "mental mutilation" of people:

Robert Owen likewise discussed this transformation when he declared in 1815, that "The general diffusion of manufactures throughout a country generates a new character . . . an essential change in the general character of the mass of the people." Less abstractly, the Hammonds [historians of the British working class] harkened back to the early 19th century and heard the "lament that the games and happiness of life are disappearing," and that soon "the art of the living had been degraded to its rudest forms."[15]

Kropotkin, too, was concerned about the effects of the new system of manufacture on human behavior. He felt in particular that the division of labor was destructive of the creative spirit.

The worker whose task has been specialised by the permanent division of labour has lost the intellectual interest in his labour, and it is especially so in the great industries: he has lost his inventive powers. . . . But since the great factory has been enthroned, the worker, depressed by the monotony of his work, invents no more. What can weavers invent who merely supervise four looms, without knowing anything either about their complicated movements or how the machines grow to be what they are? What can a man invent who is condemned for life to bind together the ends of two threads with the greatest celerity, and knows nothing beyond making a knot?[16]

THE PROTESTANT WORK ETHIC

Much has been written—both pro and con—about the so-called Protestant work ethic, a term coined by Max Weber to articulate the convergence of Protestant individualism and the emerging capitalist system. The Protestant Reformation split with medieval Catholicism over the issue of work, or, more specifically, the doing of good works and the ends to which work should strive. Under Catholicism, good works here on earth were intimately connected with salvation. In fact, the connection between the world and the afterlife was so firmly planted in medieval Catholicism that Martin Luther accused the church of being too materialistic by selling indulgences as a way for the purchasers to get to heaven.

For Catholics, work also implied a whole constellation of social ethics and responsibilities. What you did was watched by others and evaluated by the church. For Protestants, however, there were no such curbs or restrictions; faith alone could guarantee one's admission into heaven. The true believer whose salvation was predestined theoretically needed to do nothing. Disdaining the real world, Protestant theology preached that people worked because it was God's will and not for any intrinsic value the work itself might draw out. On the surface, a noble ethic seems to inspire work:

It is a logical consequence of Puritan theology: man is put in this world . . . to do what the world requires, according to its terms. He must raise children, he must work at his calling. No activity is outside the holy purpose of the overarching covenant. Yet the Christian works not for the gain that may (or may not) result from his labor, but for the glory of God.[17]

This ethic, however, left the Protestants in an ambiguous situation vis-à-vis the products of labor. They were supposed to work hard, but weren't supposed to "enjoy" work or its products. Humanity was in the world, not of it, and work should be undertaken with an attitude of what American Puritans called "weaned affections" (an ascetic attitude of deprivation and denial, which said that one worked not for personal gain or satisfaction but for the glory of God). One was not to be ostentatious in any way.

The Calvinist saint demonstrates his election by means of his industry but at the same time shows, through his limitations of personal consumption, that he realizes the incompatibility of personal display with election. Hence the tendency of the Calvinist ethic is to encourage production but at the same time to limit personal consumption drastically.[18]

At first glance we might assume that the Protestants would endorse a no-growth or low-growth economic policy. However, such was not the case. Another ambiguity in the Protestant work ethic resulted in the encouragement of unrestrained economic development. Since salvation was an "individual" activity, the governance of economic activity was also left to the individual soul. Personal ethics replaced community ethics. The individual merchant could easily argue, for example, that God had "willed" an extravagant accumulation of wealth, and in the same breath deny any personal or social responsibility for its just distribution. In practice, the Protestant Reformation freed the enterprising spirit from the constraints of worldly criticism and social responsibility, and encouraged the development of capitalism. With ethics tied to the individual, the door was opened to the excesses of our own time.

Art, too, and the process of creating generally, were severed from the question of salvation. Aesthetic expression was seen as idolatry and the creative outpouring of art and ritual characterizing medieval Catholicism was replaced by the Protestant "plain style." In many cases, churches were "purged" of their art, and many works of art were destroyed. Charges of papism were serious indeed, and ritual, iconography, and other materialistic representations were abhorred. Art did not really matter, and in fact, it could be distracting to the good Christian. Pleasure in one's work was frowned on. One worked more from "duty" than from love for the creative. Art came to be seen as nonproductive, distracting, frivolous—and finally sinful.

It is more than coincidental, I could argue, that the Protestant work ethic and modern industrialism emerged simultaneously in our history. This ethic was necessary to reconcile the human spirit to the drudgery of the factory and its machine-made products. With their "weaned affections," people were also more easily convinced that the aesthetically inferior machine-made products were a necessary evil. Denied enjoyment in the process of work or the aesthetic pleasures in its end product, the new industrial worker was weaned from the richness of the medieval world to the stark reality of the machine aesthetic.

The transition to industrial capitalism was swift and harsh. The medieval community in which economics had been embedded no longer functioned. The guilds, which Kropotkin held in the highest regard, were broken up, and the workers were forced into competing with one another rather than working co-operatively. The ethics of economic community was also destroyed as the merchant class came to power. All these transformations together—changes in time, place, and attitudes toward work—altered forever the personal, social, and economic realities of Western civilization. With the introduction of the industrial factory system, a new type of work emerged: work for wages. The machines set the standards and rhythms, the clock set the hours of work, the boss set the pace. The role of worker became more passive, less creative. He or she did a "job." For the average factory worker, pride in craftsmanship diminished. Although some craftspersons were still required by the factories (and they were paid more because of their skills), their numbers were limited. Now, however, they were rewarded for their skills in operating machines rather than for the goods they produced. In time, even skills came to be measured as extensions of the machines. Modern capitalism was off and running, as Karl Marx sat in a London library putting the finishing touches on the first theoretical challenge to the emerging economic order.

CAPITALISM AND ALIENATION: PRODUCTION

The emergence of capitalism wrought great changes at all levels of economic life: production, consumption, and the politics of community. This section will focus on the changes brought about in production. Much of the analysis will be based on Karl Marx's theories on the alienation of worker from the production process.

Any discussion of work in the modern era should begin by understanding the term *division of labor*. Labor has always been *divided*—one such division familiar to all of us is division by gender. The division of labor was often determined by the abilities and talents of the individual, relying on the "nature" of the individual to determine who did what kinds of tasks. Even slaves, for example, were sometimes assigned work based on their inclinations or talents. In other societies, the division of work was linked to social status.

In the ancient Greek philosophies we find one of the earliest expressions of the connection between work and individual needs for self-actualization. Georg Hegel expanded on this Greek notion, taking a slightly different approach that emphasized our potential for growth and development. Work was not connected to the individual's nature, but rather was the opportunity for the individual to create the self anew, and to experience the basic human ability to create. As we work, we create ourselves—the self is product of the work we do, and we realize ourselves through our work. This insight into work deeply influenced the young Karl Marx:

Marx believed that Hegel's concept of self-activity had as an important part of its meaning not only a notion of potentially beyond the given, but also a notion of creative work—work, moreover, of the very kind that the capitalist division of labour subverts and denies. . . . "The outstanding achievement of Hegel's *Phenomenology*," Marx insisted, had been that "Hegel grasps the self-creation of man as a process, . . . and that he therefore grasps the nature of *labour*, and conceives objective man (true, because real man) as the result of his own labor."[19]

Central to Marx's argument was his proposition that the division of labor thwarted this process of self-development through work. It also destroyed the collective, communal impulses in work. *Undivided* work—work that had not been broken down into its parts and distributed randomly to workers, was based on community needs and standards—work that was for *use* between people rather than for *exchange*. Work for use value was done to meet needs rather than the *wants* produced by the market. Marx called work for exchange value *alienated labor*—labor that is torn out of personal and social relationships and thrust into the abstract marketplace where it becomes just another commodity to be bought and sold.

There were other voices besides Marx's. Socialist William Morris was an early critic of the new industrial system. As part of the nineteenth-century English Crafts Movement he raised similar objections to the new economic order:

They are called "labour-saving" machines—a commonly used phrase which implies what we expect of them; but we do not get what we expect. What they really do is to reduce the skilled labourer to the ranks of the unskilled, to increase the number of the reserve army of labour.[20]

The only labor "saved" was the cost of labor to the capitalist. The system was not labor-saving for the workers.

With the advantage of an additional century of observation, our present reality confirmed Morris's early fears and suspicions about the degradation of work. In the newly emerging technological worldview, labor was subordinated to the technological process. Its connection with human intentionality was severed and the machine became the new standard, driving the whole reality. E. F. Schumacher called it a process of "de-skilling." Crafts became superfluous and the few skills learned were not transferable since in a machine reality each skill is specific to the portion of the labor that particular machine does.

The world of work of today is the product of a hundred years of "de-skilling"—why take the trouble and incur the cost of letting people acquire the skills of a craftsman, when all that is wanted is a machine winder? The only skills worth acquiring are those which the system demands, *and they are worthless outside the system*. They have no survival value outside the system and therefore do not ever confer the spirit of self-reliance.[21]

Hannah Arendt described the new alienated labor force as a product of the division of labor compounded by the burgeoning technology. This created, she felt, a new distinction between laborers and workers—one that may not have been intended: "What happened, and this is one of the ironies of the modern world, is that by dividing, subdividing, and mechanizing the tasks we have to perform we effectively eliminated what work there was, leaving only labor to be done."[22]

The process of de-skilling continues even today. Evelyn Glenn and Roslyn Feldberg explored the impact of computerization on clerical jobs, and predicted that the office worker would undergo a similar process of mental alienation that had already transformed the industrial work economy. He called the process the proletarianization of the work force, which occurs "as work is organized around manual rather than mental activities, as tasks become externally structured and controlled and as relationships become depersonalized."[23]

The computer initially was promoted as yet another labor-saving device that would free the worker for more challenging and interesting work. What it did, on the contrary, was further degrade the quality of the work environment.

The introduction of a computer rarely reduces the size of a clerical staff. . . . Although the clerk may be less directly supervised, she does not gain autonomy; the requirements of the machine replace the directives of an immediate supervisor. Her mental choices are limited to predetermined categories. She has little discretion to do the work as she sees fit or to set her own pace, since her work has to feed into subsequent stages. As these changes occur, the worker is proletarianized according to our definition.[24]

Alienation from the means of production began almost immediately as machines replaced workers, and is continuing even today as the technology is increasingly automated. This alienation was experienced by workers in several ways: Through the division of labor, work was simplified to the level of boring repetition; in some cases workers lost their jobs as the machines took over human activities; workers found themselves isolated from other workers; and finally, they lost control over the quality of the product. As work became increasingly meaningless, the workers' needs for satisfaction and integration shifted to the ends of production—consumption.

CAPITALISM AND ALIENATION: CONSUMPTION

The primary task of the capitalist is to produce things. The primary task of the people is to consume those things. Over time, these things, or commodities, have come to take on their own independent existence—what Marx first called the "fetishism of commodities."[25] Prior to capitalism, the value of work lay in its usefulness to the individual and to the community. In a commodity-driven society, value inheres in things, and we become hostage to their independent value. Set free from any societal constraints by labor or by need, things proliferate, and in their proliferation, drive the whole economy.

In fact, and speaking very broadly and tentatively, industrialist culture might be said to be an existential illustration of what Plato referred to in Book II of the *Republic* as the uncontrolled, undirected "luxurious state." Like the luxurious state ideal type, the industrialist culture represents a vast development of complex division of labor and an almost unimaginable proliferation of material goods.[26]

The United States is on the verge of drowning in a sea of garbage—the flotsam and jetsam of a culture committed to compulsive production of "stuff." We have achieved Marx's goal of "abundance"—but it is not quite what anyone had predicted. The alienation of workers from their work, leaving them only "labor" to do, and the degradation of skills as a result of the mechanized factory are only part of the story of how work has transformed culture. There is the other side of alienation to be explored: the alienation from the wealth of products that are produced by capitalism.

In many ways, the nineteenth-century critics of industrial capitalism could not have predicted the depth of this form of alienation, simply because the technological system had not achieved its present-day sophisticated level of production. By the twentieth century, Eric Gill could describe in detail the relentless compulsivity of a commodity-driven economy. His concerns about the power of things in our lives were dismissed as "romantic"—representative of only a small minority of Cassandra-like critics.

In his [Gill's] observation that the machine is primarily an instrument for producing profits (XI:10) is foreshadowed the observation that the modern economy is primarily concerned to produce *demand*. . . . Gill recognized the remorseless circularity of that unique form of modern slavery, "consumerism." (XI:11) . . . Such is the treadmill of "consumer choice" and hence it comes about that men must serve "the Economy" for the good of a society that has no higher notion of the social good than that of "free enterprise" serving consumer demand.[27]

Today, in this country we call it the American Standard of Living. It is also, I will argue in this section, the American standard by which we can gauge the present level of the degradation of work.

In recent decades, contemporary researchers have turned increasingly to studying the impact of the glut of production and consumption on traditional Marxist theory. This discussion is of central importance to political theorists because it touches on some of the basic building blocks of Marxist theory—classism, the role of abundance, and the need for some sense of connection with the product of one's work.

Like many others of his day, Marx was fascinated with the potential for freedom from arduous labor that the machines promised. For the first time in human history, our needs could be met and exceeded. Marx also implicitly supported the centralization of the means of production, and its companion, the efficiency of large-scale production. His support of mass production contradicted in some ways his criticism of the concentration of capital since it took large amounts of capital to create large factories, but he felt that in time, the workers would simply appropriate the means of production to their own ends.

Mass production by itself did not produce the abundance to meet the basic needs of the worker that Marx had hoped for. We only need to look around us at the homeless and hungry people in our communities today to see that something went wrong. The failure of capitalism to meet the basic needs of workers— despite the tendency on the part of the economy to overproduce consumer items— saw its clearest expression during the severe worldwide depression of the 1930s. Because the commodity takes on a life of its own in the marketplace, capitalism produces not basic needs, but "stuff" that people want and that makes a profit.

It did not take us long to see the power of things in our lives. One of the most eloquent challenges to industrial capitalism of the Depression era was written by twelve Southern writers. In their declaration, "I'll Take My Stand," which among other things called for a return to a simpler level of technology, their critique of consumption rings true even today:

Turning to consumption, as the grand end which justifies the evil of modern labor, we find that we have been deceived. We have more time in which to consume, and many more products to be consumed. But the tempo of our labors communicates itself to our satisfactions, and these also become brutal and hurried. The constitution of the natural man probably does not permit him to shorten his labor-time and enlarge his consuming-time indefinitely. He has to pay the penalty in satiety and aimlessness. The modern man has lost his sense of vocation.[28]

Commodity production that began as a mere trickle of goods in the 1930s has become an obscene flood. We are all encouraged, and, if necessary, manipulated, to hop aboard the merry-go-round of our contemporary consumer society. Need no longer drives our economic activities: Another imperative is operating—the need of capitalism to escalate the ever-increasing production of consumer goods, until we become what we consume.

In capitalist society, creative activity takes the form of commodity production, namely production of marketable goods, and the results of human activity take the form of commodities. . . . If a large number of men accept the legitimacy of these conventions, if they accept the convention that commodities are a prerequisite for money, and that money is a prerequisite for survival, then they find themselves locked into a vicious circle.[29]

What exactly is consumerism? Consumerism is the reification of production; it is production having a life of its own; it is part of the perpetual motion machine we have created with the mass production of goods; and in Marxist terms, it is production for exchange value instead of use value. It is also the way of life that dominates and shapes our cultural and social relations. The whole hegemony of commodity consumption is ultimately more than just a vicious circle. It takes on a life of its own, and in turn creates its own world, which comes to dominate our very reality. Guy Debord, a contemporary French Neo-Marxist, has analyzed consumerism symbolically and semiotically, calling it "the spectacle." The spectacle, as I interpret it, is the reification of the process of capitalist production to the level of an icon that we continually and obsessively worship—another way of describing the American Standard of Living. Debord describes the economy of the spectacle as "the goal is nothing, development everything," and "the spectacle is *capital* to such a degree of accumulation that it becomes an image."[30] It ultimately becomes the total reason for human existence. Debord describes its beginnings:

In a primitive economy, the commodity sector represented a surplus of survival.... However, where commodity production met the social conditions of large scale commerce and of the accumulation of capital, it seized total domination over the economy. The entire economy then became what the commodity had shown itself to be in the course of this conquest: a process of quantitative development. This incessant expansion of economic power in the form of the commodity, which transformed human labor into commodity-labor, into *wage-labor*, cumulatively led to an abundance in which the primary question of survival is undoubtedly resolved, but in such a way that it is constantly rediscovered; it is continually posed again each time at a higher level.[31]

Built into our commodity-based economy is the principle of privation or want, but privation at a higher level all the time. It is privation artificially created by the advertising industry, whose main task is to continually reinforce the spectacle to keep consumption going. The most sinister quality of this artificially created privation is its compulsive character—a hunger that is never eased, an obsession that finds no relief.

So the rise of modern advertising—along with its twin, personal salesmanship—is the most significant development of our industrialism. Advertising means to persuade the consumers to want exactly what the applied sciences are able to furnish them. It consults the happiness of the consumer no more than it consulted the happiness of the laborer.[32]

There is no connection in a consumer economy between meeting real needs and most of the products we consume. (Here I am defining consumer economics as separate from real needs for survival and the basics of food, shelter, fuel, and clothing.) However, the things we do consume stand for real needs: We can understand ourselves (and perhaps uncover our real needs), therefore, by exploring the hidden needs that lie buried in our consumption of goods and services.

A mythology has also grown up that celebrates the American way of buying. It teaches that consumption never should stop because our standard of living is an ever-expanding spiral. It will get better and better all the time. We are told by other economists that we dare not stop consuming because retail sales account for approximately one-third of all economic activity in the United States. If production and consumption should slow up, a recession will follow and unemployment will rise. The message seems to be, buy or die. These then are the twin terrors of our contemporary economy: the fear of not consuming, coupled with the constant pressure to consume unrealistically the artificial needs created by the advertising industry. The result is a society that nourishes and celebrates the obsession of buying for its own sake.

When economic necessity is replaced by the necessity for boundless economic development, the satisfaction of primary human needs is replaced by an uninterrupted fabrication of pseudo-needs which are reduced to the single pseudo-need of maintaining the reign of the autonomous economy.[33]

What is central to the spectacle, then, is its self-referencing limitlessness. The spiral of production, like its password progress, rages on without any traditional means of control over both our inner compulsions and the outward limits originally placed on our need by the environment itself. Consumption is a train running down the track without an engineer and with the throttle stuck on full. The impact of both our culture as a whole and our individual psyches is devastating:

> The pseudo-need imposed by modern consumption clearly cannot be opposed by any genuine need or desire which is not itself shaped by society and its history. The abundant commodity stands for the total breach in the organic development of social needs. Its mechanical accumulation liberates *unlimited artificiality*, in the face of which living desire is helpless. The cumulative power of independent artificiality sows everywhere the *falsification of social life*.[34]

Consumption is not just something that exists independent of us. Consumption interacts with us, and shapes us. It holds us as willing captives to our repressed frustrations and unfulfilled dreams. Consuming is, contrary to what we might think, basically a passive activity, and it is at its best in societies where repression is so endemic that the empty receptacle of the population fills itself up only with the products it buys. Implicit in the idea of a spectacle is the presence of (primarily passive) spectators. It calls forth images of mindlessness and powerlessness. We don't do anything while we are consuming; we are not creative beings acting on our environment. One of the reasons consuming works to make us feel good is because it can approximate for us the feelings of being creative.[35] However, when we go shopping, thinking we are making choices about home decorating (shall we decorate our kitchen in Early American or Modern?) we have already foregone the option of doing it ourselves.

Consuming works because it does meet some needs, however, it is ultimately only the shell of real experience. It works because it approximates a satisfaction of some of our basic needs. The advertising industry reminds us that consuming can be both an individual act ("discover the real you") and a social one ("let's go shopping"); it gives us the illusion of having control over our environment (we can decide how to express ourselves in our choices of furniture, clothing, and other matters of taste and style); and we can even create our own social space through our choices of where we vacation and the kinds of hobbies we take up.

Consumerism also impacts how we act politically. In an essay entitled "The Politics of Consumption," Judith Williamson explored the many roles that consuming plays in our lives, and concluded: "The great irony is that it is precisely the *illusion* of autonomy which makes consumerism such an effective diversion from the lack of other kinds of power in people's lives."[36] Paul Goodman agrees, asserting that the American Standard of Living is a substitute for real social and political involvement:

The anomie of middle-class people . . . appears rather as their privatism; they retreat to their families and to their consumer goods—areas in which they still have some power and choice. It is always necessary to explain to non-Americans that middle-class Americans are not so foolish and piggish about their standard of living as it seems; it is that the standard of living has to provide all the achievement and value that are open to them. But it is a strange thing for a society to be proud of its standard of living, rather than taking it for granted as background for worthwhile action.[37]

In a consumer society all social relations are reduced to the level of *commodities*—everything becomes grist for the mill of the spectacle. We become what we buy. Everything is consumer, everything becomes "appearance." We relate to one another through the medium of our things. I can recall years ago that when people came to visit, my parents gave them a tour of our house. I was always admonished to "clean my room" because people wanted to "see" how nice "things looked" when they were cleared of dust and debris. I grew up, as many of us did, believing that what things "looked like" was more important than what we thought about or felt. The appearance could become the reality.

Similarly, I recall the changes in my mother's shopping habits when "processed," or frozen, prepared food was first introduced in the grocery stores. A symbol of our family's economic status and wealth was our ability to afford store-bought food rather than the better-tasting, more nutritious home-cooked food. Mothers all over America gardened less and switched to white bread. We had "arrived" and were now successful Americans.

Consumption has also habituated us to aesthetic indifference. One of the little-noticed results of our dependence on machine technology is the loss of contact with tools of any sort. As we have come to depend more on the machine standard as a guide to evaluate the quality of goods, we have lost any external aesthetic standard by which to evaluate our purchases. We buy *Consumer Reports* to compare brands of VCRs, but we have no way of evaluating whether VCRs are a better cultural experience than a visit to a museum. We are no longer connected with a process of making. The less we actually make, the more the quality of goods can be degraded. We are tool-makers after all, and the loss of this ability may radically (and negatively) impact our ability to create.

Here once again we have the inevitable irony of history: industry, invention, scientific method have opened new opportunities, but just at the moment of opportunity, people have become ignorant by specialization and superstitious of science and technology, so that they no longer know what they want, nor do they dare to command it. . . . Certainly this abdication of practical competence is one important reason for the absurdity of the American Standard of Living. Where the user understands nothing and cannot evaluate his tools, you can sell him anything. It is the user, said Plato, who ought to be the judge of the chariot.[38]

We have seriously eroded our ability to judge the merits of the products we consume, partly because they are no longer connected with basic needs (or even our wants, for that matter), and partly because we have lost the human experience of engagement with the world through the act of production. On a more optimistic note, all hope may not be lost. We still preserve some sense of standards. Our phrase "junk food" is an articulation of our awareness that the "system" at its best does not produce quality. It is the nature of mechanized systems to reduce things to their lowest common denominator, and we can sense the fraudulent and the phony.

However, even though we have discovered a worm deep in the core of our dream of abundance, we still cling to the dubious belief that we can produce ourselves out of our problems—that somehow, technology will save us. Although we are not ready to give up our way of life and our habits of consumption, change may be forced upon us. We are learning, perhaps too late, that this compulsive cycle of production and consumption has endangered the health of our environment. The potential destruction of the environment presents some interesting ethical problems. If we do limit production, for example, what about the rising expectations of those poor people who will never achieve the American Standard of Living? Where will we cut production—capital-intensive military hardware or basic human needs? For the first time we can no longer ignore these basic questions, and the answers may well influence the survival of the human species.

CAPITALISM AND ALIENATION: THE LOSS OF COMMUNITY

The ultimate form of alienation is the alienation of the human being from community. Community is our natural context, the place in which we find our social meaning and our individual identity—through work, through sharing, through collective meaning. Capitalism destroyed this natural community and left people as isolated producers and consumers.

Men in civil society act as dissociated beings, as disconnected singulars, not *despite* their reduction to the common level of producer but directly *because* of this reduction. What men have in common—their status as producers and consumers—does nothing to unite them or to forge bonds among them; on the contrary, it is an expression, a social manifestation of their separation one from another.[39]

According to Arendt, Marx went beyond just describing the alienation of the worker from his or her work to explore in depth the impact on the social and political community. Marx always made a distinction between *exchange value*— the value determined by the marketplace where everything is reduced to the level of commodity; and *use value*—value determined by real needs expressed by the community of workers. This distinction is critical, Arendt argues, because "the much deplored devaluation of all things, that is, the loss of all intrinsic worth, begins with their transformation into values or commodities, for from this moment on they exist only in relation to some other thing which can be acquired in their stead."[40]

By insisting that value could be determined by something other than the marketplace, a human-scale measure could highlight the contradiction in capitalism. What was (and is) lost in our new economics of capitalism is some standard or set of universal rules by which value can be determined. Under capitalism, all value is relative to other products in the marketplace. Everything is given value based on the abstract concept of money.

For Marx, the value of work lay in community relations. He was deeply troubled by the massive upheaval of village life created by the factories and the enclosing of the commons, and he was anxious to maintain and enhance the connections between economics and the life of communities. According to Marx, only organized activity by the working class could overcome the alienation inherent in the division of labor.

This is not possible without the community. Only in community with others has the individual the means of cultivating his gifts in all directions; only in the community, therefore, is personal freedom possible. . . . In the real community, the individuals obtain their freedom in and through their association. . . . The [earlier kind of] communal relationship into which the individuals of a class entered, and which was determined by their common interests over against a third party, was always a community to which these individuals belonged only as average individuals, only in so far as they lived within the conditions of existence of their class. . . . With the community of revolutionary proletarians, on the other hand, who take their conditions of existence and those of all members of society under their control, it is just the reverse; it is as individuals that the individuals participate in it. It is just this combination of individuals which puts the conditions of the free development of individuals under their control—conditions which were previously abandoned to chance and which won an independent existence over against individuals just because of their separation as individuals.[41]

In this passage from *The German Ideology*, Marx was endeavoring to respond to Max Stirner's critique of *class* consciousness, which Stirner argued threatened the rights of the individual. However, in this passage Marx still has not addressed the problem of how this "community" will come about, and, in fact, he never did resolve the role of the individual in the revolutionary society of advanced Marxism. To do so, he would have had to explain the "withering away" of the class consciousness that had created the revolution in the first place, in addition to explaining how the state itself would wither away. What Marx overlooked was the fact that a community of workers (Marx's concept of class) could not substitute for the real community of people, and that it was more than work that tied people together in community.

What Marxism becomes, then, is a holding action against the grosser exploitation of workers by the system of capitalism, but it does nothing to halt the inroads of the system of technology on the human spirit and the human community. The problem was the breakdown of the network of economics and politics in community. The solution—class consciousness—did not restore the shattered community, it merely served (in conjunction with the new technological consciousness) to antagonize and hasten the commoditization of the alienated worker. Class consciousness was a product of the division of labor/technology and as such was part of the problem—not the solution to the problem. Class was not real community, but a community growing out of the world of factory work. The context in which the medieval worker was embedded, the political economy of organicism, no longer existed, and the working class was a pale shadow of the former rich community in which work was integrated with all aspects of life, not just the economic.

CONCLUSION: THE TRIUMPH OF THE SYSTEM

Change came swiftly and harshly. By the end of the eighteenth century the commons had been enclosed, and the factories were reproducing themselves across the landscape. Competition now centered on getting and keeping the job and meeting production quotas, rather than on producing a good product that would reflect the power and energy of the worker. It was not only the product that was degraded in the new market economy. The worker him- or herself was now a commodity for sale to the lowest bidder. Despite initial resistance to the new means of production, the next generation of workers was docile and resigned to the new system of manufacture. The worker was shortly to become completely "domesticated."

The decisive nail in the coffin which destroyed real work was the emerging technological reality. Marx's early theories focused on the alienation of the worker from the means of production—his tools and the budding new technologies. He also predicted that the centralization of capital would intensify the shift from human labor to machine labor, as it attempted to minimize the unpredictability of human workers, by moving more capital into fixed assets to enhance profitability. However, while he predicted this shift to machines, he could not have anticipated their ultimate power over the whole of culture. The introduction of the machines, powered by the new steam engines, began the greatest shift in both the material and ideological worlds that humanity had ever seen. Not only did the new technology change the world of work, it changed the very way we think.

NOTES

1. *The Teardrop Millionaire and Other Poems by Morris Rosenfeld*. Selected and translated by Aaron Kramer. (New York, 1955), 19.

2. Peter Kropotkin, *Mutual Aid: A Factor in Evolution* (Montreal, n.d.), 16.

3. Jacques LeGoff, *Time, Work and Culture in the Middle Ages* (Chicago, 1982).

4. Ibid., 35–36.

5. Ibid., 48.

6. Ibid., 29.

7. Ibid., 61.

8. Ibid., 118.

9. Ivan Illich, *Shadow Work* (Boston and London, 1981).

10. LeGoff, *Time, Work and Culture*, 121.

11. John Zerzan and Paula Zerzan, *Industrialism and Domestication* (Detroit, 1979), 1.

12. Ibid., 2.

13. Peter Kropotkin, *Fields, Factories and Workshops Tomorrow* (New York, 1974), 153.

14. Ibid., 154.

15. Zerzan and Zerzan, *Industrialism and Domestication*, 5.

16. Kropotkin, *Fields, Factories and Workshops*, 171.

17. Perry Miller, *The American Puritans: Their Prose and Poetry* (Garden City, NY, 1956), 171.

18. Mulford Sibley, *Political Ideas and Ideologies: A History of Political Thought* (New York, 1970), 324.

19. Paul Thomas, *Karl Marx and the Anarchists* (London, 1980), 158.

20. William Morris, *Political Writings of William Morris*, edited by A. L. Morton (New York, 1973), 105.

21. E. F. Schumacher, *Good Work* (New York, 1979), 123.

22. Hannah Arendt, *The Human Condition* (Chicago, 1958), 126.

23. Evelyn Glenn and Roslyn Feldberg, "Degraded and Deskilled: The Proletarianization of Clerical Work," *Social Problems* 25 (October 1977): 53.

24. Ibid., 55–56.

25. For a more detailed discussion of Marx's argument, see Karl Marx, *Capital: A Critical Analysis of Capitalist Production*, Vol. 1, ed. Frederick Engels and trans. Samuel Moore and Edward Aveling (Moscow, 1965), 71–84.

26. Mulford Sibley, *Nature and Civilization: Some Implications for Politics* (Itasca, IL, 1977), 39.

27. Brian Keeble, "Introductory," in Eric Gill, *A Holy Tradition of Working: Passages from the Writing of Eric Gill* (West Stockbridge, MA, 1983), 31.

28. Twelve Southerners, "I'll Take My Stand," in *American Issues 2*, edited by Merle Curti, Willard Thorp, Carlos Baker, and Joseph A. Dowling (Philadelphia, 1971), 405.

29. Fredy Perlman, *The Reproduction of Daily Life* (Detroit, 1972), 4.

30. Guy Debord, *Society of the Receptacle* (Detroit, 1977), 14, 34.

31. Ibid., 40.

32. Twelve Southerners, "I'll Take My Stand," 407.

33. Debord, *Society of the Spectacle*, 51.

34. Ibid., 68.

35. Judith Williamson, *Consuming Passions: The Dynamics of Popular Culture* (London and New York, 1986).

36. Ibid., 233.

37. Paul Goodman, *People or Personnel* and *Like a Conquered Province* (New York, 1968), 342.

38. Paul Goodman and Percival Goodman, *Communitas: Means of Livelihood and Ways of Life* (New York, 1960), 14.

39. Thomas, *Karl Marx and the Anarchists*, 55.

40. Arendt, *The Human Condition*, 165.

41. Karl Marx and Frederick Engels, *The German Ideology*, Parts I and III, translated and edited by Roy Pascal (New York, 1977), 74–75.

Chapter 4

Technology and Work

The *Kalevala*, the epic poem of the Finnish people, contains the story of the Sampo, a wondrous machine that is forged by a powerful smith. It becomes an object for contention throughout the entire poem as the people of Kaleva attempt to retrieve it from the North Farm folk.

The craftsman Ilmarinen agrees to forge the Sampo in exchange for the hand of a beautiful woman, and he calls up the powers of the four winds to help him create the wonderful machine:

> At the end of the third day   craftsman Ilmarinen
> bent down to look   at the bottom of his forge;
> he saw that a Sampo was being born,   a lid of many colors
>   forming.
> The craftsman Ilmarinen,   eternal smith,
> taps away fast,   pounds away spiritedly.
> He forged the Sampo skillfully: on one side a grain mill,
> on the second side a salt mill,   on the third a money mill.
> Then the new Sampo ground away,   the lid of many colors went
>   round and round;
> it ground a binful in the dawn,   one binful of things to
>   eat;
> it ground a second of things to sell,   a third of household
>   supplies.[1]

In another version of the story, the mistress of the farm sets the mill to grinding, filling her house with the bounty of the machine. But when she wanted the Sampo to stop, she encountered a problem:

"Enough! Enough!" she cried, at length. "Stop your grinding! I want no more."
The tireless Sampo heard not nor heeded. It kept on grinding, grinding; no matter on

which side it was placed, its wheels kept running, and flour, or salt, or gold and silver kept pouring out in endless streams.

"We shall all be buried!" shouted the Mistress in dismay. "Enough is good, but too much is embarrassment."

Forthwith she caused the Sampo to be taken with becoming care to a strong-built chamber underneath a hill of copper. There she imprisoned it behind nine strong doors of toughest granite, each of which was held fast shut by nine strong locks of hardest metal. . . . But through the keyhole of the ninth lock of the ninth door there issued a sweet delightful whirring sound as of wheels rapidly turning. The Sampo was grinding treasures for Dame Louhi's people, and laying them up for future uses—richness for the land, golden sap for the trees, and warm and balmy breezes to make all things flourish.[2]

The promise of riches and the dream of leisure—the twin fantasies of human labor—coalesce in even the most ancient of myths. How few heartbeats lie between the myth of the Sampo grinding away creating endless prosperity and the faith that our own contemporary technology will save us. It is the same story—the hubris of the human who lives by faith in his or her infinite ability to reshape the world to his or her own needs and wishes.

Throughout history, humanity has dreamed, invented, and schemed ways to ease our labor. It is what makes us human, after all, this ability to shape tools to transform the material world. Our dreams of leisure and satiety become the tools and the reality of technology. The dream of technology gives birth to the machine.

The Sampo is only one expression of our eternal search for the machine that will run itself. Over the centuries we have been delighted and disappointed with the imaginative perpetual motion machines—mechanical engineering fantasies of gears and levers, belts and pulleys that would produce energy to do work ceaselessly. It didn't matter that the laws of the physical universe had to be overcome. Somehow, somewhere, someday we felt that a machine would be invented that, once it started up, would keep running without further effort.

It seems somehow fitting that the dream of abundance created by the machines has manifested itself in the United States. As a people we have had the longest and most enduring passion for the machine. That ever-astute observer of the American character, de Tocqueville, was the first of many to comment on our passion for mechanical gadgets of all sorts. "Yankee ingenuity" is a phrase lying deep in the heart of every girl and boy who has ventured to take apart a radio or a watch. We have created a whole world of machines to complete tasks more efficiently, to substitute energy from nature for human energy, and to reap the abundance of nature.

However, we have also come to know the darker side of the machine: once set to running, it never ceases to reproduce itself. It tirelessly and endlessly produces wealth, but the abundance created mechanically has a price—it takes on a life of its own. Herein lies the dilemma of our economy: Built on the seemingly inexhaustible productive powers of the technological era, rampant consumption has not made us a happy people. In the last days of the twentieth century we are beginning to sense the sinister side of technology and its machine-made abundance. The machines grind on and on, producing more and more junk to dull our senses, and fill our land with endless streams of ever more clever products produced by ever more clever machines. We are beginning to choke in the poisonous environment, and indeed, we are on the verge of fouling our nest so thoroughly that it will be unable to heal itself.

MARXISM AND INDUSTRIAL TECHNOLOGY

Marx documented both the promise and the peril of the machines. He knew that eventually the workers would be replaced by machines and that the purpose of the division of labor was to simplify the work so that either a machine could do it or the worker would be forced to work in a machine-like manner to achieve the efficiency of a machine. However, he never anticipated the power of the technological reality to nearly destroy the human spirit. "Everywhere—in developed and underdeveloped nations alike—the speed of technological change seemed to paralyze men for its control: they became the prey of those very forces against which the classical political philosophers had warned them."[3]

The new technological reality also hindered the development of human collective consciousness—technology created a "machine consciousness" that destroyed both the occasion and the impulse for human community. Instead, the machines created anonymous, interchangeable, "individual" workers. There was "your" work and "my" work, but no longer "our" work, our social labor. Mass production created the mass mind: A functional, non-thinking automaton that capitulated without a whimper to the magic of the machines and their abundance. Viewed with contemporary hindsight, the unquestioned embrace of technological advancement was a tragic error in Marxist theory. Many anarchists, in fact, identify the source of the passivity of the working class in Marxist theory itself:

[The workers' domestication] is their acceptance of the development of capital as theorized by Marxism, which is itself the arch-defender of the growth of productive forces. In the course of this development, the proletariat as producer of surplus value has been denied even this function by the generalization of wage labour and the destruction of any possible distinction between productive and unproductive work. The once revered proletariat now become the strongest upholder of the capitalist mode of production. . . . The left all believe that the process of production, being rationality in action, only needs to be made to function for human needs. But this rationality is capital itself.[4]

The technological reality changed the worker so irrevocably, Jacques Camatte believes, that even if the worker were able to take back control of the means of production, the technology itself would continue the enslavement of the worker. We have all been domesticated by the abundance produced by the machines, and the result is that the people never rebel. Class issues also become irrelevant when even the so-called managers are held hostage by the technological system.

The new technological reality created a new community of workers—the working class—but it was a machine-made community, and as such it could not approximate real community. This accounts, I believe, for the mixed success of unionization in the United States. Despite the fact that people who worked together developed a special comradery and organized unions to control pay and working conditions, workers never developed a meaningful and effective political organization based on class consciousness. The problem with the concept of class is that, like the rest of the technological reality, it too treated the worker as a unit, as interchangeable and autonomous. It was a concept that fit perfectly with the idea of mass production. As such, Marx's concept of class only served to remind workers how far they had come from true community, and how far they had to go to reclaim that community.

THE TECHNOLOGICAL HEGEMONY

In this section I will undertake a critical examination of the broad characteristics of the overall technological system and its hegemony. Hegemony, in the sense I intend here, is similar to Antonio Gramsci's meaning: an interlocking system of authority that is both cultural and political, and that is

The "spontaneous" consent given by the great masses of the population to the general direction imposed on social life by the dominant fundamental group; this consent is "historically" caused by the prestige (and consequent confidence) which the dominant group enjoys because of its position and function in the world of production.[5]

The domination of a hegemony does not necessarily have to be identified with a particular group of people. In the sense in which I use it here, it can imply a general worldview to which a whole society subscribes. Hegemony includes all the symbols, activities, power relations, and so on that characterize the dominant viewpoint. The technological hegemony is part of the cultural reality in which we live and work, but seldom do we stop and think about its characteristics.

Henry Adams, although he didn't use the word hegemony, understood the impact and power of technology in American culture. Technology is a worldview, a reality, a habit of mind—and one that succeeded the other great hegemony which inspired the building of the great cathedrals in medieval Europe, the spiritual force of the Virgin. Adams, in his *Education of Henry Adams*, drew a powerful analogy between the dynamo and the virgin. At a turn-of-the-century world's fair, Adams first encountered the dynamo, and he describes his sense of awe: "As he grew accustomed to the great gallery of machines, he began to feel the forty-foot dynamos as a moral force, much as the early Christians felt the Cross. . . . Before the end, one began to pray for it; inherited instinct taught the natural expression of man before silent and infinite force."[6] Adams despaired over this emergent technological hegemony whose symbol, for him, was the dynamo. He mourned the loss of the inspiration the virgin had represented in medieval society. There would be, he knew, no poems to the dynamo, this new and terrifying force.

Other critics, like Samuel Butler in his utopian satire *Erewhon*, also tried to warn us about our dangerous fascination with the new mechanistic contrivances. The toolmaker could become the victim of his tools:

Man's very soul is due to the machines; it is a machine-made thing; he thinks as he thinks, and feels as he feels, through the work that machines have wrought upon him, and their existence is quite as much a *sine qua non* for his, as his for theirs. This fact precludes us from proposing the complete annihilation of machinery, but surely it indicates that we should destroy as many of them as we can possibly dispense with, lest they should tyrannize over us even more completely.[7]

It is important to understand technology in this fuller, more complex, and even spiritual meaning. Technology is not just tools and machines—technology is the whole network of tools, machines, people, attitudes, values, and products that result from the activities of this network. It is our economy and our lifestyles. It is our symbol of prosperity. It is our Sampo with the lid of many colors, the kaleidoscope of capitalism.

We have bought a package deal of far more fundamental novelness than simply a set of instruments under our control. It is a destiny which enfolds us in its own conceptions of instrumentality, neutrality and purposiveness. It is in this sense that it has been truthfully said: technology is the ontology of the age.[8]

To explain the force of this power of technology in our contemporary world, Albert Borgmann differentiated between things and commodities. Things are grounded in time and place, and they take their meaning from the cultural context out of which they emerged. It was things that the medieval craftsman produced. Things are the result of real work relations, real social relations—the worker in community. Commodities, on the other hand, are produced by devices and are shabby, inferior copies of things. In the term device, Borgmann identifies the technological hegemony: "In a device, the relatedness of the world is replaced by a machinery, but the machinery is concealed, and the commodities, which are made available by a device, are enjoyed without the encumbrance of or the engagement with a context."[9] The technological hegemony, the reality of the device, takes us from the density, complexity, and richness of the realm of things made through human connections with the material world, and substitutes a culture of alienation: (1) alienation from the process of our work (the making of things that result from the interaction of people with the natural world), (2) alienation from one another (the social context of work that, prior to the rise of factories, was the village or community), and (3) alienation from the things we produce (our aesthetic connection to the products of our labor).

Thus, as the technological hegemony solidified its Weltanschauung, work was degraded, the community was degraded, the products of work were degraded.

We created a world of *commoditization*—of ersatz work, ersatz things, and ersatz community. From the very beginning of the industrial era, the system took on a life of its own—continually feeding back to itself, self-regulating to maintain and perpetuate its objectives. "Marshall McLuhan has encapsulated this ability, indeed essential function, of all technologies in the phrase 'the medium is the message.' The transforming power of techniques is the technique not its content."[10]

As we endeavor to understand the shape of the beast, it is important to remember that technology is also more than the mechanisms that we describe. There is a tendency to want to define the technological in materialistic terms, as inert matter or as mechanical processes. We need to keep in mind as we discuss these characteristics that the technological hegemony is also people—people who believe in technology, people who get rich because of technology, people who use the technology to perpetuate certain political and ethical ends—and even people who are critical of technology. *Technology is not neutral.*

Furthermore, technology is political; that is, it acts on the political life of our society. In later chapters I will develop this argument more fully, but it is important now to plant the seeds of the idea of technology as having political force—what Herbert Marcuse called the "prevailing forms of social control."[11] In *One Dimensional Man*, Marcuse outlines the problem: "The brute fact that the machine's physical (only physical?) power surpasses that of the individual, and of any particular group of individuals, makes the machine the most effective political instrument in any society whose basic organization is that of the machine process."[12] He has serious misgivings about society's ability to first of all see, and second, to alter, its passion for the technological reality. He does not hold out much hope: "The more rational, productive, technical, and total the repressive administration of society becomes, the more unimaginable the means and ways by which the administered individuals might break their servitude and seize their own liberation."[13]

It is difficult, Marcuse argues, to believe that we are even interested in changing this apparently abundant world, since we embrace it so readily and easily. We find it difficult to believe that we are "alienated" from a technological society that serves up a banquet daily. Marcuse describes in detail just how the technological process is political and how it subtly exerts its control over people:

The productive apparatus and the goods and services which it produces "sell" or impose the social system as a whole. [They] . . . carry with them prescribed attitudes and habits, certain intellectual and emotional reactions which bind the consumers more or less pleasantly to the producers and, through the latter, to the whole. The products indoctrinate and manipulate; they promote a false consciousness which is immune against its falsehood. And as these beneficial products become available to more individuals in more social classes, the indoctrination they carry ceases to be publicity; it becomes a way of life. It is a good way of life—much better than before—and as a good way of life, it militates against qualitative change. Thus emerges a pattern of *one-dimensional thought and behavior* in which ideas, aspirations, and objectives that, by their content, transcend the established universe of discourse and action are either repelled or reduced to terms of this universe. They are redefined by the rationality of the given system and of its quantitative extension.[14]

The things that we create have so solidly taken hold in our individual and cultural lives that most writers, like Marcuse, are doubtful that we can ever make the necessary changes to bring technology as a way of life under conscious political control. I will return to this theme as I try to elucidate how the technological hegemony rules our political world. I will begin by exploring the general characteristics of the technological hegemony that rules the modern world.

Technology Is Scientific/Rational

Technological reality is the most obvious product of the scientific worldview. In some ways technology and science are two sides of the same coin, since it is difficult to imagine technology without the scientific method driving it ever forward. Science brings to technology the theoretical supports to define the rational reality—it is logical, it is predictable, and ultimately, it is explainable by the so-called unchanging laws of nature. Technology is the operational side of the coin, and the two became interdependent. The marriage of rationalism to engineering created a new way of thinking in our era: "The scientific method which led to the ever-more-effective domination of nature thus came to provide the pure concepts as well as the instrumentalities for the ever-more-effective domination of man by man *through* the domination of nature."[15]

The benefits of the marriage of science and technology are all around us, and it is difficult to accept that the price we pay for this wealth is the foreshortening of our personal creative powers, the loss of independent political effectiveness, and the destruction of alternative nonrational ways of explaining reality. Only the scientific reality is acceptable in explaining today's world. The imposition of a rational thought process has predictable outcomes:

In technique, whatever its aspect or the domain in which it is applied, a rational process is present which tends to bring mechanics to bear on all that is spontaneous or irrational. This rationality, best exemplified in systematization, division of labor, creation of standards, production norms, and the like, involves two distinct phases: first the use of "discourse" in every operation; this excludes spontaneity and personal creativity. Second, there is the reduction of method to its logical dimension alone.[16]

The closing off of portions of human knowing and experience was the direct result of the adoption of the scientific method. The adoption of the Cartesian scientific worldview made the world knowable only in its material manifestation. In response, the nonmaterial formulations either capitulated to the new worldview or began to define themselves in material terms. A religion calling itself Christian

Science and Marx's concern that his socialism be considered "scientific" reflect this deference to the new scientific worldview. Reality became more predictable, but lost its depth and richness.

Technology Is Mechanistic

True to its materialistic philosophy, the technological reality celebrates the machine. There is a preference for things mechanical and the products characterized by certain mechanical values: the values of standardization, efficiency, and optimal effects.

Standardization. We are all pleased when we can purchase parts for our Minnesota truck in California, and the weary and hungry traveler will know that McDonald's junk food will taste the same in Minneapolis as in New York City. We have come to appreciate standardization and the rather narrow and predictable aesthetics of standardization. Standardization, in fact, means predictability in terms of quality. It has also come to mean lack of expressiveness or individuality. Mass-produced items are the same, but they are not unique or special. They lack the subtlety of handcrafted goods, and they deny us the appreciation of richness and diversity.

As we moved from the medieval world of religion to the Renaissance world of science, there emerged a fascination with all things mechanical. If you knew how something worked, you could, just by observing, know its essence, its character. Philosophies such as sensationalism or utilitarianism went beyond simple mechanical models of the natural world to develop complex theories of psychology, of being, and even of political philosophy, which were predictably mechanical.

Hobbes, dispensing with the subjective half of Descartes' dualism, believed that man, like the universe itself, is a machine. "For seeing life is but a motion of limbs," he wrote, "why may we not say, that all *automata* (engines that move themselves by springs and wheels as doth a watch) have an artificial life? For what is the *heart*, but a *spring*; and the *nerves*, but so many *strings*; and the *joints*, but so many *wheels*, giving motion to the whole body." Every event has a necessary cause. "So that all the effects that have been or shall be produced have their necessity in things antecedent."[17]

In a desire to know, and through knowing to have power over the material world, we forced reality into narrower categories and more simplified descriptions. There is something about the scientific mind that wants always to clarify, to grasp meaning in mechanical, nonambiguous ways. If we can reduce a thing or an idea, or even another person, to its simplest, mechanical form, then we feel we can know it, its essence cannot elude us, and, most important, we can have power over it in the same way that we have power over the tools we create.

Efficiency. Ask anyone to justify a particular technology, and he or she will invariably reply, "We use it because it's more efficient." Efficiency in machines is characterized by simplified tasks and machine-like movements that get the job done in the shortest period of time with the fewest repetitive motions. In some definitions, machines per se are considered efficient—more efficient than people—and hence are preferred. Efficiency can also mean not wasting time, money, or energy. The resulting impatience with human ineptitude, fumbling, or even the slowness of the learning process itself creates a high level of anxiety that probably manifests itself in interpersonal violence and drug use. If we aren't "perfect," we aren't worth anything.

In his study of technological utopian novels, Howard P. Segal identified another facet of efficiency. "Efficiency is not the only machinelike virtue that technological utopians seek to inculcate. Self-control is another," he wrote. Efficiency in personal matters could be expressed through conformity, control of one's emotions, and uniformity in family relations.[18] Mechanical efficiency began in the nineteenth century as an expression of what the machines could do; but by the twentieth century, efficiency had taken on the qualities of a cult characterized by rigidity and militaristic structure. With a passion bordering on obsessive-compulsive behavior, the fascination with efficiency culminated in scientific management and time-motion studies—what some writers refer to as Taylorism. Many of us are familiar with the story and the film entitled *Cheaper by the Dozen*—a humorous application of Taylor's principles to his very large family. Unfortunately, not everyone thought Taylorism humorous. The factory workers who have been forced to endure the humiliation of subordinating themselves to the machine-like philosophy and its total control of their movements have nurtured a deep hostility to having their lives so controlled.

Optimal Effects. The search for achieving the optimal effects of each machine's capabilities was soon generalized into the culture as a whole. Down time in the factory (and in your personal life as well) was waste. Everything had to run at its peak of performance—including the worker. Similarly, "the principle of 'concentration upon effect' has perhaps the widest application of all, from doctor's prescriptions to carefully planned propaganda campaigns, since the notion of optimal effects exercises a literally compulsive hold upon the men of a technical era."[19] Optimal effects, according to Arnold Gehlen in *Man in the Age of Technology*, are effects achieved "with the most sparing means; and [we are] enthusiastic when, once 'primed,' such an effect keeps reproducing itself."[20]

Technology Is Automation: Expansion and Self-Replication

Automation is the result of the tendency of the technological hegemony to increase and multiply its process—machines are designed to make other machines, or a whole series of complex manufacturing systems are connected to one another to produce multiple products. Machine technology breeds machine technology; there is the belief that if a little bit is a good thing, more is better. There are many examples of automation—I once worked in a bottling factory which put bottle caps on bottles. The series of machines that the bottles traversed was automation. Another example is the machine that picks tomatoes. One of the dreams of automation is a factory run totally from a control board—the design and building of self-replicating systems—"combinations of computers, general and special-purpose machines that are capable of reproducing themselves—building all those same computers and machines—from raw materials and a source of energy."[21]

It is also automation that attracts some of the most vehement criticism of technology: Samuel Butler in *Erewhon* wondered satirically whether machines could reproduce themselves.

Surely if a machine is able to reproduce another machine systematically, we may say that it has a reproductive system. . . . But it is man that makes them do so. Yes; but is it not insects that make many of the plants reproductive, and would not whole families of plants die out if their fertilization was not effected by a class of agents utterly foreign to themselves?[22]

The dream of a fully automated technology (I call it efficiency for its own sake) is even closer to realization with recent advances in computer technology. What was possible to automate in the mechanical realm has been transcended by the potential for automation in the whole system of manufacture through developments in the field of artificial intelligence. However, the so-called breakthroughs may be a mixed blessing: "The ability to accomplish a task often creates the need to execute that task—often too frequently. The labor-saving computer can become the labor-making computer."[23]

All of us can think of examples of technology for its own sake; especially when we stand back and examine how dependent we are on some machines that actually take more time than doing the work by hand. Technology also creates its own artificial needs. For example, housework today is far more complex than it was a hundred years ago. As the number and kind of labor-saving devices multiplied, the level of cleanliness expected was correspondingly increased— until today we have a compulsive and obsessive fear of dirt. Judith Williamson has written a wonderfully satirical article on new kinds of dirt that were invented just to sell vacuum cleaners. The *Hoover Book of Home Management* described three kinds of dirt, and of course suggests that one buy a vacuum cleaner that removes all three:

Generously, [the book] recommends various other brand names when it comes to aspects of homecare outside its own province. But in every case, the product, whether a cleanser or a kitchen suite, is wheeled on as the "answer" to a "problem," while in fact *the product itself defines the problem it claims to solve*. (emphasis mine)[24]

Jack Miller, a good friend and fellow Luddite, talks about this tendency of technology to create "more bother." As the technology becomes more sophisticated, we are forced to deal with more and more detail: the finicky lawn mower that won't start, the constant frustration dealing with the enigmatic automobile. Similarly, John Ryan recommends that we simplify our lives.

We must learn to prefer a few essential, efficient and usable instruments to a multiplicity of luxurious, distracting, fragile and quickly obsolescent gadgets. For not only do most of even the so-called time-saving devices not make or pay for themselves, but they also need to be operated, conserved and protected; so that they can lure us into too complicated and "tranquilized" a rat race of a life. To fail to recognize this fact is to miss the point of Caesar's calling his equipment *impedimenta*; things that slow down one's progress through getting in "the way of one's feet."[25]

If we use a simple tool, our relationship with it is immediately understood. The more complex tools become, the more we have to continually tinker with them to even get them to work.

Paradoxically, Borgmann reminds us, the more highly automated the technological system is, the more "concealed" the machinery becomes. It is important to understand this quality of technology, because I believe it accounts for some of technology's seductive qualities. One of the promises of technology is that it makes things more available to us with (apparently) less effort. According to Borgmann, it's the difference between a woodstove and central heating: Both warm you, but the central heating conceals its process of production. You can concentrate totally on the outcome. It is "good" technology when "the machinery make no demands on our skill, strength, or attention, and it is less demanding the less it makes its presence felt."[26] Technology should never make itself obvious, he goes on, and the key to the level of sophistication of the technology is "the concealment and unfamiliarity of the means and the simultaneous prominence and availability of the ends."[27]

The more concealed the machinery becomes, the more we lose a sense of connection and engagement and interaction with the world around us. We also lose control of a vast portion of our lives. Advances in miniaturization of electronic circuitry mean that I can't fix my own television set. It is no longer a matter of just testing and buying a new tube: Now I need another machine to diagnose the problem. In contrast, in a simpler technology every product or function is connected in some way with its maker. The maker is known through his product; the human hand is apparent in the product. This means that the user can know how it is made and theoretically can, with the proper tools, repair it. Complex technology destroys this sense of knowing by the user.

In addition, the level of concealment is indicative of our social estrangement from one another. We no longer think of a person as we handle our new toaster or fold the sheets that someone else has made. In many cases we do not want to know the maker. In other cases, when the things don't work, we want to confront the maker about their shoddy work. This is how the machines exert their control over us. The producer or the worker disappears, and we disappear too, the more automated our world becomes. As technology becomes more automated, it grows more alien and distant from our knowledge and control. We then become increasingly dependent on the process of automation itself.

Within the cultural psyche, there is also a deep but well-hidden fear of technology. Unconsciously, perhaps, this fear comes as a result of our growing dependence on the machines, and manifests itself in our concern about loss of control over them. This well-justified fear of runaway technology is also experienced as a general speed-up of our lives.

The tempo of the industrial life is fast, but that is not the worst of it; it is accelerating. The ideal is not merely some set form of industrialism, with so many stable industries, but industrial progress, or an incessant extension of industrialization. It never proposes a specific goal; it initiates the infinite series.[28]

Mary Shelley's *Frankenstein* is a classic study of the fear of the power of science and machines and of our morbid fascination with the borderline between mechanical energy and human energy, between humanity and its tools, between control over the machines and the failure to control them. Our deep fear is that the world could conceivably come so under the control of science that we would even be able to create human life. That the resulting product is monstrous reinforces the image of mechanisms out of control. Frankenstein is the ultimate realization of the dark potential in automation.

The pro-technology people completely disregard the control issue inherent in automated systems. Cybernetics and systems science comprise, they argue, a liberatory technology—the system is so concealed that the user feels less alienated and is more free from the constraints of mechanism than ever before. This freedom is illusory, however. It is merely user-friendly control. One of the founders of systems science, Ludwig von Bertalanffy, reminds us: "Systems science, . . . centered in computer technology, cybernetics, automation and systems engineering, appears to make the systems idea another—and indeed the ultimate—technique to shape man and society even more into the 'megamachine.' "[29]

Technology Has Its Own Cognitive Style

Do machines think? Samuel Butler tried to convince us that they did:

Let any one examine the wonderful self-regulating and self-adjusting contrivances which are now incorporated with the vapour-engine; let him watch the way in which it supplies itself with oil; in which it indicates its wants to those who tend it; in which, by the governor, it regulates its application of its own strength; let him look at that store-house of inertia and momentum the fly-wheel, or at the buffers on a railway carriage; let him see how those improvements are being selected for perpetuity which contain provision against the emergencies that may arise to harass the machines, and then let him think of a hundred thousand years, and the accumulated progress which they will bring unless man can be awakened to a sense of his situation, and of the doom which he is preparing for himself.[30]

Butler's concerns have become our reality. Technology affects the way we think, and further, this particular cognitive style affects how we think about technology, and ultimately how we view social and political institutions in society.

Today we are most comfortable when we think like a machine. This machine mentality is characterized first of all by what Peter Berger calls "a pervasive quality of implicit abstraction."[31] This is the tendency to adopt the stance of the scientist doing an experiment—the neutral observer who studies phenomena in an objective manner. Second, machine thinking has a tendency to deal only with the parts of reality. It is knowledge based on a simplification of the scientific experimental method in which you isolate some phenomenon from the larger reality to study it independently of its context. The application of this mode of thinking to the everyday world creates several observable reactions: We may develop a preference for narrow-minded thinking such as one-issue politics, or we may feel unable to analyze the meaning of any specific knowledge beyond itself, e.g., seeing only the trees and remaining oblivious to the forest. This reduces our ability to understand complexity, to generalize. This, in turn, leaves us open to being manipulated.

Arnold Gehlen sees machine thinking in an experimental attitude toward life in general. This experimental attitude is characterized by an indifference to content and an overemphasis on manipulation, as one would alter ingredients in an experiment to observe changing effects, and by increased interest in formalized tools and applying them to a variety of subjects (testing hypotheses). Gehlen also observed the tendency in a scientific/technological culture to prefer mathematical methods in every field. A good example of this preference is the ascendancy of the need for data to back up our perceptions. He also criticized the growing specializations in every field, which deny accessibility to these realms of knowledge by the average person.[32]

Finally, there is a general homogenization of thought process/knowledge simply by the manner in which information is categorized and by the fact that we think everything can or should be categorized. We see this most clearly in the organization of information by the computer, and unless programming becomes more sophisticated,

the ways that computers can be used for storing and transmitting information can only be ways that increase the tempo of the homogenising processes. Abstracting facts so that they can be stored as information is achieved by classification, and it is the very nature of any classifying to homogenise.[33]

Technology Is Disconnected from Nature

Humanity has always struggled with nature. However, until the industrial revolution, that relationship was always perceived as just that—a relationship.

At the time of the Renaissance, for example, alchemy was the dominant scientific philosophy. The alchemists saw their work as completing the works of creation begun by God, and so it was a natural progression of a process begun in nature. Their science was one of finding and enhancing relationships between elements, a more cooperative science, if you will. The end of alchemy was intimately linked with the "will of God" as it revealed itself in the religious hegemony.

Paracelsus believed what was written in the bible, that everything was created from nothing; but the creation, even if entirely accomplished, was not entirely completed. He believed that the earth was created for man . . . and the completion of the creation is therefore envisaged anthropocentrically: everything was created *ex nihilo* but not in the form in which it is used by man. The necessary completion of the creation is accomplished by fire and its master, Vulcan.[34]

Thus, the role of the alchemist was to bring the human creative elements to the process of creation, and with the agent of change—fire—to complete the process begun by nature.

With the coming of the industrial revolution, however, both a qualitative change in the philosophy and practice of science, proposed by Francis Bacon, and a quantitative change in the use of technology powered by new sources of nonhuman energy, served to initiate an entirely new relationship between humanity and nature. The new scientific logic of domination replaced the biblical ethics of stewardship and responsibility. The goal of modern science was to dissect nature, to finally triumph over the unknown. The unknown could be known, and, once known, it could be brought to heel and used to a new purpose— fulfilling the will of humanity. As the religious worldview faded before the new scientific worldview, what sanctions might have been administered from a religious perspective were overridden by the scientific imperative, which offered no guidelines to limit the ends to which technology might be put.

One of the principal characteristics of the technological reality is the ability, and indeed the mission, to dominate nature. Science probes the secrets of the universe, and technology develops the tools to make them the property of humankind. Technology frees us from biological determinism. No more are we subject to the forces of nature, Mulford Sibley concludes: "As the tools become more complex, the primitively natural recedes in significance, and man often tends to believe that he has completely transcended Nature."[35]

The technological mind marvels at the creations of machines in much the same way the medieval mind marveled at the wonders of God's creations. However, technology also breeds a taste for the artificial, the mechanical. The ultimate power of technology is its ability to create something artificial that looks natural. Here is the final coup de grace: Nature became so unimportant that it could be disregarded entirely. Humanity had finally replaced God as the ultimate creator. Not only could we manipulate the natural world, we could transcend it.

As technology and science made significant impacts on the natural world, a note of arrogance was introduced into the relationship between technology and the natural world. Machine-made came to mean better; nature was dirty, impure, imperfect. The need to master the natural world was fulfilled in larger and more impressive projects: to dam the rivers, to monitor with radios the so-called wildlife, to conquer diseases. The circle has been closed, the hegemony is complete: "science, *by virtue of its own method* and concepts, has projected and promoted a universe in which the domination of nature has remained linked to the domination of man—a link which tends to be fatal to this universe as a whole."[36]

CONCLUSION—THE END OF THE DREAM

There is, however, a growing dissatisfaction with the dominant role that technology plays in our culture. We have all stood helpless in front of a machine that has taken our last quarter, and we are uneasy about the pollution of our environment. Even medicine, which for so long has been the primary raison d'être for the technological advancement, is crumbling before our eyes. We now know that medical science is not infallible: The knowledge that AIDS has no cure has struck terror in hearts around the world. Clearly, the technological system's shortcomings are becoming more apparent.

This dissatisfaction may initiate a major shift in cultural values. Where will the impetus for change originate? It will most likely come from a growing environmental movement that finally impresses on our society the destructiveness of the technological reality on the biomes; from the development of new societal values that understand that there are limits to growth; or from the ascendance of values of asceticism over the values of consumption.

At minimum, this healthy and growing skepticism about technology could begin with the establishment of new ethical guidelines to bring technology back under human control. We have already begun to identify areas of the economy and the environment where we see a need to set limits on technological expansion: In the debate over the "Star Wars" defense system, even the experts said it wouldn't work; our fear over the discovery of a hole in the ozone layer should result in a worldwide ban of the chemicals causing the environmental damage; we are establishing limitations on the application of medical technologies by establishing the right to living wills; and there is a growing anti–nuclear power movement and many others.

Finally we are beginning to get the message. The limits have been reached— and exceeded—far too many times in far too many ways. The gods have feet of clay. The emperor has no clothes. Technology doesn't work.

NOTES

1. Elias Lonnrot, comp., *The Kalevala: or Poems of the Kaleva District* (Cambridge, 1963), 61.

2. James Baldwin, "The Forging of the Sampo," *The Junior Classics*, Vol. 4, *Hero Tales* (USA, 1938), 132–33.

3. Mulford Q. Sibley, *Political Ideas and Ideologies: A History of Political Thought* (New York, 1970), 589–90.

4. Jacques Camatte, *Against Domestication* (London, 1981), 6.

5. Antonio Gramsci, *Selections from the Prison Notebooks*, ed. and trans. Quentin Hoare and Geoffrey Nowell Smith (New York, 1971): 12.

6. *The Education of Henry Adams* (New York, 1931), 380.

7. Samuel Butler, *Erewhon and Erewhon Revisited* (New York, 1965), 147.

8. George Grant, *Technology and Justice* (Toronto, 1986), 32.

9. Albert Borgmann, *Technology and the Character of Contemporary Life: A Philosophical Inquiry* (Chicago, 1987), 47.

10. Michael Shallis, *The Silicone Idol* (New York, 1984), 81.

11. Herbert Marcuse, *One Dimensional Man* (Boston, 1964), 9.

12. Ibid., 3.

13. Ibid., 6–7.

14. Ibid., 11–12.

15. Ibid., 158.

16. Jacques Ellul, *The Technological Society* (New York, 1964), 78–79.

17. Alan Wheelis, *The End of the Modern Age* (New York, 1973), 43–44.

18. Howard P. Segal, *Technological Utopianism in American Culture* (Chicago and London, 1985), 31.

19. Arnold Gehlen, *Man in the Age of Technology* (New York, 1980), 45.

20. Ibid.

21. Gerard K. O'Neill, *2081: A Hopeful View of the Human Future* (New York, 1981), 57.

22. Butler, *Erewhon*, 150.

23. Craig Brod, *Technostress: The Human Cost of the Computer Revolution* (Reading, MA, 1984), 67.

24. Judith Williamson, *Consuming Passions: The Dynamics of Popular Culture* (London and New York, 1986), 225.

25. John Julian Ryan, *The Humanization of Man* (New York and Paramus, NJ, 1972), 77.

26. Borgmann, *Technology and Contemporary Life*, 42.

27. Ibid., 43–44.

28. Twelve Southerners, "I'll Take My Stand," in *American Issues 2*, ed. Merle Curti, Willard Thorpe, Carlos Baker, and Joseph A. Dowling (Philadelphia, 1971), 406.

29. Morris Berman, *The Reenchantment of the World* (Ithaca, NY, and London, 1981), 285.

30. Butler, *Erewhon*, 158.

31. Peter Berger, Brigitte Berger, and Hansfried Kellner, *The Homeless Mind: Modernization and Consciousness* (New York, 1974), 28.

32. Gehlen, *Man in the Age of Technology*, 26–27.

33. Grant, *Technology and Justice*, 23.

34. Clarence J. Glacken, *Traces on the Rhodian Shore: Nature and Culture in Western Thought from Ancient Times to the End of the Nineteenth Century* (Berkeley, 1976), 467.

35. Mulford Q. Sibley, *Nature and Civilization: Some Implications for Politics* (Itasca, IL, 1977), 162.

36. Marcuse, *One Dimensional Man*, 166.

Chapter 5

Work and Freedom

Where there is no vision, the people perish.

—The Bible

The character of our technological world—its centralized control, its dull and mindless work, and its tendency toward so-called scientific habits of mind and action—is systematically eroding the democratic institutions of our society. Alienated, powerless, and domesticated, we turn away from human interaction and submerge ourselves in the mind-deadening drugs of television, robot-like work, and the endless parade of things to buy.

People in industrial technological societies have lost both personal and collective freedom. Our votes are meaningless exercises in choosing between Tweedledum and Tweedledee, and the best media campaign usually wins. Real issues are never explored, and our political participation is limited to voting once every four years—and only 50 percent of us still bother to do even that. The formerly sacred halls of Congress—a democratic people's check on the abuses of government—are filled with millionaires that we reelect 97 percent of the time. We have given up responsibility for government, thoughtful political dialogue and educated activism in exchange for "thirty pieces" of techno-junk— VCRs and TV dinners wrapped in non-biodegradable plastic—the modern counterpart of the Roman bread and circuses. Democracy means participation, but we retire to the living room couch each evening rather than protest the local garbage incinerator that is polluting our air.

It is the nature of the work we do and the organizational environment in which it is done that has most seriously undermined political freedom. We have become indifferent to the political life of the community, and democracy is clearly in decline. In order to begin the process of reclaiming that freedom, it is important to understand the nature of our current powerlessness.

ALIENATED LABOR AND POLITICS

The alienation of the worker from both a creative outlet and control of the process of production, coupled with the objectification of the individual in the marketplace, have had a profound impact on politics at both the theoretical and the practical levels. In this section I will examine the erosion of three basic habits of mind that must be present for enlightened political decision making and effective political action: a sense of connection, a sense of empowerment, and a sense of the whole. They also represent the important building blocks of democracy: ethical responsibility, active engagement in the political life of the community, and an informed citizenry. The absence of these qualities threatens democracy and encourages the growth of fascism and authoritarian systems of governance.

The loss of a sense of connection with the world through the process of creating. It was Marx's belief that when we interact with the material world and become engaged, the process of being engaged itself is the essence of work, which becomes, therefore, an expression and fulfillment of the self. A critical element of non-alienated work is work that takes place in a *context* (i.e., an interaction between self and the environment that sees work as a process). When work is *contextualized*, it becomes meaningful both to the individual and the social community. Contextualized work also implies interaction with other people. People who are free to communicate with their coworkers, for example, indicate greater job satisfaction. As work becomes more mechanized, the individual is alienated from both him- or herself and the product of work. According to Marx: "A direct consequence of man's alienation from the product of his work, from his life activity, and from his species-existence, is the *alienation of man from man.*"[1]

Skill is also critical to the level of engagement with the world. The more highly skilled the work, the more likely it will command attention and excitement. The loss of skill, which occurs as a result of separating work from its context and replacing individual initiative with a mechanized process, has affected both the worker's physical experience of the world and his or her social experience.

Physical engagement is not simply physical contact but the experience of the world through the manifold sensibility of the body. That sensibility is sharpened and strengthened in skill. Skill is intensive and refined world engagement. Skill, in turn, is bound up with social engagement. It molds the person and gives the person character.[2]

By extension, as the technological process simplifies work through the division of labor, the smaller the area of work on which one focuses, the more the human intellectual horizon is diminished. We become habituated to the narrower vision, the small field. The result is lower expectations both intellectually and socially. Mechanization of work kills curiosity and the attendant human impulse to become engaged, involved. If the world seems to operate in a machine-like manner, we are also less likely to feel that people can interfere or interrupt the mechanism. In the same way that we used to see the hand of God in certain activities, we now capitulate to the hand of the machine. The political implications are clear:

Those holding a reified view of the world would thus seem to be less likely to try to change it. And by the same token, those with less intellectual flexibility, those less able or willing to adopt alternative perspectives, may be less open to considering why and how the social world might be changed. This could also inhibit effective political actions.[3]

The loss of a sense of empowerment and of being in charge of one's own actions. The ability to perceive the connection between means and ends is crucial in the development of political and ethical behavior. When we are in control of the process of production, we are able to project ourselves into the world as an integrated extension of self through its interaction with the objective physical, material world. When the human being no longer controls his or her own actions and is instead subject to the actions of the machines, the self is thwarted in its process of self-actualizing. Instead, it turns inward on itself and becomes part of the machine. Disconnected from the objective world, we remain in the subjective, and by analogy we are less receptive to social activity and political action. Marx described this quality of alienated labor:

First, is the fact that labor is external to the laborer,—that is, it is not part of his nature— and that the worker does not affirm himself in his work but denies himself, feels miserable and unhappy, develops no free physical and mental energy but mortifies his flesh and ruins his mind. The worker, therefore, feels at ease only outside work, and during work he is outside himself. He is at home when he is not working and when he is working he is not at home. His work, therefore, is not voluntary, but coerced, *forced labor.* It is not the satisfaction of a need, but only a *means* to satisfy other needs.[4]

According to Marx, it is only at home that the worker feels any empowerment. Being at home, as Marx uses the term here, means having an awareness of the self in relation to work, to other people (family and community), and, most importantly, to the feeling of being free—free politically and free to structure work and meet one's own needs. Alienated work denies workers this sense of community, of connection, which Marx defines as a basic need of human beings. People grounded in an experience of being at home and in community are free to express themselves and to exercise some level of control over the objective reality.

A worker who is alienated from his or her job experiences feelings of powerlessness and meaninglessness. The division of labor gives control of the process of work to the managers. In many cases, workers have no idea how their own work contributes to the product being made. In addition, workers are often isolated from other people by such things as noise level or having to interact only with a machine. They may even lose a sense of connection with the managers, and come to feel that the machine is controlling them. If individual workers have no arena in which to exercise control, no specific goal or even reasons and purposes to work, or are ignorant of how the work they do will contribute to the community as a whole, then both work and the life of the community become degraded.

The loss of the sense of the whole, of ways in which the parts relate to one another. A culture of work based on a division of labor that breaks everything down to its component parts and then gives the individual only part of the whole process or task deadens an important political skill—the ability to make connections between means and ends. To think and act politically and ethically, we need to understand how our actions impinge on others. Without a sense of how the parts of our work are connected or how our work is connected with the work of other people, we lose the capacity to understand how any of our actions connect with and impact on others. Without this sense of connection which lies at the base of all ethical community, there is no way to evaluate our actions or those of others. When work is viewed as meaningless, a habit of mind is created in which one feels that any action, even political acts, is also meaningless. An ethical community contains a sense of responsibility and commitment to others. If workers are alienated from the product they create, there will be a corresponding alienation from a sense of responsibility.

A different but related problem centers on how a mechanistic worldview simplifies our understanding of cause and effect and of how things are related and connected in general. The reductionist logic of materialism leads us to believe that thinking is linear—that one can deduce meaning by simply understanding what went before, or that we can know the whole simply by adding up the parts. It is a simplistic view of how the world really works. This simplistic quality which Peter Berger, Brigitte Berger, and Hansfried Kellner call *componentiality* has a predictable outcome: "the separability of means and ends."[5] That separation, in turn, has a dramatic impact on politics and political thinking.

As a result, we almost unconsciously develop a preference for "logical" explanations, and we become impatient with ambiguity. We also give up the habit of mind that seeks to understand how things are connected or related. We are more interested in how reality is broken down, separated. In addition, this preference for the "easy" and "simple" explanation eventually leads us to prefer a simpler, more homogenized reality in which even people are reduced to their lowest common denominator. We prefer, according to Arnold Gehlen, people who are interchangeable functionaries:

Personal characteristics which hinder such a development appear unwanted, no matter whether possessed by a genius or by a socially maladapted individual . . . and if it is possible to say that each major social order is embodied in a distinctive, representative, proverbial (as it were) human type, the "specialist" stands for ours.[6]

One important result of the world being broken down into its parts is the breakdown of interpersonal activities and communication of a meaningful sort between workers. When people see their world in parts, they come to see people as isolated from one another. In such an alienated environment, all control of communication falls to those having the whole under their charge. In the case of work, this means management: "Accompanying the progress of accumulation of separate products and the concentration of the productive process, unity and communication become the exclusive attribute of the system's management."[7]

These three habits of mind—a sense of connection, a sense of being in charge of one's actions, and a sense of the whole—are critical to the political life of community. Where they are absent there is a low level of participation and action. The alienation from work carries over to alienation from community and the political process. In the next section, I will explore in more detail how technology shapes political culture.

THE POLITICAL CULTURE OF TECHNOLOGY

There are many qualities of an industrial/technological society that jeopardize the effectiveness of democratic political activity. The culture of technology is based on an organizational structure of oppression that is both a political structure and an economic one. As I said before, technology is not neutral. Technology is organized in such a way as to maintain control. Control, of course, is a political concept, and ultimately technology is about the accumulation of political power and control. More important, however, we must understand that "domination perpetuates and extends itself not only through technology but *as* technology, and the latter provides the great legitimation of the expanding political power, which absorbs all spheres of culture."[8] Furthermore, the technological hegemony has its own power structure and its own implicit political agenda:

Technology is not a simple tool which can be used in any way we like. It is a form of social organization, a set of social relations. It has its own laws. If we are to engage in its use, we must accept its authority. *The enormous size, complex interconnection and stratification of tasks which make up modern technological systems make authoritarian command necessary and independent, individual decision-making impossible.* (emphasis mine)[9]

Samuel Butler was one of the first individuals to articulate our unease with the technologies we have created—especially the political implications of the potential for loss of control over them. He was particularly alarmed at the tendency toward automation—the process of machines making and controlling other machines—and concludes: "I fear none of the existing machines; what I fear is the extraordinary rapidity with which they are becoming something very different to what they are at present."[10] Butler was prophetic in his understanding of the tendency and capacity of technology to become its own master and promote its own logic. Mulford Sibley too was concerned with our dependence on the machines: "Beyond a relatively primitive level, men become so dependent on machines that the machines in effect take over, direct, and sometimes destroy their creators.''[11] This fear of the potential of machines to surpass our abilities to rule them has been a staple plot in dystopian novels and films: Witness the insane computer Hal in the movie *2001* who turned on his human masters.

Our previous tools were based on simpler technologies that were largely extensions of human motor skills, and it was clear who was the real master of work. However, with the ascendance of the machine-driven technological hegemony, there was an exponential increase in the power of tools. We have created a qualitatively different reality that has impressed itself deeply on our political and social lives.

Today, we are enmeshed in an intricate web of technological systems that have grown so independent of our conscious control that we are scarcely aware of their power over our lives. Jerry Mander, in a book exploring the cultural and political impact of television, argues, for example, that technology can, in and of itself, be ideological and shape political reality:

Television has no democratic potential. The technology itself places absolute limits on what may pass through it. The medium, in effect, chooses its own content from a very narrow field of possibilities. The effect is to drastically confine all human understanding within a rigid channel. . . . What is revealed in the end is that there is ideology in the technology itself. To speak of television as ''neutral'' and therefore subject to change is as absurd as speaking of the reform of a technology such as guns.[12]

It is the self-referencing quality of technology and the political implications of that quality on the technological world that Hannah Arendt identified when she described the tendency ''to design objects for the operational capacity of the machine instead of designing machines for the production of certain objects.''[13] In other words, the mechanism of the totality of the technological reality begins to define itself only in terms of itself.

A surgical operation which was formerly not feasible but can now be performed is not an object of choice. It simply is. Here we see the prime aspect of technical automatism. Technique itself, ipso facto and without indulgence or possible discussion, selects among the means to be employed. The human being is no longer in any sense the agent of choice. . . . He is a device for recording effects and results obtained by various techniques. He does not make a choice of complex and, in some way, human motives. He can decide only in favor of the technique that gives the maximum efficiency. But this is not choice.[14]

The machine world takes on a life of its own. There are many examples of this process of self-referencing in terms of product design: The most outrageous object designed with the machine's needs in mind is, of course, the process of the development of ''hard tomato'' that Jim Hightower describes in his book, *Hard Tomatoes, Hard Times*.[15] The hard tomato, he argues, was developed through a collaboration between land grant university biologists and engineers in private enterprise interested in a mechanical tomato picker to replace the human laborer. What they created is a tomato that is both unappealing and unappetizing, but that is easily picked by mechanical means: a tomato designed to accommodate the machine.

In his study of the phenomenon he called "the industrialization of culture," Norman Birnbaum lists means by which political control is maintained through the use of various technologies.[16] Through the capacity of the machines to create massive quantities of goods, and through improvements in mass communications media in particular, domination of our society can be realized. Technology has solidified the centralization of political control:

The control of access to information, the control of the main media of communication, the command of the system of education, allows those who dominate the political order to impose their ideological will upon an intellectually inert population. . . . Moreover, in presenting the world as it is, in suppressing the possibility of critical thought (a suppression itself hardly conscious), the channels of mass communication generally reinforce that political compliance produced by routine.[17]

ORGANIZATIONAL ELEMENTS OF OPPRESSION

In this section I will explore structural characteristics of industrial/technological societies that are roadblocks to political self-expression and collective action: the centralization of decision making, the emphasis on specialization and simplification of the work process, and the passivity created by the technological process that mitigates against involvement and participation in politics.

In addition, certain organizational elements are hallmarks of a technological hegemony: large size, hierarchies, rigidity, bureaucracy. These characteristics are so pervasive that even in his study of technological utopias, Howard P. Segal found that most of the so-called ideal communities were controlled by governments that were hierarchical, centralized, and authoritarian.[18] Mulford Sibley, in *Nature and Civilization*, describes an additional characteristic of technological societies: their tendency to supersede the need for human decision making. "The machines . . . make a mockery of the decision-making process developed by human beings: since the multiplication and use of machines is the decisive factor in social change, politics itself becomes a secondary activity designed to serve the machines."[19]

Size

Large size is a hallmark of technological organization. The pursuit of increased efficiency has led to ever-larger units of organization ("economy of scale"), and of ever-more fragmented and specialized tasks. Of necessity, the larger organizations get, the more they tend to authoritarian structures. Beyond a certain size, for example, hierarchies of communication and control must be developed just to circulate information throughout the organization.

The idea that small size enhances political awareness and involvement is an ancient one. Plato argued in *The Republic*, for example, that in order to maximize the potential for the active involvement of all citizens in politics, the community should be no larger than 5,040 households. Larger communities and large organizations alienate citizens from one another and cut them off from firsthand knowledge that would enable meaningful political participation.

Hierarchy

It is a curious irony of our culture that we pride ourselves on the importance of individualism and independent thinking as part of a democratic process, while at the same time submitting to authoritarian, hierarchical work environments. The essence of hierarchy is centralized decision making. When all decisions are made from the top down by "the bosses," there is little incentive to develop the democratic habit of participating in political decision-making processes. Hierarchies tell us we have no personal role to fulfill and no contributions to make: We simply receive orders from others and act at their behest.

There are several aspects of hierarchy that are important to the relationship between work and politics. The first is hierarchy as it is expressed in the division of labor in highly automated systems.

In a simple division of labor, for example, the worker had a large measure of control over his own working conditions, i.e., the set-up and make-ready, the cleaning and repairing of machines, obtaining his own materials, and so on. Under a complex division of labor, these tasks pass out of his control and he must rely on management to see that they are properly done. This dependence extends along the entire process of production.[20]

The more the work is broken down and divided, the greater the need to establish a hierarchy to organize and coordinate the work. Where these hierarchies of labor exist, the amount of the worker's freedom over control of the work process is one of the most important criteria for determining job quality. In the 1985–1986 Hormel Meat-Packers strike in Austin, Minnesota, for example, one of the most important issues was the workers' control over their own tools—their knives.

Some of the cuts had more far-reaching effects than a loss of money. For example, the time allowed for individual workers to sharpen the knives they used was eliminated. Financially, this amounted to less than $5 per week. But henceforth they were to use presharpened knives and not take the time to do it themselves. . . . Old-timers explain that each person holds and wields a knife slightly differently. By experience they learn the precise sharpening that is most appropriate for them, and the knife becomes shaped to their individual work habit. Presharpened knives, however, are all the same. According to these experts [the long-time workers], the incidence of carpal tunnel syndrome—a nerve disease common among Hormel workers, caused by overloading certain muscles of the wrist and hand—will be increased with the use of presharpened knives.[21]

Hierarchies of kinds of labor also keep us from taking pride in our work by encouraging competition. If you think there is a better job around the corner, you will always disdain the work that you are doing, because you continually believe you deserve a better job "higher up," or with more power or money. The presence of this hierarchy also holds us hostage to the system, because as long as we believe there is a better job out there, we will support and maintain the system and do its bidding to try to get the better job, to improve our own lot.

The second hierarchy that is present in our work is the hierarchy of control—the managers have it, the workers don't. This rigid structure breeds passivity in the worker, both on the job and in the community.

Pateman argues that hierarchical, nondemocratic organizational structures socialize workers into passivity and political apathy, which is reflected in their poor turnout for elections, low levels of community service, and reluctance to participate in voluntary organizations and union, community and political activities.[22]

According to Daniel Bell, working in a hierarchical environment also breeds dependence, and affects what Bob Black calls "our aptitude for autonomy." During our whole lives we are trained to be obedient, first by our educational institutions and then by the workplace: but it is the workplace that is the most oppressive.

People who are regimented all their lives . . . are habituated to hierarchy and psychologically enslaved. Their aptitude for autonomy is so atrophied that their fear of freedom is among their few rationally grounded phobias. Their obedience training at work carries over into the families they start, thus reproducing the system in more ways than one, and into politics, culture and everything else. Once you drain the vitality from people at work, they'll likely submit to hierarchy and expertise in everything. They're used to it.[23]

Work in hierarchical structures so habituates us to passivity and compliance, Norman Birnbaum argues, that our political effectiveness is compromised.

The degree of conscious political consent required of the modern working class, in other words, is not necessarily very large: routine may be counted upon to do what is needed, and the essential aspect of routine is the acceptance of hierarchy at the workplace. Acceptance of hierarchy is even more pronounced for those in the middle class, or bourgeoisie, in administrative and professional occupations. Their very careers entail not only acceptance of hierarchy but factual complicity in its maintenance, in the actual exercise of power.[24]

Specialization and Simplification

During his visit in 1830, de Tocqueville was especially interested in studying the new political theory of democracy and its interactions with work and the new culture of industrial capitalism. One of his concerns was the impact of the division of labor on human creativity: "In proportion as the principle of the division of labor is more extensively applied, the workman becomes more weak, more narrow-minded, and more dependent. The art advances, the artisan recedes."[25] He also believed that the division of labor had a negative impact on the mental and intellectual abilities of workers:

When a workman is unceasingly and exclusively engaged in the fabrication of one thing, he ultimately does his work with singular dexterity; but, at the same time, he loses the general faculty of applying his mind to the direction of the work. He every day becomes more adroit and less industrious; so that it may be said of him, that, in proportion as the workman improves, the man is degraded. What can be expected of a man who has spent twenty years of his life in making heads for pins? and to what can that mighty human intelligence, which has so often stirred the world, be applied in him, except it be to investigate the best method of making pins' heads?[26]

Hannah Arendt made a distinction between specialization and the division of labor. The division of labor "presupposes the qualitative equivalence of all single activities for which no special skill is required," and is based on the perception of work as simply quantities of labor power that can be added together.[27] It assumes that every worker has the same value, and that labor value is determined by combining like quantities. Specialization, on the other hand, is determined by the finished product itself "whose nature it is to require different skills which then are pooled and organized together."[28] She goes on to draw out the political implications of these two different perceptions of the worker:

The formation of a labor collective where the laborers are socially organized in accordance with this principle of common and divisible labor power is the very opposite of the various workmen's organizations, from the old guilds and corporations to certain types of modern trade unions, whose members are bound together by the skills and specializations that distinguish them from others.[29]

In other words, it is difference that distinguishes the laborer under a division of labor from the worker who is valued for his or her individual skills. The standard of a machine economy is *sameness*—the standard of a free economy is *diversity*. Only in a situation of the specialization of labor, where the worker comes willingly to coordinate his or her effort with others, can we have true democratic political activity. The worker under the division of labor does not have the same freedom to choose whether to bring his or her labor into cooperation with others; he or she is probably not even aware of how his or her work relates to the tasks of other workers. Under the division of labor the workers do not bring themselves to the task as whole creative beings. Instead, they merely bring their labor power, the lowest common denominator of the work force. Further, because they see nothing of themselves in their work, they develop no moral or ethical commitment to their work.

There is a moral dimension to this problem; for only open-ended action, reinforced by its own successes, willing to take diverse risks and to assimilate past experiences and failures, can engage deeper and more personal levels of motivation, appeal to an individual's moral core. Yet the specialized tasks, made necessary in such great numbers by the industrial-bureaucratic system, do not require enough inner strength and capacity for growth to evoke a feeling of personal worth.[30]

In such an environment, as so many of us know, the image of the self as valuable, empowered, and capable is never allowed to come into being, and we leave on tasks each day feeling more diminished and powerless. When every aspiration is thwarted, we cease to aspire—for ourselves, for others. Disconnected and fragmented, we cease to care, and an ethical paralysis sets in.

THE DESTRUCTION OF COMMUNITY IN THE INDUSTRIAL ERA

In an ideal society, the individual is embedded in a web of meaningful social relations. Unfortunately, the modern industrial era was predicated on the destruction of traditional community. The network of cultural, economic, social, and political institutions we call community were replaced by the so-called modern individual, who him- or herself became a commodity in the market. These autonomous individuals found themselves living in a society characterized by anonymous social relations. Isolated and severed from traditional community, people gradually lost the skill of participating in political activity. For Wendell Berry, the problem can be traced to the division of labor, which he calls "specialization."

What happens under the rule of specialization is that, though society becomes more and more intricate, it has less and less structure. It becomes more and more organized, but less and less orderly. The community disintegrates because it loses the necessary understandings, forms, and enactments of the relations among materials and processes, principles and actions, ideals and realities, past and present, present and future, men and women, body and spirit, city and country, civilization and wilderness, growth and decay, life and death—just as the individual character loses the sense of a responsible involvement in these relations.[31]

The machine also severed the relationship between work and community. According to Eric Gill, the introduction of the machine destroyed the personalized character of work and threatened the long-standing belief that work was intended to meet specific human needs, and as such, was a function of community. Once work was no longer seen as an exchange between people to meet a human need, the ethical community languished: "If all necessary things are to be made by machinery and with as little human labour as possible (for this is admittedly a necessary corollary), then we should be deprived of any necessity to serve our fellowmen."[32]

Gill believed that work was based on the biblically inspired ethic of "the necessity of personal service—the service of men by one another."[33] If this personal contact between people (made through the creation of one's products for another person's use) were to be replaced by the activities of machines, then the biblical injunction to "do unto others" would be short-circuited, and the moral and ethical woof and warp of the community would be destroyed.

Seldom do the workers of today connect what they make with their friends, family, or neighbors: They produce only to get their paychecks. Production is for the market, not the community, and not even for the workers. All social relations are subsumed under the ethics of the marketplace. St. Thomas Aquinas's injunction against generalizing the ethics of the marketplace to the human community as a whole still rings true today:

Again, if the citizens themselves devote their lives to matters of trade, the way will be opened to many vices. For, since the object of tradesmen leads especially to making money, greed is awakened in the hearts of the citizens through the pursuit of trade. The result is that everything in the city will be offered for sale: confidence will be destroyed and the way opened to all kinds of trickery: each one will work only for his own profit, despising the public good; the cultivation of virtue will fail, since honour, virtue's reward, will be bestowed upon anybody. Thus, in such a city civic life will necessarily be corrupted.[34]

Wendell Berry, like Aquinas and Gill, is concerned about the effect of the machine on community. In a technological society, obedience is more highly valued than cooperation, and allegiances to products and multinational corporations come more easily than ties to family and neighbors. This warped sense of loyalty is central to the corporate mystique which is perpetuated at the highest levels of management: family, community, friends—all take second place to the demands of the system.

The enlargement of industrial technology is thus analogous to war. It continually requires the movement of knowledge and responsibility away from home. It thrives upon the disintegration of homes, the subjugation of homelands. It requires that people cease to cooperate directly to fulfill local needs from local sources and begin instead to deal with each other always across the rift that divides producer and consumer, and always competitively.[35]

The political life of community is especially corrupted by the loss of our decision-making powers to the technological imperative. The power to make choices—real choices—is one of the essential characteristics of a democratic process. To be able to choose is a basic American "right"—a misnomer born of the capitalist imperative to consume. The reality of industrial technology, however, is the denial of choice and diversity in favor of standardization and similarity. We are constantly reminded by the advertising industry that there are many choices to be made, but if television programming is any guide, the average American is well aware that many of the choices we make are between two evils. A general cultural malaise and political passivity often result: When we come to see how little our decisions really mean, we simply cease making them, or defer to the so-called experts whom we believe run the system.

It is difficult to resist the lure of political passivity. The more control we lose over our work, the more habituated we become to non-participation generally. This is not a conscious process, and there are other factors in the culture that contribute to the paralysis. Langdon Winner, writing about the impact of television on the political process, outlines just how the television machine destroys our political participation.

Public participation in voting has steadily declined as television replaces the face-to-face politics of precincts and neighborhoods. The passive monitoring of electronic news makes citizens feel involved while releasing them from the desire to take an active part, and from any genuine political knowledge based on first-hand experience. *The vitality of democratic politics depends on people's willingness to act together—to appear before each other in person, speak their minds, deliberate, and decide what they will do.* (emphasis mine)[36]

Balancing democratic rights are democratic responsibilities. A sense of responsibility is critical to the democratic process and to the life of a community. According to Gill, if the worker is not freely engaged or connected with his or her work, and responsible for it, he or she won't know how to "follow through" and "stand behind" the work. "He who is free is responsible for his work. He who is not responsible for his work is not free."[37] Gill continues:

The real distinction between tools and machines is discovered in the sphere of control and responsibility. Who is responsible for things made or the deed done?—and deeds done, when viewed in themselves and not simply as means to ends, are also to be regarded as things made. Who is responsible for the thing made?[38]

Gill was also critical of individual ownership of the means of production: Since industrialism was introduced to meet the needs of the masses, he argued that the means of production should be nationalized as a "public service." "Of its nature it is not private ownership. Is it not obvious then that the claim to private profits from public services is preposterous and can only be made by fools or knaves."[39] Like Marx, Gill wanted the workers to control the means of production, not only for economic reasons but also to enhance the quality of work and ensure a sense of political responsibility: "For it is only as persons that we serve one another, and when personal control is divorced from ownership, it is only with great difficulty that men retain responsibility for the form and quality of what is done or produced."[40]

CONCLUSION: WORK AND FREEDOM

The quality of our work lives directly influences our experience of freedom. It may be instructive at this point to return to Hegel's definition of work—the self-actualizing activity of the individual to realize her or his fullest potential. The person (as subject) acts on the material world (as object) to transform him- or herself to a new level of self-hood. Marx retained this intentionality in his arguments—to work is to be, and a critical component of being is to be free. In order to be free, one must be able to plan, to act, to change the world. We must intend to be free; we are not made free by accident or by the external world changing us. What makes us human is that we intend to be, and one of the most important ways to express our humanity—to be—is to do good work, and through the doing of good work, to achieve freedom.

Until such time as our society commits itself to rejecting technology's ethic of efficiency, little will change. We must seek value beyond the machine, and the needs of the worker and of people in our communities must come before the needs of the system. Clearly we must begin the task of reclaiming good work to help us better carry out the political activities of a free people. As long as we remain victims of technology and the technological bureaucratic structures of oppression, we remain unfree and powerless. To be truly free, we must reaffirm quality over quantity, process over product, handwork over machines, and the worker over the system.

NOTES

1. Karl Marx, "Economic and Philosophic Manuscripts (1844)," in *Writings of the Young Marx on Philosophy and Society*, translated and edited by Lloyd D. Easton and Kurt H. Guddat (Garden City, NY, 1967), 295.

2. Albert Borgmann, *Technology and the Character of Contemporary Life: A Philosophical Inquiry* (Chicago, 1987), 42.

3. Michael Schwalbe, *The Psychosocial Consequences of Natural and Alienated Work* (Albany, 1986), 154.

4. Marx, "Economic and Philosophic Manuscripts," 292.

5. Peter Berger, Brigitte Berger and Hansfried Kellner, *The Homeless Mind: Modernization and Consciousness* (New York, 1974), 26–27.

6. Arnold Gehlen, *Man in the Age of Technology* (New York, 1980), 147.

7. Guy Debord, *Society of the Spectacle* (Detroit, 1977), 25.

8. Herbert Marcuse, *One Dimensional Man* (Boston, 1964), 158.

9. T. Fulano, "Uncovering a Corpse: A Reply to the Defenders of Technology," *Fifth Estate* 15 (1981): 6.

10. Samuel Butler, *Erewhon and Erewhon Revisited* (New York, 1965), 144.

11. Mulford Q. Sibley, *Nature and Civilization: Some Implications for Politics* (Itasca, IL, 1977), 174.

12. Jerry Mander, *Four Arguments for the Elimination of Television* (New York, 1978), 46–47.

13. Hannah Arendt, *The Human Condition* (Chicago, 1958), 152.

14. Jacques Ellul, *The Technological Society* (New York, 1964), 80.

15. Jim Hightower, *Hard Tomatoes, Hard Times: A Report of the Agribusiness Accountability Project on the Failure of America's Land Grant College Complex* (Cambridge, MA, 1973).

16. Norman Birnbaum, *The Crisis of Industrial Society* (London, 1969), 81.

17. Ibid., 72.

18. Howard P. Segal, *Technological Utopianism in American Culture* (Chicago and London, 1985), 30.

19. Sibley, *Nature and Civilization*, 176.

20. Daniel Bell, *Work and Its Discontents: The Cult of Efficiency in America* (New York, 1970), 9–10.

21. Fred Halstead, *The 1985–86 Hormel Meat-Packers Strike* (New York, 1986), 5–6.

22. Don Mankin, "Autonomy, Control, and the Office of the Future: Personal and Social Implications," in *The World of Work*, ed. Howard F. Didsbury, Jr. (Bethesda, MD, 1983), 167–68.

23. Bob Black, *The Abolition of Work* (San Francisco, 1986), 5–7.

24. Birnbaum, *Crisis of Industrial Society*, 68.

25. Alexis de Tocqueville, *Democracy in America*, ed. and abr. by Richard D. Heffner (New York, 1956), 218.

26. Ibid., 217.

27. Arendt, *The Human Condition*, 123.

28. Ibid.

29. Ibid.

30. Gehlen, *Man in the Age of Technology*, 50.

31. Wendell Berry, *The Unsettling of America: Culture and Agriculture* (New York, 1977), 21.

32. Eric Gill, *Christianity and the Machine Age* (London and New York, 1940), 66.

33. Ibid., 64.

34. St. Thomas Aquinas, *On the Governance of Rulers (De regimine principum)*, Book 2, translated from the Latin by Gerald B. Phelen (Toronto, 1935), ch. 3, 123.

35. Wendell Berry, *Standing by Words* (San Francisco, 1983), 73.

36. Langdon Winner, "Mythinformation," *Whole Earth Review*, January 1985, 27.

37. Eric Gill, *A Holy Tradition of Working: Passages from the Writing of Eric Gill* (West Stockbridge, MA, 1983), 97.

38. Eric Gill, *The Necessity of Belief: An Enquiry into the Nature of Human Certainty, the Causes of Skepticism and the Grounds of Morality, and a Justification of the Doctrine That the End Is the Beginning* (London, 1936), 88.

39. Eric Gill, "Ownership and Industrialism," in *Sacred and Secular &c* (London, 1940), 184.

40. Eric Gill, *Christianity and the Machine Age* (London and New York, 1940), 34.

Chapter 6

Women and Work

Early one fine spring day, the Little Red Hen decided to bake some bread. Her first task was planting the wheat seeds. She went around the barnyard seeking a helper: "Who will help me plant the seeds?" she asked.

"Not I," said the rooster.

"Not I," said the cow.

"Not I," said the pig, and the horse and all the other animals in the barnyard. So the Little Red Hen did the planting herself.

After the wheat had grown, the Little Red Hen had to harvest the grain. Once again, she went around the barnyard seeking assistance: "Who will help me harvest the grain?"

"Not I," said the rooster.

"Not I," said the cow.

"Not I," said the pig, and the horse and all the other animals in the barnyard. So the Little Red Hen did the harvesting by herself.

When the grain was all harvested, she repeated the same process when she needed to grind the corn and when it came time to bake the bread. And in each case, none of the other farm animals would help her in her labors. Finally, when the bread was baked, she asked one last time: "Who will help me eat the bread?"

"I will," cried the rooster.

"I will," cried the cow.

"We will," shouted the pig and the horse and all the other animals. But their cries went unheeded as the Little Red Hen and her chicks sat down to enjoy the freshly baked bread.

—From an old folk tale

Women do two-thirds of the world's work, they receive only 5 percent of the world's income, and they own less than 1 percent of the world's assets. This should, by all accounts, give women special leave to share their insights on the world of work. This is not the case, however, since most studies of work concentrate only on work for wages, ignoring or discounting the unpaid work done in all cultures, most of which is done by women.

The story of the Little Red Hen is the story of women's work: work to ensure the family's survival and meet its need for food and feeding, planting and cooking; work done out of necessity—no matter how you feel and whether or not you have help; and work that is unpaid. Women's work is caring for children, and it is making clothing. In some cultures it is still education. In the United States it is doing the laundry and the shopping, inventorying the groceries, and having the telephone repaired. It is everything, it is thankless, and it is expected.

CONTINUITY AND CHANGE IN WOMEN'S WORK

Across all cultures and throughout historic time, women and men have divided up the tasks that are needed for survival of the family (generally an extended family) or tribal unit. The earliest and most ubiquitous division of work is the sexual division of labor, where tasks are assigned by gender. In most cultures, this division is fairly obvious: Men do the heavy work or work that takes them away from the family or social unit (such as hunting), and women take care of the children and the family's basic needs (those institutionalized tasks that are aimed at providing the support for the continuation of the family, such as gathering food, firewood, and water, and maintaining the dwelling).

Work in pre-capitalist society was conducted within a web of social relationships. Most work was performed for use in the immediate community, for a known group of people. The industrial revolution tore apart this fabric of social/work relations, and by the end of the nineteenth century, the split between work done at home and work done in the factory was formalized into the theory of separate spheres for men and women. From the very beginning of the industrial revolution, women were excluded from the newly emerging production economy for two primary reasons: First, they were not perceived to be economic heads of families, and second, men actively worked to keep them out because women were paid lower wages. Under the putting out system, contracts for work were negotiated with the male heads of households. Women and children worked, in theory, for men, and as "hired hands" they were paid less because the male wages also went to their support. When women entered the wage economy, the capitalists, of course, insisted that women's work was still worth less.

In the domestic industry, the father or husband collected the wages for the family's work; each worker's contribution was not priced separately. . . . When hosiery making became a factory industry, however, women and men earned individual wages. The ideology which constructed women as merely supplementing the wages of the households to which they belonged, and which envisioned women as economically dependent on men, allowed capitalists to pay women less than men for the same work. This, of course, thrust women into direct competition with men for jobs.[1]

Although women held the majority of factory jobs at the onset of the industrial revolution, they were never really considered equal members of the work force. Occasionally, in model communities like Lowell, Massachusetts, which were specially designed to totally control the lives of their female workers, young single women were recruited to work in the mills. However, women's work in factories was never seen as permanent. By and large, as soon as they married most women were expected to leave outside work and remain at home, where they took up the tasks of homemaking, child care, and housework.

As men were forced into the factories, women were "left behind" to take over the household economy, and they continued to operate in this informal, less structured, and more cooperative work environment for nearly a century until they, too, were finally forced into the production economy. Because women were less acculturated to the factory/wage system, they still retain, I believe, habits and styles of work that are significantly different from the work style imposed on men by the new factory system. By studying women and the way they work, we have a unique opportunity to examine pre-technological styles of work, which may provide some clues toward altering the current shape and quality of work.

In this section I will explore the characteristics of three distinct economies in which women work: the production economy, the survival economy, and the service economy. In some cases, economists have collapsed the survival and service economies into a single entity which they call the reproduction economy. The work of women has traditionally fallen into this reproduction economy, although in the twentieth century the service economy is gradually being moved out of the control of women and into the public sphere, where it comes under the control of men and the wage-labor economy.[2]

Women's work, the work of reproduction, or what I call the survival economy, has always been the most significant and critical human economic activity. Anthropological studies in simpler economies based on hunting and gathering have shown, for example, that the bulk of a family's dietary needs were generally provided by the gathering work done by women. The extra protein that might be available through men's hunting activity was unpredictable at best. Clearly, across both cultures and historical time, women have been central to the reproduction economy.

At the dawn of the technological/industrial age, the primacy of reproduction and the importance of that work to the family unit was still recognized in the male worker's demand to be paid a "family wage." As families came to be more dependent on wages to meet their survival needs, and as the economy shifted to a consumer economy where even survival items needed to be purchased, the male workers demanded a wage that was sufficient to care for the whole family, with the woman staying at home. Whether this was money received in recognition of her contribution to the economics of the family, a symbol of how unimportant her contribution was since the extra money may have been for *his* work which the family could no longer count on at home, or whether it was a symbol of what Thorstein Veblen called conspicuous consumption (pay to support an idle wife) is an interesting question. In any case, Heidi Hartmann concludes: "This 'family wage' system gradually came to be the norm for stable working class families at the end of the nineteenth century and the beginning of the twentieth."[3] Other historians disagree, however, arguing that while the family wage was on every union wish list, it was actually achieved by only a small percentage of the work force.

Since women who worked in the production economy were so poorly paid, so another argument went, the family wage allowed them to remain outside the wage system and take care of the reproduction economy. "Hence the labour movement quite logically developed the tendency to calculate the desirable minimum wage in terms of the earnings of a single (i.e., in practice male) breadwinner, and to regard a wage-working wife as a symptom of an undesirable economic situation."[4] In any case, the middle-class myth of making enough money to have one person stay home seems to be just that—a myth. As we have moved into a consumer society, more and more women have been forced into the wage/production economy. Probably not so coincidentally, breadwinner wages are on the decline, and it now takes two wage earners to maintain a lifestyle that one income supported just 25 years ago, and what we call the minimum wage today doesn't even support an individual, let alone a family.

The transition from the survival economy to the production economy was a fairly abrupt one. I would like to describe a general scenario of how the economic transition may have taken place. Initially, women and men work together to farm, to care for animals, and to weave cloth to earn money for items they are not able to produce themselves. The cash income from weaving is unpredictable, and is seen as extra income for the family. With the advent of the factory system, the production work—the weaving—is taken out of the cottage, and the male has to go to work in the factory because the family still needs the cash to buy those items it cannot produce itself. The man's contribution to the shared survival work is now missing, and more of the survival work falls on the shoulders of women. In addition, because of the man's absence, the woman cannot do everything, and the family now has to turn to the cash economy to have more of its basic needs met; for example, they may have to quit farming and buy the wheat to make their bread.

As more of the family's survival needs have to be met by the purchase of goods and services in the production/cash economy, there is an increasing need for more cash. The cost of survival has gone up and dependency on the wage system has been established. The only way to get the extra cash now is for (1) the woman to go to work for wages; or (2) men's wages to increase. Since the capitalists pay women less, the second option is the only viable one. Whose work the wage replaces seems to be the central question on which the economic independence of women turns.

As men moved into the factory in the production economy, women were relegated to the home or reproductive economy. In retrospect, this sexual division of labor seemed the natural one because of women's necessary role in caring for young children. In Eric Hobsbawm's study of working-class iconography, for example, he discovered that even the visual symbols reflecting the status of women's contribution to the economy of the family have changed over time. In the era of utopian socialism at the onset of the industrial revolution, for example, images of utopia emphasized the relationship between women and the abundance of nature. Ceres was the goddess of communism, symbolic of abundance and plenty. Even today the iconography of communism incorporates the sickle. As the production economy became male-dominated, however, the iconography changed: "The image of utopia increasingly shifted from one based on natural fertility to one based on technological and scientific productivity. . . . However iconographically nature/fertility prevailed over technology, certainly until 1917."[5]

Although initially they were the majority of factory workers, women were quickly consciously excluded from the production economy. Male factory workers did everything they could to perpetuate male preeminence in the wage-labor system rightly fearing that women would drive down the level of wages. They also developed so-called moral reasons why women and men should not intermix in the work force.

Often it was the technology itself that created hostility between the sexes. Some of the hostility directed toward women should have been directed at the new technologies and machines that replaced men. Capitalists knew that whenever workers could be replaced with machines, profits were increased. As a result, new technologies were developed by the factory owners as quickly as possible to replace the more skilled workers. In many cases, there was good cause for male resentment: As the technology increasingly automated work, highly skilled, higher-paid men were replaced by less-skilled and lower-paid women.

Marx and Engels were well aware of the negative impact of the emerging capitalist economy on women's economic status. They laid the blame for that gender's isolation and oppression on the division of labor by sex in the nuclear family, and called for women to reject the oppressive institution of the family. Liberation for women could be achieved, they argued, by women entering the wage-labor market and abolishing the separate work sphere of the nuclear family. Once all work had entered the marketplace, domestic chores would also become public work and women would be freed from economic oppression. This conclusion assumed, of course, that domestic work would be as highly valued, say, as work done by a skilled mechanic—a highly unlikely possibility given the subordinate status of women and women's work. History has also shown us that industrialization did not free women from domestic chores.[6] Instead, domestic work continued to be unpaid labor done primarily by women, as women who entered the wage-labor system quickly discovered that they now had two full-time jobs.

Everywhere, the new production economy served to increase women's work and at the same time deny them economic control. The changes that capitalism made in the lives of women can still be observed today. In so-called developing countries (countries which are pursuing a capitalistic development), women are losing long-held positions of power and decision making:

Initial attempts to explore gender and development policies showed that women's status in many Third World countries had declined and that part of the problem was the change accompanying technology's transfer to new social contexts. While men had also been affected, crucial differences in the experience of the sexes resulted in more erosion of women's status. Women were denied their customary rights to land, excluded from agricultural development projects, and deprived of access to new tools, techniques, and training on the same terms as men.[7]

WOMEN AND THE ECONOMICS OF SURVIVAL

Real women's work is survival work. It is an economy of subsistence, of self-sufficiency. Women's work has always concerned the business of survival, the perpetuation of human society. In a recent interview, Ann Kanten, a farmer and a former deputy commissioner for agriculture in Minnesota, reflected on women's commitment to ensuring survival:

During my visit to Africa, I was so impressed by the strength of the African women— their physical strength, as they carried water, logs and such on their heads and backs, as well as their dedication to survival and everything that meant. It's women's responsibility to ensure the very survival of their families, of their children. . . . In our culture, that is not only women's responsibility. Still, our primary concern as women is for our families' survival. Many of us who live on the land in this culture have turned into the fighters. And more and more, women are the ones addressing the survival issues, the policy issues. . . . Women are fighting to keep their farms. It's in that way that we share a lot with women on any continent. Fighting for that piece of land. Fighting to keep the family together.[8]

Survival issues are increasingly becoming the American way of life as women from many different sectors of the culture are confronted with the realities of poverty, lost jobs or farms, and homelessness. In order to survive, there are some basic needs that must be met. In the following sections I would like to explore a variety of survival issues which are central to the development of effective economic survival policies.

Survival Issue: Access to Resources

Several years ago I was visiting with a friend of mine from South Africa. She had come here to study at the university where I work, and was having a hard time living on an extremely limited income. One day in frustration she exclaimed: "You can't do anything in America without money!" I asked her what she meant, and she went on to talk about the difference in many African countries between the two economies: the wage economy, and the survival economy. There were still vast tracts of land, she told me, where you could go, build a house, and survive "without a job." Most Americans probably could not conceive of a commons—areas of land or portions of the economy of overabundance where they could make their own way with some semblance of dignity and pride.

We must make access to ownership of land—both homes and farms—a major goal. A survival economy is premised on the understanding that the society as a whole has access to natural resources in order to achieve self-sufficiency. The status of women is also connected to the maintenance of an economic commons. Lourdes Beneria and Gita Sen reported in their study of the impact of economic development on the status of Third World women that historically, as land held in common was converted to private property, women lost status and became dependent on male wage earners.[9] We could, by analogy, speculate that a similar loss of power might have occurred when commonly held lands in England and Europe were fenced in and converted to private ownership.

Survival Issue: Toward a New Economic Philosophy

In many ways, the survival economy is similar to the low-technology economies outlined by E. F. Schumacher, Ivan Illich, and others. Most home workers or domestic laborers operate on a survival ethic: seeking the best way to use limited resources, endorsing the ethics of getting by, making do, and stretching a meal to feed everyone—always keeping in mind the bottom line, the economic limits beneath which the family cannot go. In its judicious use of available resources, women's survival economics is similar to the example of Buddhist economics as outlined below by Schumacher:

Thus, if the purpose of clothing is a certain amount of temperature comfort and an attractive appearance, the task is to attain this purpose with the smallest possible effort, that is, with the smallest annual destruction of cloth and with the help of designs that involve the smallest possible input of toil. The less toil there is, the more time and strength is left for artistic creativity.[10]

The survival economy is an economy of doing (production for use), not having, and provides a more viable alternative to the capitalist economy based on production for consumption.[11] It takes basic materials and converts them directly to use by the family. In the survival economy, bigger is not better, especially as size relates to our ability to initiate economic change. Small production groups allow people to stay in control and assure that needs are addressed at the level of articulation. According to Schumacher, "Action is a highly personal affair," and small groups can create the most effective economics.[12]

People can be themselves only in small comprehensible groups. Therefore we must learn to think in terms of an articulated structure that can cope with a multiplicity of small-scale units. If economic thinking cannot grasp this it is useless. If it cannot get beyond its vast abstractions . . . and make contact with the human realities of poverty, frustration, alienation, despair, breakdown, crime, escapism, stress, congestion, ugliness, and spiritual death, then let us scrap economics and start afresh.[13]

Further, the survival economy is based on the development of simpler technologies—what Schumacher calls "appropriate" or "intermediate" technology and what Ivan Illich calls "convivial" tools. This is technology that is human-centered and enhances participation by the worker. An excellent example of an appropriate technology is the sewing machine. It makes the work of sewing much easier while the worker retains absolute control of the creative process of making clothes.

Finally, the survival economy is a people-centered economy. Schumacher calls it "production by the masses" rather than "mass production."

The system of *production by the masses* mobilises the priceless resources which are possessed by all human beings, their clever brains and skillful hands, *and supports them with first-class tools*. . . . [It is] designed to serve the human person instead of making him the servant of machines. . . . One can also call it self-help technology, or democratic or people's technology—a technology . . . which is not reserved to those already rich and powerful.[14]

Survival Issue: The Real Politics of Housework

There is another economy in which women work—unpaid women's housework. Ivan Illich described women's domestic work as a good example of what he calls "shadow work"—work that is done in support of a worker in the wage-labor system. According to Illich, the capitalist economy could not survive without someone to do this unpaid work:

Homo economicus has never been sexually neutral; from the beginning *he* was created as a couple, as *vir laborans*, the workingman, and *femina domestica*, the hausfrau, *homo industrialis* was made. In no society that developed toward the goal of full employment has shadow work not grown apace with that employment.[15]

Shadow work is not what I am calling survival work, although some housework is in this category. Shadow work is *consumption* work, which only exists when "the social conditions for subsistence living" have been destroyed, and time and energy must be spent in consuming goods and services the family previously provided for itself.[16] It comprises those tasks which must be done to maintain the (primary male) worker.

Women's serfdom in the domestic sphere is the most obvious example today. Housework is not salaried. Nor is it a subsistence activity in the sense that most of the work done by women was such as when, with their menfolk, they used the entire household as the setting and the means for the creation of most of the inhabitants' livelihood.[17]

While a return to a survival economy looks appealing at first glance, women need to proceed with great caution. It is a seductive minefield of economic and ideological subtleties and women must be wary of finding themselves with even more work to do. The role of misogyny in shaping our economic choices and directions cannot be discounted. According to John Mack Faragher:

The regulation of the sexual division of labor [in Midwestern rural communities in the nineteenth century] was achieved through the perpetuation of a hierarchical and male-dominant family structure, linked to a public world from which women were excluded. . . . Men were free to pursue the work of the public world precisely because the inequitable division of labor at home made them the beneficiaries of women's and children's labor.[18]

However, if men and women both were committed to making the shift from housework to survival work—and sharing that responsibility—we would have the beginnings of truly revolutionary economic change.

Converting shadow work to survival work will necessitate reclaiming housework. The feminist community has always had an ambiguous relationship, however, with women who define themselves as homemakers. Feminists by and large have defined success for women as success in the production economy, and both men and women belittle housework as unproductive and inefficient. Whatever women think about housework, however, they continue to be responsible for it. Anger over having to do housework is articulated as a decided hostility toward those female traitors who embraced housework with either acceptance or active approval.

I suspect that part of women's ambivalence over their role occurred because, while housework was perceived as being degrading, it also offered women an outlet for self-expression, creativity, and meaningful work. Giving up the role of homemaker (especially in cases where many of the tasks women performed still met basic survival needs) was probably as difficult for women as was giving up the role of farmer for men. In both cases, there are people struggling to articulate the centrality of the intimate connection between work and freedom.

Reclaiming housework makes good economic and political sense. However, it is interesting that the organization Wages for Housework has had only limited impact in the United States. Since its founding in 1972, Wages for Housework has organized worldwide to "petition every government to count the contribution to the economy of all women's work, so that it is recognized and reflected in every Gross National Product."[19] The group's thesis is a simple one: Once women's contribution to the economy is recognized, women will be in a stronger position to make policy changes that will benefit them and their families. At the World Conference of the U.N. Decade for Women in 1985, the group won passage of the following statement:

The remunerated and, in particular, the unremunerated contribution of women to all aspects and sectors of development should be recognised, and appropriate efforts should be made to measure and reflect those contributions in national accounts and economic statistics, and in the Gross National Product (GNP). Concrete steps should be taken to quantify the unremunerated contributions of women to food and agricultural production, reproduction, and household activities.[20]

John Kenneth Galbraith, writing in the 1970s, agreed: "Women's household work in the United States would, if counted, amount to as much as 24 percent of the US GNP."[21] Selma James argued that counting the value of women's work will give women not only economic power but political power as well:

power which can be measured by refusal in the private sphere and organisation in the public one. We have to learn anew the lesson of the women's movement: the personal is political. Now we can see its roots in the entire social, political and economic structure of society. The personal, private work of women is the foundation of the public, the economic, political and social power relations which are the very nature of the world we live in.[22]

In order to make those economic development and political decisions informed ones, we must clarify precisely what we mean by survival issues. Third World women have always seen survival economy issues as separate from wage-labor issues, and have rightfully focused their political energies on the survival needs of food, shelter, water and fuel. For many of these women, the struggle for survival included the struggle for political freedom. Elvia Alvarado, a Honduran woman who worked as an organizer of peasant women farmers, commented recently on her own struggle with survival issues. For a while, she began, the Catholic church had funded her program.

Then all of a sudden the church took away all the funds. Why? They said there was no more money, but we don't think that's what happened. . . . They wanted us to give food to malnourished mothers and children, but they didn't want us to question why we were malnourished to begin with. They wanted us to grow vegetables on the tiny plots around our houses, but they didn't want us to question why we didn't have enough land to feed ourselves. But once we started getting together and talking to each other, we started asking these questions.[23]

Unfortunately, women in the United States do not see survival issues as separate from wage issues—probably because they no longer do survival work. From a feminist perspective, economic analysis is rudimentary at best, and the predominantly liberal economic agenda is vague and unfocused. Individual economic issues within the wage-labor system demanding equal pay and comparable worth salaries are put forth. What is also striking about the feminist economic agenda in the United States is the quality of abstraction that characterizes economic discussions. At no point yet has the American women's movement determined just what women want money *for*. The movement has not gone deep enough in its analysis of the economy. Equal pay, in minimum wage jobs, for example, may not provide enough income to meet the needs of men or women. Despite so-called concern about the feminization of poverty, it is more handwringing than real political activity in support of expanding benefits to those who may need them. Feminist theoreticians haven't even addressed the obvious: Welfare—in some states—is a good economic idea for women and children.

In 1987 in Vermont a mother with two children (one in school) and no significant assets was entitled by law to $544 a month in ANFC [Vermont's family assistance program, Aid to Needy Families with Children] and $103 a month in food stamps, for a net tax-free cash income of $7,764 a year. By contrast, the same woman, working as retail clerk for $4.86 an hour for fifty weeks a year, would earn a gross income of $9,718. When Social Security taxes, earned-income tax credits, work-related expenses, and child-care costs are taken into account, the working woman enjoys a usable income of $6,281 a year, almost 20 percent less than she can get from welfare alone—not even counting school-lunch and Medicaid benefits. Even if this woman got food stamps while working ($951), her usable income would still be less than if she refused work altogether and remained on welfare. It is a rare spirit who will work forty hours a week to be able to enjoy only 80 percent of what he or she can get for not working at all.[24]

Tremendous political energy is wasted because we fail to see that survival economics is a more basic political issue. Instead of demanding "equal opportunity exploitation"—that is, basically accepting the premise of the capitalist system which is, in principle, exploitive of both men and women—we need to be asking those basic economic questions about who is eating and who isn't.

Even the current national disgrace—homelessness—has not been addressed by the women's movement. Homemaking apparently does not extend to demanding housing policies that ensure that every American has a decent place to live. In her latest book, *Women, Culture and Politics*, Angela Davis is a rare voice speaking out on the issue of housing:

The United Nations declared 1987 to be the Year of Shelter for the Homeless. Although only the developing countries were the initial focus of this resolution, eventually it became clear that the United States is an "undeveloping country." Two-thirds of the 4 million homeless in this country are families, and 40 percent of them are Afro-American. . . . Presently, under New York's Work Incentive Program, homeless women and men are employed to clean toilets, wash graffiti from subway trains, and clean parks at wages of sixty-two cents an hour, a mere fraction of the minimum wage. In other words, the homeless are being compelled to provide slave labor for the government if they wish to receive assistance.[25]

Nonetheless, no voice is raised by the women's movement to counter these tendencies. The term homelessness is a euphemism to cover up the deeper economic reality, that we do not have access to land as a place to garden, farm, or even build a house. In fact, home ownership, which used to be considered de rigueur for Americans, is an increasingly elusive goal.

In their demand to enter the wage economy as equals to men and their fight for their economic rights within that system, American women rejected the social nature of survival work. Where women formerly had a tradition that called for a more community- or family-based ethic, they have rejected this ethic in favor of the ethics of a society committed to individualism. Unfortunately, *as* individuals they have no political or economic power. European feminists did not make the same mistake. Building on the economic gains made by socialism, European women have achieved some success in securing the basics of the survival economy over and against the wage-labor system: Paid parental leave, child care, and universal medical insurance are benefits enjoyed by most European capitalist societies including many of the Eastern Soviet bloc countries.[26] The United States is a glaring exception among the so-called developed nations. Because socialists made these issues societal issues and not just women's issues, European feminists have also had a more noticeable impact on the political process in their countries—particularly in a strong peace movement and the Green environmental movement.

THE SOCIAL NATURE OF WOMEN'S WORK

As capitalism expanded and the economic lives of men and women went in separate directions, men and women began to express different styles of work. In the factories, men worked up to fifteen hours a day in a primarily male world. It was a world that encouraged competition between men, and that isolated them from communication and interaction with each other. Women, however, still continued working in a community of family and other people with whom they often worked cooperatively. In this section I will explore some special characteristics of women's work—originally the work style of both men and women— that strongly influence the manner in which work itself is done.

1. Women's work is social. It is work that is generally done with other people: husband, children, neighbors. As late as the latter half of the nineteenth century, for example, Finnish women in Minnesota were still doing collective gardening, moving from one garden to another until all were weeded. In a society based on survival, whether the primary economic unit is the nuclear family, the extended family, or some other nonfamilial human grouping, survival always takes place in community. Survival is not an individual undertaking, it occurs with other people.

2. Women's work is varied. Variety is the spice of work life, and anyone who has ever done survival housework on a regular basis knows that there are infinite numbers of tasks that can be ordered in any way the houseworker might wish—a little bit of laundry, a little bit of sweeping, a little bit of gardening. Diversity characterized the pre-capitalist economy.

In the pre-industrial or proto-industrial economy (peasant farming, artisanal production, small shopkeeping, cottage industry, putting-out, etc.) household and production were generally a single or combined unit, and though this normally meant that women were grossly overworked—since they did most of the housework and shared in the rest of the work—they were not confined to one type of work.[27]

3. Women's work is done to meet a specific family or community need and includes such tasks as keeping the family fed, housed and clothed, and also what we now call the service economy—teaching, social work, and nursing. It is characterized by purpose and intentionality. Women's work is work that is done for the good of the social/family unit. It is work done for use value rather than for exchange value:

The point of a woman's production was to meet the needs of people. Even when women realized cash from the sale of their produce, this cash would be converted into something usable within the home. *Value*, within the household component of the family economy, was *use value*. Measurement and quantification were only minor aspects of women's production. In the household sphere, social relations determined a person's rights to goods and services.[28]

4. Women's work is cooperative, not competitive. Women's work is perhaps the finest example of selfless or shared work. By this I do not mean that women do the work as an expression of martyrdom or without any personal satisfaction. I also do not mean that women are better because their work is selfless. Because so much women's work is done to meet specific needs and not for exchange of products in the marketplace, it has a distinctive quality of an exchange between people and can serve as a model for all work. It is highly personalized work and, precisely because it is unpaid, it can serve as an inspiration for developing a renewed sense of work as the sharing between people. It is also work that receives its reward (or should) through recognition of its contribution to the life of the community. When our work and our time become available for any price in the marketplace of contemporary capitalism, we systematically destroy the cultural context of work. Without a context that honors our work, the only ethic that remains is the ethic of me for myself. As our work enters the marketplace, it becomes degraded. It can be bought and sold at the cheapest rate. Just as prostitution (sex for pay) is a degradation of the sexual relationship, work for wages is a degradation of the survival economy.

Women's work, therefore, is characterized by cooperative ethics, not individual ethics. It speaks not of rights but rather of responsibilities. According to Gita Sen, even today we still retain this sense of community in our economic expectations of the working class family.

The most basic unit of the network is the working-class household. Within the household, one finds resource pooling and reciprocity over time, the sharing of work and consumption, and the support of those with weaker social claims on subsistence. This is the meaning of the working-class family *to the working class*. It is the reason why attacks on the family strike few resonant chords among the working class.[29]

5. Women's work is contextual. There are several meanings of this word. It means that work is social, but it also means that the work itself is in a context, it has a purpose in the community and it is generally connected with the maintenance of social relationships. It includes much volunteer work. Hanna Papanek gives an example of this kind of contextual work—"the politics of status maintenance" is her term for work that solidifies the family's status in the community. It includes things such as cooking for potluck suppers, sending Christmas cards, and buying gifts for birthday parties.[30] As more and more women enter the production economy, this contextual work either does not get done or it enters the service economy. Today we can hire someone to answer our phones, walk our dog, or cater a meal, but even though the task gets completed, the network of social relations that resulted from that sharing of work is lost.

WOMEN, WORK, AND POWER IN COMMUNITY

Emerging from the culture of women and women's work, then, are certain social and ideological frameworks that are integral to the development of a post-industrial survival economy. In addition to skills that will need to be reappropriated, people who live in a survival economy will be guided by a set of moral and ethical principles that preserve the integrity of work, its role in family and community, and its role in the political life of that community. Carol Gilligan, in *A Different Voice*, has argued that women live within a different moral environment from men.[31] They are, for example, far more acculturated to taking responsibility for family. By extension, therefore, they have the potential for better skills in the subtle negotiations of cooperative social and political living. Women's more highly developed sensitivity to caring for others suggests the potential for a greater attentiveness to concepts of stewardship and reciprocity as well.

The Personal Is the Political

To be political, is, after all, to act, and for women, political action has often arisen from the context of their social experience. The essence of the concept that the personal is the political means that in the company of others, the insights into how power operates between people are deeper, less abstract, more personal/intimate, more meaningful. Women pay much more attention than men to subtle differences in people and in the environment. Politics is understood in a more contextual way—a deep, human way; an intimate, personal and painful way. Furthermore, because of women's major role in a survival economy, they are better able to communicate economic need and see that it gets articulated in the community's political sphere.

For some women, the phrase, the personal is the political, has meant only identifying and acting with other women. In its deepest meaning, however, it means action from the place of woman—action from the moral certitude of care and responsibility in cooperation with others. Because most women have remained outside the wage labor system, they share a richer social reality than do most men, and thus probably have more highly developed skills in creating collective experiences in which people can maximize their mutual energies. "The personal is the political" takes on this symbiotic understanding—we can only be our most personal when we are our most political, and to be political is to act collectively, in community with others.

The Philosophy of Empowerment

Many contemporary feminists have proposed a collectivist political theory based on a philosophy of self-actualization. It is offered up as an alternative to patriarchal, hierarchical authoritarian structures. The key to empowerment is the understanding that power needs to be decentralized—that otherwise it becomes corrupted. When everyone has a share in power, control and exploitation cannot occur. Paradoxically, the more power is spread around and shared, the less there is a need for power in the traditional, imperialistic sense. If everyone has power, no one has power over another. Power is placed in everyone's hands and no longer can be institutionalized in one individual or one role.

Authority and Decision Making

While it is true that women have been oppressed by the patriarchal social order, the patriarchy has not intruded, as capitalism has, into the world of women's work. When women did encounter organizational power structures, they experienced double oppression. In order to survive in this environment, many women developed sophisticated passive aggressive behaviors. At the same time, they nourished every opportunity to enhance personal freedom—however small. Often, this opportunity was in her housework—a small sphere of control if it is true, but a valuable one, although its value went unappreciated in the culture as a whole. The housewife, we recall, basically worked independently (except that she worked for a husband) and in cooperation with family and neighbors. She did not, as did the men who went into the wage system, work for someone. Even when she did go into the wage system, because she had to do both jobs—work at home and work for wages—she still retained control over the process of her home work, including its timing, its order, and its end products. To be sure, there were some tasks that were driven by necessity and had to be done—cooking, taking care of children, the demands of gardening—but by and large, the housewife was (as was the whole family in pre-capitalist society) her own boss.

Women are also less psychically dependent than men on the production economy, probably because they have always seen their employment for wages as temporary or part-time and they had other avenues for achieving ego gratification and self-esteem. With more women who are single parents entering the production economy, however, that sense of independence will be replaced by the same dependence on the system that male workers experience. Knowing that the survival of both the individual and the family is linked to keeping a job is a strong incentive to keep quiet and do what you're told.

Women and Action

Throughout history, women have, in moments of political activism, exhibited the fiercest and swiftest actions—what Eric Hobsbawm called the "moral economy of the crowd."[32] Women, he observed, make a direct connection between survival and political action. During the French Revolution, the march on Versailles saw women taking direct action to correct social injustice. Meridel Le Sueur tells a similar story of women in Minneapolis during the Depression. They leaned on the window of a large supermarket until it broke. They then went into the store, taking off the shelves "only what they needed." They apologized to the store owner, and promised him that when the economy got better and they could feed their families, he would be paid for all the food that had been taken.[33] In the *Summa Theologica*, St. Thomas Aquinas articulated a similar ethic in his question "Is it stealing to take bread if you are hungry?" He replied, in good scholastic form, that no, it is not a crime, and that the greater crime is his or hers who does not share their food with the hungry.

CONCLUSION: WOMEN'S WORK IS NEVER DONE?

It is in the reproduction economy that women still maintain the largest degree of control. Because reproductive work is generally unpaid or underpaid, there has been little incentive for the system as a whole to bring this work into the production sphere—in most cases this is work that will be done anyway, and women have little choice about the matter. However, for the sake of argument, I will suggest that women are in control of the survival and service economies, and that there is potential for making changes in the economy as a whole through women expanding their power in this area.

The first order of business will be for women to begin the process of developing public policy that readjusts the priorities of the whole economy. Women must take up the reproductive economy as their own responsibility, and begin to develop federated ways of reaching consensus on a modern moral economy of the crowd. Basically, of course, this involves building networks of women and men nationwide to start developing policies and procedures to alter the whole infrastructure of our society: the responsibilities for the care of children, housing, education, food, fuel/energy, and more hidden resources of the community like roads and utilities. All of the community's survival issues must become women's issues, for it is only when women have reclaimed the survival economy that they can reclaim themselves.

NOTES

1. Sonya O. Rose, "Gender Segregation in the Transition to the Factory: The English Hosiery Industry, 1850–1910," *Feminist Studies* 13, no. 1 (Spring 1987): 178.

2. Renate Bridenthal, "The Dialectics of Production and Reproduction in History," *Radical America* 10 (1976): 6.

3. Heidi Hartmann, "The Unhappy Marriage of Marxism and Feminism: Towards a More Progressive Union," in *Women and Revolution*, ed. Lydia Sargent (Boston, 1981), 21.

4. Eric Hobsbawm, "Man and Woman in Socialist Iconography," *History Workshop Journal* 6 (1978): 130.

5. Ibid., 138.

6. Eleanor Leacock, "History, Development, and the Division of Labor by Sex: Implications for Organizations," *Signs: Journal of Women in Culture and Society* 7 (1981): 474–91.

7. Susan C. Bourque and Kay B. Warren, "Technology, Gender and Development," *Daedalus* 116 (1987): 174.

8. Zoe Diacou, "An Interview with Anne Kanten: 'I'm a Farmer, I'm a Woman, and I'm Angry,' " *World Women News* 1 (1989): 10–11.

9. Lourdes Beneria and Gita Sen, "Accumulation, Reproduction, and Women's Role in Economic Development: Boserup Revisited," *Signs: Journal of Women in Culture and Society* 4 (1981): 289.

10. E. F. Schumacher, *Small is Beautiful* (New York, 1973), 57–58.

11. Ivan Illich, *Shadow Work* (Boston and London, 1981).

12. Schumacher, *Small Is Beautiful*, 65.

13. Ibid., 75.

14. Ibid., 153–54.

15. Illich, *Shadow Work*, 23.

16. Ibid., 21.

17. Ibid., 14.

18. John Mack Faragher, "History from the Inside-Out: Writing the History of Women in Rural America," *American Quarterly* 33, no. 5 (Winter 1981): 550.

19. International Wages for Housework Campaign: *Wages for Housework*, pamphlet, 1985.

20. "Women's Time Is Not Money," *Connexions* 30 (1989): 2.

21. Selma James, *The Global Kitchen* (London, 1985), 12.

22. Ibid., 21.

23. Kate Klingner, "Elvia Alvarado, Honduran Peasant Activist," *World Women News* 1 (1989): 8.

24. Frank Bryan and John McClaughry, *The Vermont Papers: Recreating Democracy on a Human Scale* (Chelsea, VT, 1989), 206–7.

25. Angela Y. Davis, *Women, Culture, and Politics* (New York, 1989), 8.

26. Sheila B. Kamerman, "Work and Family in Industrialized Societies," *Signs: Journal of Women in Culture and Society* 4, no. 4 (Summer 1979): 632–650.

27. Hobsbawm, "Man and Woman in Socialist Iconography," 130.

28. Deborah Fink, *Open Country, Iowa: Rural Women, Tradition and Change* (Albany, 1986), 37.

29. Gita Sen, "The Sexual Division of Labor and the Working Class Family: Toward a Conceptual Synthesis of Class Relations and the Subordination of Women," *Review of Radical Political Economics* 12, no. 2 (Summer 1980): 81.

30. Hanna Papanek, "Family Status Production: The 'Work' and 'Non-Work' of Women," *Signs: A Journal of Women in Culture and Society* 4 (1979): 777.

31. Carol Gilligan, *In a Different Voice: Psychological Theory and Women's Development* (Cambridge, MA, 1982).

32. Hobsbawm, "Man and Woman in Socialist Iconography," 131.

33. Neala J. Schleuning, *America: Song We Sang without Knowing—The Life and Ideas of Meridel Le Sueur* (Mankato, MN, 1983).

Chapter 7

Good Work: Working Together

The creation of good work must take place in community, and the creation of community is dependent on people working together. As we have seen, the marriage of capitalism, the new technologies, the centralization of work in factories, and the division of labor all served to alienate the worker from both community and work. Reclaiming that integration is central to redefining and recreating a culture conducive to the health and well-being of people and the earth. In this chapter I will focus on the relationship between workers' rights, work, and community. I will also explore non-alienating political and economic activities that serve to build the self-esteem of individuals and empower them with the skills to build community.

WORK AND RIGHTS

For most Americans the world of work is exploitive, repressive, and absolutely barren of creative activity. As we seek to create an alternative to this oppressive environment, we must begin by outlining some basic principles compatible with a new cooperative economy. There are several important political and social issues to be addressed before we can set out new moral and ethical guidelines: Do we—as individuals, families, or some other economic unit—have the right to a job? What gives us that right? Do we have the right to meaningful work, the right to expect others to support us, or the right to survival? In democratic societies, we tend to focus on individual rights over and above any claims that community might have in guiding our thinking and action. What is the relationship of work to community? Who has priority over the profits of work? In our new economic world we will pay special attention to the convergence of individual rights and communal expectations.

When we talk about rights in the following sections, we will be using that term in a specific sense: as a natural right. Over the centuries, natural law and natural rights arguments have fallen into disfavor. With the rise of the modern state, we have come to rely on contractual rights, or positive law, rather than natural law. In the modern state, individuals are given rights as part of the social contract. A natural right is a right based on the understanding that all human rights exist only as a function of the human community. There are no rights, for example, that the individual has over and against the rights of people as a whole. What is right is what benefits the community, and, by the same argument, the environment.

Natural rights also presume a counterpart: an obligation on the part of the individual to the larger community. This does not mean that there is no room for the expression of individual will, or that groupthink will prevail. As we have seen, self-expression is an important component to human growth, and true community is the environment most conducive to developing free, self-actualized individuals. In the undifferentiated group, the individual is repressed; in community, the individual is fulfilled.

The Survival Economy

There are many ways to conduct the economic life of communities. In this section I will argue for the establishment of a survival economy, or what Christopher Merrill calls "a household mode of production": an economy based on the belief in a commons to which people would have access in order to survive. This survival economy would guarantee to everyone the resources for basic survival.

The commons is both a place and an idea. Prior to the industrial era, and even today in many Third World countries, there were always lands that were held in common for all to use: the town commons even existed briefly in the United States in the seventeenth century. At the dawn of the industrial era, the commons was enclosed, fenced off from communal use, and converted to private ownership. It created, as we might imagine, an incredible upheaval in European society. The enclosure in England, for example, was accompanied by widespread resistance, but there was little even such organized groups as the Diggers could do to reverse the trend. The Diggers were an organization comprised of unemployed men who appropriated for themselves land held in common in England in 1648. They claimed people had a natural right to the basic means of production. The appropriation of commonly accessed land to private ownership continues today. Just in the past few years, for example, farmers in the Philippines have been evicted from land their families have farmed for centuries. Dole Pineapple Company "bought" the land from the government. The land was "for sale" because it had never been deeded to the illiterate people who depended on it for their very survival.

This idea of the commons, of the right to commonly held resources, is at the heart of many revolutionary movements worldwide. It generally appears as a call for land reform. It is also a reiteration of the primacy of labor over capital in its rejection of private ownership of the means of production. Since the seventeenth century, as capitalism and colonialism spread worldwide, the concept of private property replaced the traditional practice of collective ownership—or, in effect, no ownership—as the lands were fenced in. One of the basic under-pinnings of a capitalist economy is the right to private property, and, in particular, the right to private ownership of the means of production.

In an economy based on the idea of the commons, however, another more cooperative ethic operates. Here, the principles of cooperative ownership or access to resources supercedes private ownership. Pope John Paul II, in a recent papal decree, for example, endorsed labor's right to access natural resources:

Christian tradition has never upheld this right [to private ownership of property] as absolute and untouchable. On the contrary, it has always understood this right within the broader context of the right common to all to use the goods of the whole of creation: The right to private property is subordinated to the right to common use, to the fact that goods are meant for everyone.[1]

From this basic right to the resources needed for survival, all other economic rights proceed.

It is important, however, to understand that the right to survival does not assume the right to rampant exploitation of other humans or the material resources of the earth. I will explore these rights in another context, but it should be noted that the second rule of conduct in the new economy will be stewardship of the earth. Only when the health and balance of the environment is secure will human life be secure.

The survival economy is also characterized by the right of persons to apply their human effort to the resources of the commons—the right to work itself and to the income generated by that work. The first economic priority will be the reproduction economy in order to meet the need to sustain the worker and his or her family. This priority would exist outside the wage system, and, as much as possible, even outside the money system. In recent research into the early American economy, Merrill traced the shift from a survival economic mode, which he labeled the "household mode of production," to a commodity mode based on the wage-labor system, machine production, and capitalism. Although the actual existence of a household mode of production in early America is a hotly debated issue among historians on the Left, I will accept the possibility of the existence of such a mode of production since it has, and does, exist in many other societies. Our interest is not whether it existed in the past, but whether the principles that shape it might be applied to a similar survival economy in the future. Whatever the case, in order to create a new economic order, we need to understand the economic and political forces that brought us to our present state of technological gridlock. Armed with insights into these phenom-ena, we might more clearly see our way to a transition to a survival economy.

A survival economy is characterized by work that is embedded in social relationships. Merrill's research was directed at uncovering evidence of an early American economy prior to industrialization that was characterized by "the presence of traditions, secure in their own 'rationality,' which resisted a commercial orientation."[2] This economy did not have a "money relation." Instead, individuals "constantly cooperated in their work,"[3] and "personal relations in cooperative work govern[ed] the exchange of products rather than the reverse, as is the case in a commodity mode of production."[4] Instead of a market economy, Merrill found an economy based on a quasi-medieval craft economy that was characterized by the control of work by individual craftspersons: "Most articles that artisans made were what were known as 'spoken' or 'bespoken goods'; that is, made to order for a customer."[5] In addition, most other economic activities, he argues, were direct exchanges of labor to get the work of the household done.

The craftsperson who produced only at the request of an individual need has, according to Denise Pym, a contemporary counterpart—the self-employed person who sees his or her work as part of relationships in a community: "He exhibits some reluctance to exchange his products and skills, which he sees as part of himself, merely for money. . . . He often prefers to barter and exchange his products and skills among friends and associates because these activities provide the basis of more lasting and meaningful relationships."[6] Douglas Harper's loving and gentle study of the mechanic embedded in the social relations of his community is a similar study of the social relationship of work.[7] I can recall having similar feelings recently when someone asked to buy some of our firewood. I could imagine giving it away, but I couldn't imagine setting a price on such hard work. In a survival economy it is work that is exchanged, not just the product. The product stands for the social relationship.

Merrill also argues that the profit motive was absent in the household mode of production, and, instead, the economy was regulated "by social need."[8] When needs drive the economy, this also provides a built-in restraint to production. He continues:

Production is planned with one eye on the needs of one's own household, and the other on the needs of neighboring households. A household produces use-values for itself, and use-values for others. The latter, of course, is a necessary condition for any exchange. But, unlike the situation in capitalist or simple commodity production, the use-values-for-others are not use-values in general which become use-values for no one if the supply turns out to be greater than the demand. Instead, the use-values for others in household production are use-values for someone, produced for specific persons to meet their specific needs.[9]

This is the intimacy of community work; the intimacy of two individuals gauging the work needs of one another and then collaboratively meeting those needs. If there is right to be found here, it is the right to share one's work in cooperation with others at a subsistence level. There is, then, by extension the right to self-sufficiency and survival outside the wage system, based solely on one's membership in community.

Controlling the Means of Creation

Our ability to control the way the work itself is carried out and shaped is as important as having a supportive community in which one's work is honored as important and useful. Ordinarily, when we talk about the means of production, we automatically equate that term with machines. We need to understand, however, that means are also more than machines—more than buildings, tools, or other fixed capital. Means of production are the whole process as well—and the essence of creativity is control of the process of making.

Creativity thrives best in an environment where the individual feels a strong connection between his or her work and self-expression, where work is closer to its original meaning of calling. A calling is what you want to *be* rather than what you do in a job. A calling is generated internally, whereas the job is driven by the market.

A career is the opposite of a calling. The packaging or commoditization of work into careers is the accepted norm for young college students who go to school not for learning but to get a job. They carefully package themselves to be a sought-after product in the economy. Several years ago I met a young woman who was a student majoring in computer science and minoring in anthropology. One day she confessed to me that she hated computer science. Her real goal in life was to graduate in computer science, get a well-paying job, and then go to graduate school in anthropology, which was her real passion.

An important part of creativity is having control of resources, and a workplace where control of resources is in the hands of workers requires a political restructuring of work relations. According to John Cotter, "Access to resources is an issue of organizational structure, since structural arrangements formally determine the degree to which employees can influence decisions, policies, and procedures relevant to their work."[10] In recent decades, Catholic economic philosophy has also addressed this important issue of control of the work process. In 1961, Pope John XXIII called for the establishment of cooperatives throughout the economy, expansion of the principles of workers' rights to include shares in the ownership of privately owned firms and "a voice and a share in the running and development of their business[es]."[11]

Controlling the Outcomes of Production

Another right (which was also central to Karl Marx's analysis), is the right to control the production process in order to ensure equitable distribution of the wealth our work creates. The idea of the redistribution of wealth to the whole community is not a new one, nor is this concept the sole property of Marxists and radicals. In his "Encyclical Quadragesimo Anno" (Reconstructing the social order), Pope Pius XI called for an equitable distribution of wealth:

Wealth, therefore, which is constantly being augmented by social and economic progress, must be so distributed amongst the various individuals and classes of society that the common good of all . . . be thereby promoted. In other words, the good of the whole community must be safeguarded. By these principles of social justice one class is forbidden to exclude the other from a share in the profits.[12]

In addition, the amount distributed should be fairly determined. Pius XI established three principles governing what he called a "just wage": (1) the wage should be adequate to support the worker and the worker's family; (2) the just wage would be determined based on the state of the business ("but technical and economic inefficiency is not to be considered an excuse for reducing wages"), and (3) "The level of wages must be adjusted to the public economic good. . . . Wages should be so regulated . . . that as many as possible may be able to hire their labour and receive suitable reward for their livelihood."[13] Under a survival economy, of course, there will be no profits, and wages will reflect the equitable redistribution of wealth.

Miscellaneous Issues

There are many rights that workers and communities should delineate as they develop a more just and equitable economy. Some are already in existence, or at least readily apparent—rights to a safe and healthy work environment, limits on hours worked, and others. Pope John Paul II, for example, admonished the state to ensure workers rights in such areas as a just labor policy, unemployment benefits, sufficient remuneration to maintain a family, the right to rest, a pension, and the right of association (unionization).[14]

There is one other area to explore in terms of workers' rights: the right to work in general. According to John Thompson, the so-called "right-to-work" legislation that many states have implemented is merely a "right-to-scab," and has nothing to do with worker rights. The rights guaranteed by this kind of legislation are the rights of corporations to require that work continue in unsafe working environments, and to control whether workers can form unions or other associations:

More importantly, it proclaims that workers are worth less. It advertises that the state and its citizens have determined that workers deserve less pay, less protection, and less respect. . . . It is the public self-flagellation of a society saying that it will abandon any of its institutions designed to enhance the quality of life and the dignity of its citizens. . . . If I repudiate unions, and I reject the concept of solidarity with my coworkers, will I dare stand alone[?] . . . Once I have started down the road of undercutting my neighbors will I know when to draw the line?[15]

If there are no jobs—because they are exported to areas in the world where labor can be more easily exploited or because machines replace human labor—the right to work will take on increasing importance. Already there is a case to be made for the right to a just wage. More and more workers are being thrust into low-paying jobs in the service area, and these jobs are increasingly part-time and without benefits. The trend is clearest in rural areas where low-paying jobs predominate and whole towns become colonized by large corporations. What began in Appalachia is now spreading to rural areas nationwide. In the town where I work, for example, the largest private employer has built his personal fortune of over 300 million dollars on the part-time labor of college students and women. The town has become what one developer called "a $3.75 an hour town."

One of the most pressing problems in today's economy is structural unemployment. Despite lip service paid to schemes to reeducate workers who are displaced by mechanization and automation, few services are available—either counseling or financial assistance—to assist workers in retooling or exploring new careers. Many are counted for a while among the unemployed—at least until their benefits run out. After that, they are relegated to the shadow world of workers who have "become discouraged"—a euphemism for the truth that they are unnecessary to the economy. Further, even if they do find other employment, most victims of structural job loss never regain the income level they received before their jobs were eliminated.

However we resolve this problem, we must begin with the basic premise that all people—even the permanently unemployed—have the same rights to survival as employed workers. One obvious solution would be to simplify our technology, thereby creating many new jobs. At the very least, in those cases where the community consciously votes to automate one or another area of work, displaced workers could also be guaranteed another job, or education for a new line of meaningful work.

WORK AND COMMUNITY

One of the least studied phenomena of the industrial world of work is the relationship between work and human kinship. Only organizations such as the medieval guilds, some contemporary fraternal and sororal societies, and religious communities even begin to approximate the richness of some of those lost human relationships. One of our greatest losses has been that of the experience of work as physical closeness between people. Like the fit between the hand and the tool, work is at its best when it brings us into intimate contact with one another. Among guild members, for example,

Throughout the day there was the closeness of man to man, the sense of one another's existence, and the exchange between the experienced workers and the novices: the meeting of eyes, the showing and the watching, the speaking and the listening. How different from the usual factories and workplaces of today, where little is "handed" from man to man, where eyes rarely meet, and the human voice cannot always rise above the noise of machinery; where men in their isolation from one another begin to feel a kinship only with their particular machine.[16]

When Marx first conceived of the working class, he was probably envisioning just such a community of guild members. Indeed, in Marx's time, there was the intimacy of working with real neighbors and relatives. Workers in the nineteenth century did not commute—they lived near one another and probably shared a life beyond the hours spent in the factory.

By the twentieth century, however, work and community had been split asunder. Workers often don't know one another outside work, and are actively discouraged by management from having any social interaction during work hours. In some cases, human contact is not just discouraged but actively forbidden, and whole work environments are designed to isolate workers from one another.

More important, however, work is no longer physically grounded in a community. We are a culture of commuters, and that mobility has had consequences for both work and community. Wendell Berry writes, "When people do not live where they work, they do not feel the effects of what they do."[17] The profound rupture between work and community results in degradation of the environment of work and the loss of a sense of connection with and responsibility toward the community. "Once," Berry goes on, "some farmers, particularly in Europe, lived in their barns—and so were both at work and at home. Work and rest, work and pleasure, were continuous with each other, often not distinct from each other at all."[18] Good work requires the reintegration of work and the sense of place, of belonging, that characterizes community.

The Failure of Individualism

Economic success in the United States has, by and large, been linked to the twin cults of individualism and entrepreneurship. It only took a generation or so for the ethic of me first to quickly replace a community-based work ethic. As individuals we could rise, and as individuals we would fall. Even Ralph Waldo Emerson, who many people erroneously interpret as an advocate of unbridled individualism, was highly critical of the greedy, raw capitalism he saw emerging in the nineteenth century:

The general system of our trade, . . . is a system of selfishness; is not dictated by the high sentiments of human nature; is not measured by the exact law of reciprocity; much less by the sentiments of love and heroism, but is a system of distrust, of concealment, of superior keenness, not of giving but of taking advantage.[19]

The only collective institution to survive was the nuclear family, and it too had nearly disappeared by the end of the twentieth century.

However, individualism didn't really work. It worked for people who had good skills, special talents, and a great deal of money, but it did not work for many groups in our society: old people, children, differently abled people, or people that society shut out deliberately—people of color, the poor, the sick or mentally ill. The dark side of individualism meant that many people found themselves isolated and made responsible for their own plight, and put to shame for their inability to "pull themselves up by their bootstraps" when times got tough. Every time a farmer lost his or her farm, it was his or her own fault because he or she was a bad manager, and not because of uncontrollable economic forces. In the nineteenth century, one financial panic after another broke the small businessperson and the farmer; well into the twentieth century (and even today for that matter), people living in poverty were blamed for their plight.

By the twentieth century, people had grown even more distant and isolated. The Great Depression psychologically broke many strong individuals who believed that somehow they were responsible for their poverty. Both the division of labor and the growing urbanization hastened the isolation of individuals from other community members, from their work, and from control of the economy; contributing to the general fragmentation of society.

Alan Bloom, in his controversial analysis of American education, pinpoints American individualism as the cause of the isolation and alienation endemic in our culture today: "Everyone has his own little separate system," he writes.

The possibility of separation is already the fact of separation, inasmuch as people today must plan to be whole and self-sufficient, and cannot risk interdependence. Imagination compels everyone to look forward to the day of separation in order to see how he will do. The energies people should use in the common enterprise are exhausted in preparation for independence. What would, in the case of union, be a building stone becomes a stumbling block on the path to secession. The goals of those who are together naturally and necessarily must become a common good; what one must live with can be accepted. But there is no common good for those who are to separate. The presence of choice already changes the character of relatedness. And the more separation there is, the more there will be.[20]

This nearly compulsive need to be individual and independent is epitomized by the whole co-dependency movement which developed in the 1980s and focuses on eliminating dependent relationships. Every relationship is methodically investigated for its unhealthy ties—usually with the help of a well-paid therapist. Predictably, unhealthy dependencies are usually discovered that must be severed. The whole movement inadvertently creates people who are paranoid, isolated, and suspicious of any human interdependence. Instead of focusing on ferreting out the pathologies in our relationships, we need to help people form positive, interdependent relationships.

The belief in individualism grew in importance in the United States at the same time that some of the last vestiges of community were being destroyed. The same era saw the emergence of consumer capitalism, and the environment of the consumer—the faceless mass market—replaced the community of people at work. In an article entitled "Advertising America," Susan Benson explored the concurrent creation of the "American consumer" and the destruction of traditional cultural networks of interdependence. It was an effort spearheaded by the newly formed advertising industry:

In their efforts to undermine class struggle the prophets of mass consumption proposed not rampant individualism but a perverse sort of collectivism, a homogenized, conformist view of the good life under the guidance of corporate America. The social glue of the mass society was composed of habits of consumption. . . . If you consumed correctly, you became part of the Great American Consensus. The way "in" was at once democratic and totalitarian: it was open to everyone with the price of admission, but woe betide the person who failed to scrape up the cash.[21]

The consumerization of the culture also penetrated the world of women's work. Benson argues that part of the destruction of women's more cooperative, communal economy—a process she calls the "proletarianization of household work"—can be attributed to the role that advertising played in destroying not only the culture of sharing between women, but also their culture of communication with each other.

The efforts to revise the consciousness of women as consumers have meant the colonization and trivialization of these cultures, reducing their traditions of reciprocal aid and support to whispered hints about how to make laundry whiter-than-white, or how to ensure a family good health and good humor by servicing them with appropriate products. The loss for women, wherever the captains of consciousness succeeded, was not just in the degradation of their household labor, but also in the degradation of their ties to other women and hence the loss of a semi-autonomous sphere of feeling and action in which women could define for one another what it meant to be a woman. In a sense, the contemporary women's movement has been picking up the pieces from the onslaught of consumer culture by recreating female support networks.[22]

It was probably a similar process that destroyed the pre-industrial cooperative community of men's shared work. We were all reduced to the empty and uncreative role of consumers when we ceased to share our work with one another.

Clearly, the need to reestablish the social basis of community is imperative. Forms of organization based on cooperative principles work because there is a basic human need for social connection. Indeed, this need is so central to human existence that we might suggest that it is a right that is central to our being—the right of association with others. Because our society is so individualistic, however, we are skeptical of cooperative efforts and fearful of losing ourselves in anonymity of the group. We are partially correct in these perceptions: There is no intimacy in being part of a mass which is why organizing people around their membership in a class is so difficult.

American culture has always turned on the uneasy tension between the individual and community, the self and others. Too often, I'm sorry to say, the community has suffered in order to shore up some macho sense of the supremacy of the individual. Ideally, we would find a balance in our social organizations that would enhance both the freedom and self-determination of the individual and the preservation of values enhancing the common good. As we create a new economy, we will have to find a way to reconcile these tensions. There is, fortunately, a long tradition in anarchist literature that seeks to honor both a healthy individualism and a new consciousness of community and connection.

Participation and Action

Participation is critical to the development of meaningful economics and to effective political action. In a recent article, Bertil Gardell reviewed the research on the relationship between the work environment and workers' participation in non-work environments such as family and leisure activities.[23] He was especially interested in looking at political participation. Most of the studies found that a lack of control in the working environment could be correlated with less activism in political arenas.

Taking greater control over their work also empowers individuals to extend the application of democratic principles beyond the workplace, enhancing the development of politically responsible, self-conscious individuals generally. According to Michael L. Schwalbe, the division of labor shapes us into people who are unable to act, crippling us politically and ethically: "If a lack of role-taking demands in work can diminish an individual's propensity to role-take, this might diminish his propensity to take the well-being of others into account before acting."[24] Being political means acting politically. Greater participation in a creative process enhances moral development, in other words. The more control we have, the more we become habituated to acting responsibly. To enhance role taking, the division of labor must be reversed and control of the process of work must be returned to the worker.

Work should be with and for others. Production has to become part of relationships with other people; it needs to emerge from the community and return back to the community. This is the basis of the new work ethic, and indeed, we cannot stress enough the importance of a participatory ethic to a democratic work process. The more people participate in their work environment, the more they take pride in and ownership of their work and the better the work itself becomes. Simone Weil has argued that products themselves should have "value and social utility" so that the workers will see the efforts of their work enhancing the life of the community.[25]

The essence of participation is an emphasis on action. The active person is a free person. In the same way that the more control one takes of the task, the more one puts oneself into the work, the more the involvement in organizations and groups is also increased. In his study of the anarchist collectives in Spain during the 1930s, Gaston Leval described the importance of a high level of participation and activity:

In the village collectives in their natural state, and in the small towns where everybody knew one another and were interdependent, liberty did not consist in being a parasite, and not interesting oneself in anything. Liberty only existed as a function of practical activity. *To be is to do*, wrote Bakunin. To be is to *realise*, voluntarily. Liberty is secured not only when one demands the rights of the "self" against others, but when it is a natural consequence of solidarity. Men who are interdependent feel free among themselves and naturally respect each other's liberty. Furthermore so far as collective life is concerned, the freedom of each is the right to participate spontaneously with one's thought, one's heart, one's will, one's initiative to the full extent of one's capacities. A negative liberty is not liberty: it is nothingness.[26]

It is difficult for Americans to set aside our knee-jerk anticommunism long enough to explore this idea of solidarity as interdependence. Our individualism, we feel, is threatened by any suggestion of cooperative efforts with others. It is even more difficult to understand that the two concepts—individualism and solidarity—are merely two sides of the same coin. We cannot be truly free individuals if that expression of self does not come out of community.

Re-creating the Work Environment

The work environment can be consciously structured to enhance self-suffi-ciency, and control by the worker. While structural changes alone will not guarantee greater freedom in work, the size of the work group and the organi-zation in which the work group operates is especially critical.

To begin with, experience has shown us that large organizations aren't able to offer the intrinsic rewards that a small organization can offer: control over the work process, a role in decision making, or other humane qualities. In a decentralized environment made up of many small organizations, the individual has much more freedom in decision making, and hence greater control over his or her work. To move to a participatory system in which work can be more meaningful, we must scale down tremendously.

Size is also important if we are to regain control over the means of production and reverse the concentration of capital. It requires huge amounts of money to centralize production, and the concentration of capital leads to the concentration of power as well: "If one realizes that the immense capital requirements *are* a principle of exclusion, are totally incompatible with any idea of justice or equal-ity, then one will systematically search for cheaper ways of doing things."[27] The decentralization of capital will also encourage creativity by making it easier for more people to become involved in the research and experimentation process and the development of new products.

The size of the work group is also important to keep abuses of power be-tween individuals to a minimum. Working in small groups or collectives "restricts the area in which any individual can dominate," and also places a "limitation on the extensity of authority."[28] On the other hand, when power is concentrated in centralized and hierarchical structures, this formalized concentration of power can more easily be exercised impersonally and independently. Power which is cut loose from its social bonds invariably becomes abusive. This potential for abuse accounts for the anarchists' long-standing suspicion of large institutions.

Finally, size is important in terms of the level of intimacy, and hence effectiveness, that can be achieved by a group: "The Collective is a recognition of the practical limits of conversation."[29] There is a necessity for face-to-face communication and participation for an organization to be truly effective, and personal, or small group conversation is an active and interactive style of communication. Meetings, on the other hand, which are more formal and also more necessary in large groups, are just the opposite: Someone is in control, and all communication is channeled through one person—the facilitator, or a process—Roberts Rules of Order. In contrast, the informality of a conversation encourages more active participation by collective members.

Finally, as we restructure the individual factories and work sites, we must still keep in mind that in today's work world power also resides in the system of work itself—the capitalist/technological/bureaucratic hegemony. It will not be easy to dismantle this organizational leviathan.

Formal organization engaged with modern technologies, entirely apart from the further coercions of capitalist ownership, contains pressures toward a machine form of organization which mirrors the mass delivery apparatus, whether it be service or production oriented. . . . Taming this beast thus represents an organizational challenge which must be met if one is to create freedom in work.[30]

CONCLUSION: WORKING TOGETHER

The sense of being together as workers is critical to changing the world. We have all had the experience of working intensively on a project, of becoming totally engaged with the process of creativity and making that experience, that process, a vital part of ourselves. Similarly, when you work with your neighbor, with another person, you can share together that same sense of vital engagement. We all become our best selves through the process of fixing, making, and creating together. We know that the factory system and the division of labor rob us of this experience of interconnection and interdependence, and when we no longer work together, it is hard to make politics together. Our task, then, is to re-create that collective environment, which is founded on the spirit of human solidarity.

It isn't enough to just think about these things; we must begin to act. We can begin by changing our own world, actions, and thinking. There are many kinds of collectives, many ways to nourish solidarity, and to act, to begin, is the first and hardest step to take.

NOTES

1. John Paul II, *Encyclical Laborem Exercens* (On human work) (Washington, DC, 1981), 31.

2. Michael Merrill, "Cash Is Good to Eat: Self-Sufficiency in the Rural Economy," *Radical History Review* 14 (Winter 1977): 46.

3. Ibid., 54.

4. Ibid., 58.

5. Ibid., 59.

6. Denise Pym, "The Other Economy as a Social System," in *Why Work: Arguments for the Leisure Society*, ed. Vernon Richards (London, 1983), 141.

7. Douglas Harper, *Working Knowledge: Skill and Community in a Small Shop* (Chicago and London, 1987).

8. Merrill, "Cash Is Good to Eat," 63.

9. Ibid.

10. John Cotter, "Ethics and Justice in the World of Work: Improving the Quality of Working Life," *Review of Social Economy* 40 (1982): 397.

11. John XXIII, *Encyclical Mater and Magistra* (Christianity and social progress), May 15, 1961 (Washington, DC, 1961), 28–31, para. 91–103.

12. Pius XI, "Encyclical Quadragesimo Anno" (Reconstructing the social order), May 15, 1931, in *Five Great Encyclicals*, (New York, 1953), 141, para. 57.

13. Ibid.

14. See John Paul II, *Encyclical Laborem Exercens*.

15. John Thompson, "The Right to Scab," Oklahoma *Observer* 18 (10 September 1986), 1.

16. D. M. Dooling, ed., *A Way of Working: The Spiritual Dimension of Craft* (New York, 1986), 62–63.

17. Wendell Berry, *The Unsettling of America: Culture and Agriculture* (New York, 1977), 52.

18. Ibid., 53.

19. Ralph Waldo Emerson, "Man the Reformer," *Dial*, April 1841, 526.

20. Alan Bloom, *The Closing of the American Mind: How Higher Education Has Failed Democracy and Impoverished the Souls of Today's Students* (New York, 1987), 117.

21. Susan P. Benson, "Advertising America," *Socialist Review* 43 (January/February 1979): 147.

22. Ibid., 153–54.

23. Bertil Gardell, "Reactions at Work and Their Influence on Nonwork Activities: An Analysis of a Sociopolitical Problem in Affluent Societies," *Human Relations* 29, 9 (1976): 885–904.

24. Michael L. Schwalbe, *The Psychosocial Consequences of Natural and Alienated Labor* (Albany, NY, 1986), 153–54.

25. Simone Weil, *The Need for Roots: Prelude to a Declaration of Duties toward Mankind* (New York, 1952).

26. Gaston Leval, *Collectives in the Spanish Revolution* (London, 1975), 346.

27. E. F. Schumacher, *Good Work*, (New York, 1979), 55.

28. *The Anti-Mass: Methods of Organization for Collectives*, Anon., circa 1970.
29. Ibid.
30. C. George Benello, "Putting the Reins on Technology," *Changing Work* 7 (1988): 32.

Chapter 8

Good Work: The Art of Work

> The victory won by the man of wisdom is also won by the man of good work. That man sees indeed the truth who sees that vision and creation are one.
>
> —*The Bhagavad Gita*, 5.5

"We have no art, we do everything as well as we can," is a quotation attributed to an anonymous member of an Oceanic tribe. In its simplicity and its depth, it suggests that work is art, and the results of work should be aesthetically pleasing products. The statement also suggests that art is not something separate or special—it is part of our everyday lives. To us as a "civilized" people, it sounds too good to be true. We dismiss the statement because it comes from a "primitive" tribe, or we believe it to be too romantic and unrealistic.

However, it is we who are primitive in our attitudes. We are heirs to a culture that has denied the integration of work and art, and this has been detrimental to our experience of both. Although both have suffered, it is work and its alienation from art that are the focus of this chapter.

THE AESTHETICS OF WORK

Ordinarily we associate the word aesthetics with esoteric theories of art. However, aesthetics has a much broader meaning: While beauty may be one facet of a theory of art, the study of aesthetics can also include exploring the artful process of making or creating—or what we call work. Work is, or should be, a creative act. The difference between whether something is made with love, care, feeling, and a sense of responsibility, or made shabbily and indifferently, is one aesthetic consideration. Aesthetics also raises the question of quality: how well something is made, and how the process of making affects the end product.

Finally, aesthetics is concerned with general ambiance, or an attitude of wholeness and completeness.

In contemporary American society, culture has been reduced to art, to the
works of artists in museums, concert halls, and libraries, which are patronized
by non-artists in their leisure time. Thus, both culture and art are divorced from
work, from the everyday lives of most people, and from action. They are received
passively in moments of leisure—a collection of consumer products to be used
at discretion and then disposed of when the world seems to call for action.

How much excellence in "the arts" is to be expected from a people who are poor at
carpentry, sewing, farming, gardening, and cooking? If you believe that you can have a
culture distinct from, or as a whole greatly better than, such work is not just illogical or
wrong—it is to make peace with the shoddy, the meretricious, and the false.[1]

To reclaim good work, then, we need to reclaim a sense of the aesthetics of
our work, and how the products we produce are not only useful in our communities, but contribute artfully to our daily experience of work. There is a need
for art in community. A line in the "Why Cheap Art Manifesto" written by the
Bread and Puppet Theater of Glover, Vermont, proclaims: "Art is food. You
can't eat it, but it feeds you."

In the sections that follow I will explore what I feel are meaningful aesthetic
components of good work. Each of us may have explored one or all of these
qualities independently, but together they make up a holistic way of looking at
how we go about the task of doing our work—both individually and culturally.

The Aesthetic Need for Work

Human beings need to work, but they need a particular kind of work—work
that allows them the fullest expression of their humanity. Adolpho Vazquez, in
Art and Society: Essays in Marxist Aesthetics, points out that Marx was interested
in the concept of art as a "higher" form of labor, the creation of our essential
humanness: "Man is human to the extent that he creates a human world, and
art is one of the highest expressions of this humanizing process."[2] We are human
because we have this need to create art through our work, to actualize our nature
through the ongoing creation of reality.

In other words, if man as a truly human being is above all a creative being, then art is
one of the spheres wherein he realizes this creative power repeatedly and limitlessly.
Because it is a creation, the work of art is always unique and artistic endeavors are always
somewhat like adventures; art is not only a reflection of reality, but a creation of a new
reality. Thanks to art, that reality of human or humanized objects created by labor is
ceaselessly extended and enriched and our relationship with reality is at once enriched
and deepened.[3]

Kurt Vonnegut, Jr.'s *Player Piano* is an excellent treatise on this need to continually create and re-create, and to transcend our reality through work. The story is set in a computerized, automated society of the future, where only a few people actually work—the engineers. They too, are on the verge of displacement by machines, and they form the Ghost Shirt Society—recalling the desperate attempt of the Sioux in the nineteenth century to resist cultural destruction. The Ghost Shirt Society develops a manifesto of the rights of workers, including the following:

Men, by their nature, seemingly, cannot be happy unless engaged in enterprises that make them feel useful. They must, therefore, be returned to participation in such enterprises. . . . I propose that men and women be returned to work as controllers of machines, and that the control of people by machines be curtailed.[4]

The displaced workers eventually revolt, and in Luddite fashion they destroy the entire city and the machines that have replaced them. However, the revolution is lost, and as the leadership of the Ghost Shirt Society prepares to surrender, they encounter a group of people attempting to repair a soft drink machine. One of the men is successful in getting the machine to work. "The man had been desperately unhappy until then. Now he was proud and smiling because his hands were busy doing what they liked to do best, Paul supposed . . . replacing men like himself with machines."[5] Vonnegut poignantly reminds us of the irony in our creativity: The human ability to create tools and machines to make our lives more pleasant also bears within it the seeds of our vocational self-destruction. Vonnegut also seems to imply that, robbed of the ability to create, we will destroy.

A Sense of Completion/Accomplishment

There is, in work of any sort, the need to comprehend it in wholes. I recall asking a painter friend of mine how he knew when a painting was done. His reply was: "When it works." In the process of painting the parts, there was always the need to understand and express the whole, and to see it emerge from the process itself and result in a completion. In order to achieve this aesthetic sense of completion or closure, we must be in charge or in control of an entire production from start to finish. However, how many of us leave our work each day feeling complete, finished? The automobile industry understands this need for completion. The assembly lines have been dismantled, and teams of workers now build entire cars. Although workers have no real control over the process of that work, the integration of tasks does meet the need for closure.

The Art of Efficiency

The quality of "taking pains" described by Thorstein Veblen has been gradually replaced in our society by a machine standard of efficiency. The machine is primarily concerned with time and quantity—not a job well done. Veblen proposed a return to a standard of true efficiency—the effective and economical use of time and materials. He wrote: "Efficient use of the means at hand and adequate management of resources available for the purposes of life is itself an end of endeavour, and accomplishment of this kind is a source of gratification."[6] Haste makes waste, says the old adage, and when speed and quantity are not motivators, one can literally take the time to do a good job—what Veblen called "the disposition to do the next thing and do it as well as may be."[7] If we take the time to do a job well, however, our work will probably no longer be profitable in a capitalist market. Profit, however, is also a relative term. We may find, for example, that the cost of time may be cheaper than the cost of energy to run a machine.

A Quality of Restraint

The idea of prudential production is not new—in fact, it is a rather old idea. Prudence is, as we have seen, inconsistent with a consumer society. Nevertheless, it is necessary that we begin to develop prudence not only as a political concept, but as an aesthetic one too. The question we need to ask is, "How much is enough?" Furthermore, we must ask that question with the intention of finding ways of nourishing a new aesthetic based on restraint. Such an aesthetic would articulate a new kind of efficiency such as Veblen suggested—the idea of using the materials of work in the most prudential way with a minimum of damage to the environment.

Veblen also describes restraint in another way: "The instinct of workmanship will commonly not run to passionate excesses."[8] Production created just for mindless consumption, we must begin to tell ourselves, is wasteful of both materials and time. It also sets up an endless loop of escalating wants. Mulford Sibley wrote:

The kind of culture associated with industrialism, technological progress, and the "conquest of nature" tends also to be connected with the stimulation of human desires for more and more material goods. Psychologically, it would seem, when it is *possible* technologically to do anything, it tends to be difficult not to do it. . . . It is here that the classical position offers perhaps its greatest challenge to the modern ethos. Why should we go faster simply because we *can* do so? Why should we indefinitely replace human labor with machines, leaving the displaced workers with little meaning in their lives?[9]

On this question of why turns the meaning of the modern world. Sibley and others argue for a return to classical attitudes on controlling technology and enhancing the aesthetic sense of boundaries and limits. Whether you call it moderation, the golden mean, or intermediate technology, it boils down to drawing distinctions between our needs and our wants—a question seldom asked in a consumer society such as ours.

Restraint is further characterized by a strong sense of the appropriate, a sense of how the parts fit with the whole. It is an essentially conservative attitude that seeks to understand all potential impacts that technology may make on a given social, political, and environmental ecology. In some Native American tribes, this cautionary quality is institutionalized in political discourse. It is a particularly valuable tool in assessing the merits of technological advances and their impact on the environment. As the community debates a variety of issues, one person is designated to speak on behalf of the generations of the future: How will this decision affect grandchildren seven generations hence? Had our culture asked this question about nuclear energy, it probably would never have been approved.

Human-Centered Work

Being in control of the means of production is not only an economic need— it is an aesthetic one as well. Michael L. Schwalbe, basing his philosophy on that of Margaret Mead, argues for a return to what he calls "natural labor":

It is labor that expresses and satisfies an individual's own impulses, that demands use of human capacities for imagining, role taking, and problem solving, and that results in a creative advance in nature—a more satisfying and better life-sustaining relationship between humans and their environments. Aesthetic experience is the subjective moment of natural labor; the creative advance of nature is its objective moment.[10]

Schwalbe sees these ethical issues as key to developing a new moral imperative on work that moves beyond the satisfaction of aesthetic ends. He concludes: "It seems natural labor itself, without some set of guiding values, is not sufficient to overcome the dehumanization of labor under capitalism."[11]

The ability to center ourselves in our work is crucial to nourishing good work. Douglas Harper, in his study of a mechanic in a small northern New York community, defines this state of being as "kinesthetic." It is a merging with the materials of making, a powerful knowing and being:

Married to the knowledge of materials, [the kinesthetic sense] . . . produces a working knowledge that stands in stark contrast to the working knowledge produced by formal education. The kinesthetic quality of Willie's working method shows how his shop is premodern, a multidimensional dialectic of the theoretical and the empirical. Willie's training has been informal and years-long, and it has trained the hand and the eye as well as the mind. The result is more than the sum of its parts. It seems mysterious to those who do not have it. Working without such knowledge, a mechanic fights materials rather than communicating—reading their messages. . . . Gaining the kinesthetic sense, however, reduces the gap between the subject—the worker—and the object—the work.[12]

In *The Theory of Business Enterprise*, Veblen describes how machines have displaced human intentionality in the work process, thus effectively destroying the human element in work. In addition to denying us a sense of involvement with work, the machine also asserts its own mechanistic aesthetic on our sensibilities. This aesthetic serves to dampen the creative, the playful, the artful impulses so central to good work. The machine aesthetic especially cultivates the rigid qualities of precision, the expectation that everything moves in an orderly manner, and that cause and effect should and can be measurable.[13] What results is a mind that is narrow, highly intolerant of ambiguity, and easily manipulated by facts and figures.

Arnold Gehlen identified a whole range of impacts mechanization has had on our thought processes. According to Gehlen, the principle of total requirement—''the avoidance of running idle, of dead weights, and of unexploited energies''[14]—leads to an exploitative attitude generally, and a disdain for anything unproductive—such as older workers and children. The need for optimal utilization moves the worker from one job to another, denying him or her consistency of work and possible aesthetic satisfaction. We become, literally, extensions of the machine. Already such principles as standardized measurement and the interchangeability of parts are, according to Gehlen, ''well in evidence in the want ads, with their exact defini ions of the required qualities and quantities (including age).''[15] This mechanical universe is the opposite of an artful universe which emphasizes connection, meaning, and intentionality.

An important aesthetic consideration, then, should be the necessity for connection and relationship with one's work—or else we tend to objectify one another and all of our personal, interpersonal, and cultural pursuits. To resist the mechanization of the self and the tendency toward standardization, we need to nourish our sense of diversity and multiplicity. To counter the tendency to enjoy the mathematical and predictable, we need to expand and celebrate the spontaneous. To resist the tendency to automate our interpersonal relationships and our understanding of others, we need to remember that efficiency is relative to the capabilities of individuals—not a standard imposed on us by the machine.

The Place of the Imaginative Sense

The industrial mechanical process has a profound influence on another aesthetic component of work—the human need for imaginative thinking. In *Education Through Art*, Herbert Read argued:

that there exists in the whole process of industrialization and technological invention a tendency to destroy sensuous perception and imaginative experience, the very faculties upon which our scientific knowledge of the nature of things finally depends. In short, technology (and the automatism that goes with it) tend to destroy human sensibility, and it is upon human sensibility that what is human in us survives. . . . The technological revolution lacks any moral or aesthetic foundation.[16]

The free play of imagination is critical to the creation of good products and ultimately of culture itself. As E. F. Schumacher has argued, the technologies we choose should ensure maximum control by the craftsman. The most important distinction is that between a tool and a machine: A tool "enhances a man's skill and power"; a machine leaves humans "in a position of having to serve the slave. The carpet loom is a tool, a contrivance for holding warp threads at a stretch for the pile to be woven round them by the craftsmen's fingers; but the power loom is a machine, and its significance as a destroyer of culture lies in the fact that it does the essentially human part of the work."[17] The more control we give to the machines, the less imagination enters into the process of work, because the machine process is a static one—not self-renewing. The loss of the imaginative sense over time results in a cultural reduction of creativity as a whole.

An important quality of the imaginative sense is subtlety. The standardization demanded by the machine results in a general leveling of all taste and discrimination. We can buy the same McDonald's hamburger anywhere in the world, and it is this fact that impresses us more than its nutritional value. We seek out IBM-compatible word processors and curse foreign imports for which we can't get parts. Genetic engineers focus efforts on cloning rather than exploring genetic diversity, and we grow increasingly intolerant of anything different. A groupthink mentality emerges as the cultural norm, and our growth both as individuals and societies is narrowed and constricted. This impoverishment of the imaginative sense stifles future creativity and destroys the problem-solving skills so necessary to species survival. We become dependent, childlike, and easily manipulated.

Process Is Our Most Important Product

One of the greatest needs today is the reintegration of work into our total experience. The industrial revolution separated our work from the process of our daily lives, and in the process destroyed the family and our sense of connection with our work. At some deep level, I resent the eight-hour day because it keeps me from other tasks that may need doing. Often I sit at my desk, wishing I were home cutting wood, or fixing gutters after a heavy rain. On the other hand, when I'm home, I'm thinking up solutions to problems at work. In any case, I'm often in the wrong place at the wrong time to get a task done in a timely, efficient manner. The industrial mentality measures our pay by the hours we give to the machine or the bureaucracy. As an alternative, I would rather see us learn to trust our own work styles and use our own judgment to appropriate the hours of the day or week in the most effective manner.

When I work at home, I find I accomplish more in less time. Part of this has to do with the fact that I can break up tasks: I can write for two hours ("easy" work) and carry wood for two hours ("hard" work). I don't get stale at anything, and each task energizes the next. A more important factor, however, is my freedom to control the process and pace of my own work—to be my own boss. Efficiency for me is not only wise use of materials and time, but the ultimate freedom to find the best process.

My husband, Mike, has a highly developed mechanical sense, and I have often wondered at his quick understanding of how something works and, when it doesn't work, his ability to fathom its intricacies and fix it. He is fascinated with tinkering, with making a machine do its job. However, sometimes I have seen him "waste time" (in my mind) to go out of his way to get a machine to do a task when it would have been a more efficient use of time to perform the task by hand. Take our "weed-wacker" machine as an example. When you add up all the hours spent tinkering with it, repairing it, earning the money to buy it, the cost of gas and oil to run it, the probable damage to hearing, and potential minor damage to plant life—I wonder if a scythe might not have been the more efficient tool?

A Quality of Feeling and Caring

We don't often think of work as giving us a good feeling or enhancing our feelings toward one another. However, feeling may be the least tangible and most important of our aesthetic considerations. It is not only a question of how we feel about our work, but our ability to feel at all. The tendency in our culture to deny and suppress feeling is a direct effect of the modern technological worldview. With the mechanization of work has come depersonalization and a general coarseness of sensibility.

Until recently, women have been in charge of feelings in our culture (and, interestingly, were outside the industrial world by and large until the 1970s), and the feminine consciousness, with its qualities of nurturance and sensitivity, according to Lewis Mumford, holds the key to reclaiming our connection with feelings. Mumford's search for the antidote to mechanism and militarism led him to Henry Adams, a turn-of-the-century critic of the modern industrial world. Adams distilled for him the essence of the conflict between machine and feeling in the metaphor of the dynamo and the virgin:

He saw that the males of his society, who had transferred so many of their once autonomous activities to machines and automatons, did not have sufficient life-sense to save the race. In their blind pride over their scientific facilities, they would cling to the insensate mechanisms they had created, making them go ever faster and faster, though incapable of applying the brakes, changing the direction, or choosing the destination. Anticipating that desperate strait, Henry Adams, at the end of his own career, turned to another countervailing form of energy, the energy of life, the energy of erotic love, reproduction, and creation; he sought a counterpoise to chaos by invoking woman's faith in her own creativity, in the ramifying, formative processes of life, above all those of sex, love, motherhood.[18]

The quality of caring and feeling is basic, I believe, to the work we do—it permeates all aspects of work. It underlies our desire to work well, it drives the need to take pains with our tasks, and it connects us in an intimate way with the products we create and the people we create them for. As our work is infused with this caring, nurturing quality, we will become more insistent that the patterns of the modern workplace change.

More important, it is necessary for us to cultivate this quality of caring to keep us from destroying our environment. The main impetus of technology was to dominate nature, to impose the mechanical world over the natural world. When we cultivate the nurturing attitude in our work, we will then begin to see more clearly the impact of our work on the larger environment. Nurturing requires paying attention to the consequences of our actions. To nurture a child, for example, requires a heightened attentiveness and awareness of not only the child but of the total environment that could potentially impact on that child. Nurturing also means paying attention to the past and the future both—again, using the nurturance of the child as an example, to properly care for the child means to know when the last meal was, and where the next one will come from. It is attention to detail, diversity, complexity, and interrelationships in the environment. Nurturing also implies an awareness of the integrity of the person, the community, or the environment that one is nurturing. It results in a "relational ethic"—through the process of nurturing, I become connected and hence care more.

Creating Collective Meaning

Work and art are two sides of the same impulse in humanity—the desire to express the experience of being together in a creative way. Christopher Caudwell, in his study of the origins of poetry, found its source to be in the community. He described the aesthetic relationship between art and human cooperation in this way:

Sweetened with a harvest song, the work goes well. Just because poetry is what it is, it exhibits a reality beyond the reality it brings to birth and nominally portrays, a reality which though secondary is yet higher and more complete. For poetry describes and expresses not so much the grain in its concreteness, the harvest in its factual essence—which it helps to realise and which are the conditions for its own existence—but the emotional, social and collective complex which is that tribe's relation to the harvest. It expresses a whole new world of truth—its emotion, its comradeship, its sweat, its long-drawn-out wait and happy consummation—which has been brought into being by the fact that man's relation to the harvest is not instinctive and blind but economic and conscious. Not poetry's abstract statement—its content of facts—but its dynamic role in society— its content of collective emotion—is therefore poetry's truth.[19]

Using the poem as an example of work raised to the symbolic or iconic level, Caudwell sees the poem as an expression of how work unites us in community. The world of work is the world emerging from shared work as it creates community. Through the poem (or any work of art), we understand and experience the collective nature of our shared work.

Implicit in art is the human desire to integrate the experience of the world, to make sense of things, to bring things to closure by creating symbols, images, and artifacts that articulate meaning. However, according to Yi-Fu Tuan, because people in a technological culture no longer create artifacts and things (the machines do it), they no longer create the reality around them and therefore they have lost the ability to integrate and make sense of reality.

The human made object no longer stands for clarity, for something that we can understand intuitively and spontaneously. . . . Our mind cannot rest in a manufactured world that has no overall plan, but rather must grapple with that world, must try to resolve its perplexing amorphousness at the level of intellectual comprehension while knowing that the task is unrealizable.[20]

Ideally, work connects us with our reality, and the products we create help shape and furnish that reality with known objects. The lack of integration of meaning or synthesis in American cultural attitudes toward work and consumption leaves us searching for an aesthetic that will counterbalance the high-tech world of capitalism. David Shi, in his recent book *The Simple Life*, outlines the history of a "moral equivalent" to capitalism and technology—an American experience he calls in his subtitle, "Plain Living and High Thinking." Woven throughout his book is a description of the "other" America—an America fulfilling the Puritan call for restraint in the material world in order to participate more fully in the spiritual and ideal. This was the moral economy of the Puritans, the Quakers, Ralph Waldo Emerson, and Henry David Thoreau, and the real world of Scott and Helen Nearing; but it remained a minor voice in the great orchestra of consumption. He concludes:

Simplicity is more aesthetic than ascetic in its approach to good living. Money or possessions or activities themselves do not corrupt simplicity, but the love of money, the craving for possessions, and the prison of activities do. Knowing the difference between personal trappings and personal traps, therefore, is the key to mastering the fine art of simple living. . . . The good life, as Aldo Leopold pointed out, "boils down to a question of degree."[21]

ART AND POLITICS

One of the astounding realities of our modern world is that images of work have virtually disappeared in our culture. Not only is work no longer the subject of art, but when it is, that activity is no longer viewed as art. It becomes, instead, tainted with politics.

Since the 1930s, the dominant culture has ridiculed the works of artists who choose to portray work or explore issues surrounding work. What came to be called proletarian art was not considered real art. The attempt to formulate a radical aesthetic began in the turn-of-the-century socialist movements, but really flowered in the 1930s. In this new aesthetic, art was to be defined in social rather than formalistic terms—not art for art's sake, but art inspiring collective human enterprise.

Criticism of this social realism was aimed at two levels: the actual content and the politics that content represented. While critics of proletarian literature, for example, focused on so-called literary criteria such as subject matter, conflicts between rational ideology and fictional art, and the lack of symbols in proletarian art, they also felt a need to criticize the presence of political ideology in works of art, particularly communism. Because some communist art celebrated work and the worker, any art depicting work was therefore suspect because it might be political art. Real art, they argued, succeeds precisely because it is not political.

However, as Richard H. Pellis and others have pointed out, these critics generally were shouting into a vacuum. A whole generation of artists wedded creativity with political activism. The Left had a remarkable impact on American art and aesthetic theory. During the 1930s in particular, social realism dominated every field: photography, theater, art, and especially literature, and according to Pellis,

those who rejected proletarian literature were usually on the defensive. No matter how eloquently they celebrated the universality of art or the writer's dedication to this craft, they seemed unable to grasp that these ideals were simply less appealing to intellectuals at present than the desire to play a more direct role in American life. For most writers during the depression, the problem was not how to remain free but how to become more committed.[22]

By the 1950s, images of work and working people virtually disappeared from the culture. The government's House UnAmerican Activities Committee did its work well, destroying the last vestiges of proletarian art and consciousness from cultural artifacts—film, theater, and literature all succumbed to the relentless attacks on collective consciousness wherever it emerged in art.

Look at television today. No one works except women doing housework and farmers driving combines in the commercials. Work in these ads is there to be escaped or made easier. Characters in sit-coms have jobs, but you seldom see them working. "Roseanne" is an exception, but even there the worker is trivialized. What work you do see is done by professionals—nurses, doctors, lawyers, police officers—not factory workers or file clerks or data entry people. The work itself is never at the center of the plot, just as "real" work is peripheral to our "real" lives after 5:00 P.M.

The absence of the iconography of work from our society probably reflects several things: our disdain for work, our desire not to work, the absence of meaning of work in our lives. Where we do see images of real work—often on public television documentaries about Third World countries—it is seen as alien, foreign. Were we to present work as it is in the United States, one wonders how it would sell.

CONCLUSION: ART AND FREEDOM

Our work has been stolen from us, its creative energy destroyed, its artistic qualities compromised. Aesthetics is sacrificed daily not only to the standardization of the machine but also to the profit motive that presupposes overproduction and a need for mindless consumption. Although Marxism has traditionally advised us to "wait until after the revolution"—then we will have time for art and aesthetic questions—we should seriously examine this advice.

Good work and good art are, at their finest, revolutionary. According to Wendell Bradley, the key to our collective freedom lies in developing our aesthetic sensibility: "As a faculty that responds to the unity and completeness of experience it is an eminently social quality. . . . We are made more fully human as we develop aesthetically through a process of deeply mutual living."[23] Where good art and good work flourish, freedom is realized because

People who are motivated aesthetically value freedom too highly to be easily controllable. . . . The will to freedom, that is the will to do away with coercive power, begins with a vision of a better world that remains true even in temporary defeat. A communal-aesthetic temperament can help organize this vision into a spiritual unity that can stand up against domination, iron progress and the myth of the machine.[24]

Cultural and aesthetic transformation should go hand in hand with economic reappropriation. We need to begin now to develop a blueprint that will transform the oppressive conditions of work today into aesthetic experiences of the first order. Each of the above aesthetic qualities represents not only abstract values, but real possibilities to transform the nature of our work and our society as a whole. Our task is to apply these criteria to the work that we do—whether that work be writing a book, performing in a play, or building computers. Indeed, we have a responsibility bordering on an imperative to evaluate our work in aesthetic terms. Do I perform my work mechanically, technically? Do I emphasize special effects or technical wizardry at the expense of substance, content, or human interaction in my work? Am I really in control of my work, and, if I were, how would it be different and how would I be different? Few of us are immune from the subtle influences of machine capitalism and its demands to surrender self and artistic work to the market mentality.

What is the nature of our work? Our task is to reclaim the intrinsic unity of work and art. This is possible. Work as art is the true reality. These aesthetic qualities, if practiced, will create a new world—a world characterized by intimacy and connection—work with art, people with one another, and means with ends.

NOTES

1. Wendell Berry, *Standing by Words*, (San Francisco, 1983), 87–88.
2. Adolpho Sanchez Vazquez, *Art and Society: Essays in Marxist Aesthetics* (New York and London, 1973), 102.

3. Ibid., 105–6.

4. Kurt Vonnegut, Jr., *Player Piano* (New York, 1970), 284–85.

5. Ibid., 318.

6. Thorstein Veblen, *The Portable Veblen*, ed. Max Lerner (New York, 1972), 318.

7. Ibid., 320.

8. Ibid.

9. Mulford Sibley, "The Relevance of Classical Political Theory for Economy, Technology and Ecology," *Alternatives: Perspectives on Society and Environment* 2 (1973): 31.

10. Michael L. Schwalbe, *The Psychosocial Consequences of Natural and Alienated Labor* (Albany, NY, 1986), 52.

11. Ibid., 152.

12. See Douglas Harper, *Working Knowledge: Skill and Community in a Small Shop* (Chicago and London, 1987), 131–32.

13. Thorstein Veblen, *The Theory of Business Enterprise* (New York, 1904). See chapter 9.

14. Arnold Gehlen, *Man in the Age of Technology* (New York, 1980), 45.

15. Ibid.

16. Herbert Read, *Education through Art* (New York, 1956).

17. E. F. Schumacher, *Small Is Beautiful* (New York, 1973), 55.

18. Lewis Mumford, "Apology to Henry Adams," *The Virginia Quarterly Review* 38 (1962): 215–16.

19. Christopher Caudwell, *Illusion and Reality* (New York, 1977), 38.

20. Yi-Fu Tuan, "The Significance of the Artifact," *Geographical Review* 70 (1980): 471.

21. David E. Shi, *The Simple Life: Plain Living and High Thinking in American Culture* (New York, 1985), 280–81.

22. Richard H. Pellis, *Radical Visions and American Dreams* (New York, 1973), 186.

23. Wendell Bradley, "Power, Aesthetics and Community," unpublished paper, 7.

24. Ibid., 8.

Chapter 9

Good Work: The Ethics of Caring

The work of the world is common as mud.
Botched, it smears the hands, crumbles to dust.
But the thing worth doing well done
has a shape that satisfies, clean and evident.
Greek amphoras for wine or oil,
Hopi vases that held corn, are put in museums
but you know they were made to be used.
The pitcher cries for water to carry
and a person for work that is real.
                                —Marge Piercy from "To Be of Use"[1]

Throughout human history we have studied work and its meaning in all aspects
of culture. The last two chapters were devoted to an examination of good work
from political and aesthetic perspectives. Two basic propositions resulted: good
work must be done both with others and for others, and good work emerges
from an aesthetic process of making. Ultimately, however, the aesthetics of good
work must address the question of quality and how we are to define it.

Good work is also characterized by certain moral, ethical, and political principles: the right to survival, control over the means of production, the presence
of a sense of calling, the right to the profits of one's work, and other principles
consistent with creating a work environment that enhances human freedom and
builds community.

This chapter will highlight the important notion of quality in defining good
work: work as a way of life that creates meaningful opportunities for high quality
self-expression, work that is driven by a passion for quality, work that allows
the worker to experience a sense of wholeness or oneness, and work that uses
appropriate technologies to ensure the continued high quality of both the individual and the environment.

GOOD WORK: EXPRESSING THE SELF

Good work is ultimately about creating a way of life. It is not something you go to, like a job; it is a way of being, a way of articulating how one experiences the world. "When a man undertakes to create something," wrote Paracelsus, "he establishes a new heaven, as it were, and from it the work that he desires to create flows into him."[2] Experienced in this way, a sense of rightness permeates the work activity and the individual is, in turn, empowered, i.e., having the power to act, shape, create his or her own world.

Paradoxically, to do good work is also to lose the self in the involvement and engagement with work in order to find the self in work—either in the end product of work, or in the process of doing work. E. F. Schumacher defines good work both as "work that is good for the worker"[3] and as work that is done "in service to, and in cooperation with, others, so as to liberate ourselves from our inborn egocentricity."[4] There is in good work a powerful integration of the mind and body, the intellectual and the physical, the individual and the community. Work humbles and exalts—we wonder at the ends of work as we submit to the necessity of doing it.

Good work is further characterized by such qualities as a sense of commitment, activities that generate purposeful actions, and close attention to the synergy of means and ends. Work has to have meaning beyond itself and beyond our individual selves. Satisfaction comes with knowing that there is meaning beyond just the making of money, or the doing of things just to be done with them. Good work also takes pride in the results of work and the carrying through of the individual's intent to completion.

Work is also good when it stimulates both the mind and the body. Since most of us do so little physical or hand work today, we have lost the ability to enjoy this particular side of work. While we have replaced physical work with our current culture of exercise and running, we still lack the final integration inherent in good work and a sense of completion—the feel of the product in our hands, the sight of the garden weeded or the wood stacked. There is nothing creative about jogging! For a while, in the 1960s, we did revive craftsmanship and pride in handmade goods or home-baked bread. However, the crafts revival faltered on the tide of handmade goods produced by people in Third World countries. The consumer market was flooded with lower-priced items and the American craftsperson could not compete. In a consumer society, where things are more important than human relations, it is more desirable to consume crafts than to honor the process of making them.

The loss of the sense of integration through handwork may also impair basic human development functions. According to Schumacher, "Various types of physical activity in which neuromotor capabilities interact with mental processes to strengthen both are the most dangerously neglected components of modern education."[5] We do know that one specific motor skill—eye-hand coordination—is no longer acquired primarily by making things. Instead, young people (primarily men) sharpen their concentration, focus, and coordination by playing video games. While skill can be developed this way, its only source of satisfaction lies in further manipulations of a machine.

It is also important that we see ourselves as creators, makers. Why is this so? To create is to empower the self. People who create things are more self-confident, and therefore more likely to act in a political or social way. They understand the connection between means and ends, and through controlling what you do, you can achieve your objectives. Good work is work that allows us to control the entire process of that task: conceive of the task to be done, determine how it will be done, and, when it is completed, see it put to use. According to Schumacher, the division of labor denies us this satisfaction:

Satisfaction [in work] is lacking because a "sense of consequence" is lacking in specialized and fragmented activity in which we deal with only one piece of a process which leads either to a remote or even really undesirable achievement; and because the sense of responsibility is not engaged within productive activity.[6]

A sense of calling is also an essential ingredient of a creative work experience. To be called is to be taken out of the self, to be drawn to a larger reality, a broader mission, a public responsibility. The concept of a calling was associated historically with a religious impulse and it had both personal and ethical connotations. The concept transcends this narrow religious association, however, and should be reclaimed and expanded to more general usage.

In early American Puritan society, to be called meant to live out an intensely personal intentionality through one's work. John Cotton, reflecting on the meaning of calling in his Puritan community, likened it to a process of self-fulfillment. There were three principal requirements of a calling: "He would see his calling aiming at the public good; he would see gifts for it and an open door for his entrance into it; he would not come unto it by deceit and undermining of others."[7] For most people today, however, work is not a fit between self, job and community, but rather the means to buy enough freedom to pursue one's calling after five o'clock.

A calling, then, is driven by both public and private ends. However, it is best characterized by the presence of talents, or gifts, that are consecrated to good and noble ends: "to enable every one of us to use and thereby perfect our gifts like good stewards."[8] A calling is, in essence, true ethical individualism.

GOOD WORK: A QUALITY OF SPIRIT

Unfortunately, the sense of the sacred, of spirituality, in contemporary American culture is most often experienced as a reverence for the scientific and technical. This decidedly modern religion defines itself first and foremost as separate from nature. It exalts the rational, the material. In a perverse way, it celebrates work—the work of the machine, the work of subduing nature. According to Wendell Berry, however, it is an unsatisfactory spirituality. To revitalize a sense of the spiritual in our culture, Berry believes, we need to recapture an awareness of something beyond the material world, something larger than the individual, in order to create the kind of culture that nourishes good work. Good work, he insists, exists only as a part of something, when we have a sense of a larger environment or context. For Berry, that greater something is nature. For others, it may be religion, or human community.

The role of the sacred in human experience is especially problematic when we attempt to situate that impulse in the material worlds of work and community. We ordinarily understand the spiritual as a sense of transcendence, an expression of abstraction away from the real, material world. Spiritual in its religious formulation is cosmic, ethereal, otherworldly even; the spiritual in nature is animistic, contemplative, integrative. Our own era has seen the emergence of a new religious expression: worship of the machine and the artistry of technology. According to Lev Chernyi, all of these expressions of the spiritual—the religious, the animistic, the scientific—fail to achieve true spirituality because they "involve a reification of experience which suppresses *the priority of that which is directly lived* in favor of fetishized abstractions that are viewed as more important and fundamental" [emphasis mine].[9] Chernyi is interested in laying to rest all expressions of spirituality—including presumably those calling themselves "new age"—that propose transcendent solutions to the world's problems. Instead, he opts for a

relativistic, situated discourse which takes place between humans in community without any claim to finality. The pretense to absolute or (unsituated) objective knowledge is always totalitarian. For the countertradition, on the other hand, rationality is always seen as an outgrowth of life and nature—reflecting its origins rather than prescribing the nature of reality. . . . It is always bound to finite living, social and historical beings, their desires and their worlds, not to any supposed transcendental realities in which everything is perfectly unreal.[10]

It is through the transformation of good work, I believe, that we can begin to develop a true spirituality, and one can only approach that greater spiritual awareness by grounding work in human community and environmental place. The American experience has been just the opposite, however: the good American is the person free to move about. We don't want to be stuck—we want to be ready to move quickly to take advantage of new opportunities. We have not learned that the grass is never greener. We have not learned that the frontier doesn't exist. Being "grounded" is not a pleasant experience for the average American (isn't it interesting that we use the same term to punish our children, teaching them early in their lives that mobility is a central American ethic). We must relearn how to locate ourselves in the various contexts in which we live: our physical place, the community of friends and neighbors through which we move, the history of our personal lives and our communities.

Good work at its best can reward the worker with this more grounded feeling of transcendence beyond the self that gives peace of mind. Oneness, or holism, is a function of context, of being with others, of knowing where one belongs. When we are at one, we have peace of mind. Peace of mind is a deeply spiritual need, a need that transcends specific religions and yet seems to be central to many religious philosophies. The feeling of transcendence can be both a personal sense of renewal and a means of reaffirming the connection of self to the community, to the earth, to something greater than the self.

I found one of the deepest and most beautiful insights into good work in a book on aesthetics and philosophy with the unlikely title of *Zen and the Art of Motorcycle Maintenance*.[11] Robert H. Pirsig wants us to understand that work is the highest expression of the human being—and it is best understood as existing on the finely balanced edge of our interaction with the world. What we do is how we are: How we acquit ourselves in the qualitative sense can be known through our work.

Peace of mind isn't at all superficial to technical work. It's the whole thing. That which produces it is good work and that which destroys it is bad work. The specs, the measuring instruments, the quality control, the final checkout, these are all *means* toward the end of satisfying the peace of mind of those responsible for the work.[12]

Work as art, work as being: in the act of doing the spiritual is experienced. The business of good work is the business of making peace with the materials of work: the clay of the bowl, the words written on the page, the bread dough rising in the pan. Work is the knowledge of when the bread is done and the clay can no longer be shaped.

The experience of the sacred also requires stepping out of time, and the doing of good work can enhance this feeling of timelessness. Taking time to do good work is also a revolutionary act when you recall that one of the first triumphs of the new capitalist system was the harnessing of time to work. When the worker takes the time to do a task well, it is an act of rebellion. As we saw earlier in this book, the preeminence of the factory owner came when he or she could control the time and motions of work. Real work is free of both constraints. It allows for immersion in the process of making and freedom from the limits of the clock. Capitalism has even tried to convince us that the time stolen from the worker does not really affect the quality of our lives:

The great myth of our work-intense era is "quality time." We believe that we can make up for the loss of days or hours, especially with each other, by concentrated minutes. But ultimately there is no way to do one-minute mothering. There is no way to pay attention in a hurry. Seeing, as Georgia O'Keeffe said, takes time. Friendship takes time. So does family. So does arriving at a sense of well-being.[13]

Taking time to do good work also makes a statement about the level of involvement with the task. Concentration, engagement, taking pains, and total absorption are all ways of saying the same thing: the process of making is all-consuming. Quality work is work that results from the total engagement of the worker/artist with the means of production. It is work we care about, it is work in which we lose ourselves in order to find the sense of the whole. Through this doing of good work we can also participate in a spiritual sense of balance, a sense of rightness with the world. According to Pirsig, when we have achieved this transcendent awareness of the unity of the self with work, we approach the ultimate good, which he calls "Quality."

Zen Buddhists talk about "just sitting," a meditative practice in which the idea of a duality of self and object does not dominate one's consciousness. What I'm talking about here in motorcycle maintenance is "just fixing," in which the idea of a duality of self and object doesn't dominate one's consciousness. When one isn't dominated by feelings of separateness from what he's working on, then one can be said to "care" about what he's doing. That is what caring really is, a feeling of identification with what one's doing. When one has this feeling then he also sees the inverse of caring, Quality itself.[14]

GOOD WORK: THE ETHICS OF TECHNOLOGICAL MAKING

Good work should also have a care for the consequences of its creation and our choice of tools is an ethical consideration. There have been serious moral and ethical consequences of our society's decision to become dependent upon machine technology. We wanted machines because they made more faster. We chose an ethic of expansion rather than an ethic of setting limits, and as a result have seriously jeopardized the health of the entire planet. Clearly, our relationship with machines must undergo a critical transformation.

To begin, we could introduce the concept of the appropriate. How do we decide what technologies are appropriate, and what is the context of that appropriateness? Deciding the appropriate use of technology will be one of the most important political issues facing us in this century. What technologies we use and how much they should produce will be determined by a host of mitigating factors, but the final outcome will undoubtedly be to curb their expansion.

Something is appropriate when it takes account of its environment, its surrounding reality. Determining what is appropriate is a process of analyzing the tool in its reciprocal relationship, seeking always to maintain balance in the whole. In order to apply the brakes to our runaway technology and create an appropriate technology, for example, our society will have to adopt ethical guidelines that are circumscribed by the health of the physical environment. Garrett Hardin, in his essay "The Tragedy of the Commons," wrote, "The morality of an act is a function of the state of the system at the time it is performed."[15] What will work in one era, or in one context, he goes on to argue, may not necessarily be generalizable to all situations. In our own time, the balance has been dangerously skewed toward technology, and care for our environment must now take priority.

One of the most obvious places we could begin is to evaluate technologies for their safety. At the turn of the century, union demands resulted in the passage of a whole body of legislation to ensure a safe work environment. Even today the Occupational Safety and Health Administration (OSHA) still stands as a symbol of our society's vigilance and care for the work environment. Not unexpectedly, OSHA is the bane of capitalists both large and small, and its effectiveness is often subject to the winds of political ideology.

It will be more costly to make the work environment safe, and priorities will have to shift from the harmful production processes we have to those compatible with healthy human and natural environments. Real change will require efforts beyond the power of regulatory agencies, however. Controls of technologies must revert to the local environment where the impact can be most directly assessed. No one wants a nuclear waste dump in their community. Each community could establish an environmental group or committee whose responsibility would be to coordinate the establishment of ethical guidelines. Beyond the local community, a federated organization could monitor and recommend adaptations that affect broader concerns or impact on whole ecosystems.

Our ethics also have to extend beyond our nation's borders. We can no longer allow "our" corporations to do in other countries what is unethical or illegal here. Harmful agricultural chemicals like DDT, for example, are still heavily used in other countries. Although their use is banned in the United States, these chemicals have been found on some imported fruits and vegetables. One of the great technological horrors of our time was the production and sale of a life-threatening technology—the Dalkon Shield intrauterine contraceptive device (IUD)—to Third World countries. These IUDs, which U.S. District Judge Miles Lord called "deadly depth charges" in the wombs of women, were marketed to unsuspecting women worldwide.[16] In other cases, companies that were forced to shut down operations in this country because they create environmental pollution have simply moved across the border into Mexico. We must cease buying into the myth that there is such a thing as a transnational corporation that is free and independent of any ethical restrictions and begin to require them to be socially and environmentally responsible wherever they do business.

Under such a system in which ethical constraints would apply, product or production process safety would be evaluated in terms of impact on both human beings and the environment. Further, we need to begin the process of evaluation even before products are produced by asking whether the use of a particular natural resource will harm the environment in some significant way. Although we already make some of these decisions much more could be done. For example, we could expand requirements that strip-mined land be restored to ecological health, and we could refuse to allow clear-cutting in forests. We will also need to evaluate the renewability of resources and make appropriate decisions to ensure that resources last as long as possible.

Once we commit ourselves to a process of evaluation of technologies, how do we begin? After all, *appropriate* means different things to different people. A poster produced for the 1985 meeting of the Non-Governmental Organizations (NGOs) on the U.N. Decade on Women, held in Nairobi, Kenya, proclaimed,

"If It's Not Appropriate for Women, It's Not Appropriate." It made reference to the tendency of First World countries to introduce technologies that are designed to encourage cash cropping rather than subsistence farming. These new technologies are marketed primarily to men. Technology should be designed to meet local, particular economic needs—not introduced into an environment haphazardly. *Appropriate*, for our purposes, will be defined as a nice fit between the tool, the hand that will use it, and the economic and physical environment in which the tool will be used.

Technologies introduced inappropriately into new environments can have disastrous results. In a recent study of economic development in Bangladesh, the author explored the impact of the introduction of certain post-harvest agricultural technologies on women's declining economic status. Some of the findings are quoted at length below.

Firstly, the mechanized post-harvest activities are done by men and as such women are losing control over the family's agricultural output which they had previously exercised when goods were being processed by them. Secondly, as their works are being taken over, they are being pushed to more labour intensive and poorly paid jobs. . . . With the increased rice production there has been a rapid increase in mechanical milling of rice, due to which nearly 2 million women have lost a traditional source of productive employment which accounted for over 16 percent of total household income of landless families. Evidences further indicate that a mechanized mill may displace up to 200 women from *bari-based* employment [the household, or survival economy]. Considering the importance of female income for household survival this loss is very significant. A survey carried out in 4 villages reveals that 50 percent of the employed women in the same derived their entire income from post-harvest activities and 44 percent had a combined source of income from post-harvest and other household works.[17]

What is important to note here is that Bangladesh has opened a debate on the applications of new technologies introduced into their culture. We Americans, on the other hand, seldom question how technologies impact us, probably because we are unaware of them as technologies. We live in the midst of the machines, and we have little understanding of how they may affect us.

It is critical, therefore, that we begin to unravel these complex networks that we call technology. The hidden devices described in chapter 4 that Albert Borgmann has pointed out to us must be uncovered. We need to educate ourselves to the many ways in which the technological process affects both people and the environment. Knowledge, in this case, will give us power—the power to control the many manifestations of technology. Once we have an understanding of how the technology works, we can begin asking ourselves such questions as: Do we really need this process, this thing? Can the same work be done with a simpler technology? Does this technology put people out of work?

What we do about technologies will ultimately affect the very nature of work. C. George Benello reminds us: "Any efforts to create freedom in work must bring the present technology under control."[18] It is not only a matter of control:

The technologies that we are making ever more complex must be simplified and should be redesigned to increase worker involvement. According to Hirschhorn:

The more complex the machinery, the more complex are the possible varieties of machine failure. There are moments when only human intelligence can diagnose and correct unforeseen breakdowns. To prevent catastrophes [such as the Three Mile Island accident], machinery must be designed to permit human intervention, and workers must be trained as problem solvers, not merely machine tenders. . . . This suggests an entirely new definition of work in a post-industrial setting. Skills can no longer be defined in terms of a particular set of actions, but as general ability to understand how a system functions and to think flexibly in solving problems.[19]

We must also uncover the hidden costs of technologies, and recalculate the cost/benefit formula to include things such as costs of disposal of materials (such as plastics or radioactive waste), costs to society to care for the unemployed worker who is displaced by new technologies, costs of depletion of natural resources, and others, to arrive at the true and total costs of any given technology. We will likely decide that certain technologies are not worth using because they are not cost-effective.

The development of a new ethic—one based on the idea of limits and boundaries—is central to controlling the growth of technology. Arnold Gehlen argues, however, that it will be difficult to impose restraints on a system of production that is currently operating on the maxim of limitless production. Asceticism is antithetical to consumer capitalism, and our society is accustomed to instant gratification of its wants. We have no experience in setting limits.

What men fear are not the monstrous destructive energies of the atomic nucleus, but their own; not the H-bomb, but themselves. They sense, rightly, that they cannot count on an internal constraint upon the use of a power one holds in one's hands to emerge suddenly in the final state of a development, whose main tendency for two hundred years has been exactly to remove such constraints, to foster and enhance a purely objective, rational, and technical concern with effectiveness.[20]

The issue of control of the technology is different from control of the means of production, but the two can go together. Benello believes we should get control of the factories first, and then, "What should or should not be produced is after all a relative decision, to be democratically arrived at."[21] I have some difficulties with his position, because I don't believe that the decision can be left to the workers in that one factory only. If the only job in town is building bombs and the alternative is no work at all, a community would probably continue in counterproductive activities. A federation of worker-owned collectives could be charged with addressing these broader ethical issues, assuming that responsibility only when workers do not act in the best interest of the society as a whole. Whatever mechanism we use, however, one thing is clear. We must stop producing and consuming and consciously lower our standard of living—not just temporarily, but forever. Twenty years ago, it would have been difficult, if not impossible, to find a majority of people in the modern industrial world to sit down and vote altruistically to reduce their level and complexity of consumption. Today, however, we have a new, urgent incentive—fear of the total destruction of the ecosystem. It is quite apparent that some processes in our technological reality are truly destructive of both people and the environment, and short of the always-hoped-for miracle of technology solving its own problems, I think we have to begin to make hard decisions between good and bad technologies. There will be little change if we gain control of the means of production only. Our first decision needs to be what our society should produce, and what technologies we want to keep to achieve those ends. There is little point in taking over control of a factory that puts motor oil in plastic bottles that pollute the environment.

Mulford Sibley has devoted much thought to the role of technology in society. Sibley outlines four basic ethical propositions to establish and maintain appropriate technologies:

1. Technology ought to be subject to general public policy direction; . . .
2. [We] need to develop the will and the skill essential to establish institutions through which public direction can be attained;
3. Our goal ought to be a society in which we seek neither to "return to nature" nor to allow an indefinite development of division of labor and complex technology; . . .
4. [We should] keep clearly in mind the centrality of spiritual development and the merely instrumental character of material goods.[22]

Sibley is especially concerned with the second proposition: the development of a political process by which we can evaluate technological applications. Currently, we have no institution in our society that monitors technology in terms of its appropriateness. Once we have determined the process by which the decision will be made, we need to then determine the criteria by which technologies will be evaluated. Sibley proposes the term "selective technology" to refer to the criteria by which societies choose which technologies to introduce. Many criteria could be applied: a technology's relative complexity, its costs in energy or raw materials, or its environmental damage. Sibley is especially interested in developing criteria that affect what he calls "traditional labor patterns": "political or public policy limits must be placed on expansion of the division of labor. Beyond a certain point, division of labor runs counter to human integrity or wholeness."[23]

We have to look at setting limits in other ways, too. As technology has expanded, it has grown more complex. Sometimes the complexity is due to businesses wishing to increase their percentage of a market, not to improve the product. Since the basic technologies are the same (for example, all microwaves operate on the same principle), the only way you can set up difference (and hence imply that your product is better), is to make the product more complex, for example, put more buttons on the blender or the microwave.

Sometimes complexity is introduced by designing the technology to expand control over some phase of the production process itself. An excellent example of this process is the introduction of computerization into automobiles. Now, the average mechanically inclined individual no longer can work on the car—it must be taken to the service station where there is a machine that can diagnose the problem better than the human. This gives the factory control over the repairs and despite the increased ease in repair that accompanied this transition to computerization, the price for the repair has not gone down. The mechanic's income is gone (as are mechanics, we might expect), but the price of parts has increased. It is interesting to me that prices never seem to go down because of technological advances. The price of cars hasn't gone down now that robots are working in the plants—the profits just go up, thus concentrating in even fewer hands the value of our labor.

It isn't just the cost of technology that's important here—what we have lost to technological centralization is our basic ability to subsist—either by ourselves or collectively. The more complex technologies become, the more dependent we are on a whole host of actions—each one hinged on the one before. The more the machines do for us, the more dependent we become on them and the less we do for ourselves and each other. We no longer need each other, and our actual work is stolen from us by the machines.

Paradoxically, as technology has grown more complex it has also reduced the diversity in our world. Cars, for example, are highly complex, but we no longer have the option of taking the train, and hybrid seed corn cannot grow without the addition of chemicals to the agricultural process. We may have reached the point in our relationship with machines equivalent to that of the medieval scholars who debated how many angels could dance on the head of a pin: We have created complexity to the point of irrelevancy, and it might even be humorous were it not so dangerous a trend.

Another way we can gain decision-making control over technology is to begin demanding "consumers' authority over production."[24] We can begin making distinctions between essential and nonessential goods and services, and then evaluate those goods and services along a predetermined axis of changes we want to make in technological production. Consumer rights advocates never question whether a product should be produced; they are concerned only with the product's quality or reliability. Other criteria we could adopt include establishing standards of production that assess the product's potential for damage to the environment, how it benefits the society, or how it allows the worker to feel satisfied in his or her work: what William Ophuls calls the ethics of "sufficiency, frugality, and stewardship instead of growth, profligacy, and exploitation." What should be abundantly clear is that we can no longer run an economy on the belief that there will "always be more."[25]

We might think of giving priority to other values—human values—as well.

Ophuls suggests we might promote the value of such personal qualities as prudence (self-control, forethought, provident use of resources) and individual self-restraint when it comes to the use of goods and services. Instead of seeing economics as the driving force of culture, we should explore such non-economic values as good work, personal happiness, adequate social services, and so on, which emphasize "the primacy of the spiritual and intellectual over the material, the intrinsic superiority of love over hate, the suspicion of complexity and so on."[26]

CONCLUSION

Finally, we must come to understand that good work is something that each of us must do. Most of us do not want to hear that we "need" to work—we have all been raised with the belief that the machines will do it. However, without our active engagement in the world of work, we are left in the position of individual and collective paralysis—unable to act in any way. We must reclaim our work and reaffirm the connection between our hands and our brains, and the results of good effort. As Grace Lee Boggs and James Boggs remind us below, we are at a crucial point in our relationship with work:

Work is a necessity for the human personality. But man/woman has struggled for so long against compulsory work that we have lost the notion that if we didn't work, we would not exist as humans. We exist at the historical conjunction of the highest point of the mass struggle against labor and the technological revolution which eliminated the old reasons to work. So we have to reaffirm that people have to work, but they don't have to work in the old way and for the old reasons. We can't look for a new way or for new reasons unless we believe that there are human reasons for working.[27]

A passion for work, a passion for quality, a passion for meaningful collective effort—it is passion that must be reawakened in the American psyche for good work to be realized. As we come to the end of our search for good work, there is the barest hint of optimism that change will come. Deep in the American character there is a sense of rightness, of justice, that will triumph over the broken promises of consumer capitalism. The dream of good work is still alive.

NOTES

1. Excerpt from a longer poem "To Be of Use," in Marge Piercy, *Circles on the Water: Selected Poems of Marge Piercy* (New York, 1973), 106.
2. D. M. Dooling, ed., *A Way of Working: The Spiritual Dimension of Craft* (New York, 1986), 94.
3. E. F. Schumacher, *Good Work* (New York, 1979), 120.
4. Ibid., 3–4.
5. Ibid., 165.
6. Ibid., 190–91.

7. John Cotton, "A Christian Calling," in *The American Puritans: Their Prose and Poetry*, ed. Perry Miller (Garden City, NY, 1956), 175.

8. Schumacher, *Good Work*, 3–4.

9. Lev Chernyi, "The Cult of the Sacred," *Anarchy: A Journal of Desire Armed* 24 (March–April 1990): 21.

10. Ibid., 21–23.

11. Robert M. Pirsig, *Zen and the Art of Motorcycle Maintenance: An Inquiry into Values* (Toronto, 1975).

12. Ibid., 288.

13. Ellen Goodman, "Learning a Lot By Doing Nothing," Minneapolis *Tribune*, 30 August 1988, 8A.

14. Pirsig, *Zen and the Art*, 290.

15. Garrett Hardin, "The Tragedy of the Commons," *Science* 162 (13 December 1968): 1243–48.

16. Miles W. Lord, " 'A Deadly Depth Charge in their Wombs,' " Minneapolis *Star and Tribune*, May 18, 1984, 15A.

17. Salma Khan, *The Fifty Percent: Women in Development and Policy in Bangladesh* (Dhaka, Bangladesh, 1988), 71.

18. George C. Benello, "Putting the Reins on Technology," *Changing Work* 7 (Winter 1988): 23.

19. Larry Hirschhorn, "The Soul of a New Worker," *Working Papers Magazine* 9, no. 1 (January/February, 1982): 44, 45.

20. Arnold Gehlen, *Man in the Age of Technology*, (New York, 1980), 101.

21. George C. Benello, "The Challenge of Mondragon," *Black Rose* 12 (Winter 1986/1987): 29.

22. Mulford Q. Sibley, *Nature and Civilization: Some Implications for Politics* (Itaska, IL, 1977), 195–96.

23. Ibid., 185.

24. Giovanni Baldelli, *Social Anarchism* (Chicago and New York, 1971), 36.

25. William Ophuls, *Ecology and the Politics of Scarcity: Prologue to a Political Theory of the Steady State* (San Francisco, 1977), 9.

26. Sibley, *Nature and Civilization*, 195.

27. Grace Lee Boggs and James Boggs, *Revolution and Evolution in the Twentieth Century* (New York, 1974), 242.

Chapter 10

Good Work: Making Change

> Every perspective on economic life ... must be shaped by three questions:
> What does the economy do *for* people? What does it do *to* people? and how
> do people *participate* in it?[1]

The event we call the industrial revolution and its economic structure, which
we call capitalism, changed human patterns of work quickly and brutally. We
have seen its fruits of human degradation, and we know that it doesn't work
anymore. Both the socialist and the capitalist industrial societies are experiencing
broad unrest and disenchantment even to the point of revolution, and we are on
the verge of major global change. While it is true that change comes slowly and
subtly, it also comes predictably. We can discern the outline of a new world, a
new hegemony, all about us, and there is much we can do to direct the course
of this change. In this chapter I will examine the nature of change, summarize
what must change, and begin to outline and sharpen a vision of a future in which
good work will take place.

PRINCIPLES OF SOCIAL CHANGE

In order to create an environment in which good work can be realized, we
need to address a major restructuring of society at all levels. The magnitude of
this change is difficult to comprehend. Many years ago, in a lecture on the
Reformation, historian David Noble addressed a similar magnitude of change.
To understand the transformations that took place during the Reformation, he
said, we should remember that people "didn't just go to bed Catholic one night,
and wake up Protestant the next morning." Change, he insisted, was subtle and
complex, and took place over a long period of time.

Once we appreciate the magnitude of changes required, how does change come about? How are we to destroy the dominant way of life in the United States—the hegemony of corporate capitalism? It is, after all, the American way. As Robert Dahl so perceptively reminded us, the hegemony exists because we want it to, because we support it, and because we believe in it:

> The greatest obstacle to democratization and reducing inequalities in the United States is not . . . an elite of wealthy men, or even that military-industrial complex so much referred to these days, but rather the military-industrial-financial-labor-farming-educational-professional-consumer-over and under thirty-lower/middle/upper class complex that, for want of a more appropriate name, might be called the American people.[2]

We are, it seems, our own worst enemies. Our first step toward change, then, should be to look deeply into the mirror of our own lives. While it is difficult to accept that we may somehow be "responsible" for our own plight, part of empowerment is stepping into and "owning," without self-blame, the reality in which we live. This will not be easy—it is easier to blame the "other" or find conspiracies to explain the state of the world. It is not a matter of deciding whether you are part of the problem or the solution—it is understanding that both are intertwined, and it is only when we see ourselves as partaking in the action that we can be empowered enough to initiate change. If change happens outside our reality and control, we will be paralyzed with inaction.

Knowledge and insight into our contribution to maintenance of the hegemony, and the structures of power that perpetuate it, leads us to the next step in social change: altering the reality of that hegemony. If Antonio Gramsci is correct, once we begin to withdraw consent from the corporate hegemony and challenge the structures of power, change will have already begun. The process of change, then, begins by gaining knowledge about the structures of oppression; understanding that change comes from the known world, not from an alien, external stimulus; and that change requires collective action.

The Dynamics of the Corporate Hegemony

Just as knowing how a machine works is critical to fixing it, we need to know how hegemony is maintained and reinforced in order to dismantle it. In his analysis of institutional power, William Dugger describes what he calls the corporate hegemony:

> in the family, the school, and then in the corporation proper, individuals are shaped by the roles they play in each institution, and each institution is itself linked to the corporation. . . . This institutional shaping produces the motives, goals, ideals, and means of the individual.[3]

According to Dugger, there are four mechanisms that serve to maintain this hegemony: subreption, contamination, emulation, and mystification. Hegemony is maintained, first of all, by undermining diversity of perspectives and destroying the independent status of institutions through a process of subreption. Steve Hickerson's description of the subreption of the legal profession is an excellent example of this process. The legal profession, he argues, has lost sight of its original commitment to defend individuals against the power of various societal institutions and has gradually shifted its loyalties and its guiding principles to serving as handmaidens of the corporate elite.[4] Second, contamination occurs when the corporate mindset pervades all our thinking. It is reflected in our constant concern with the bottom line and in today's college students who no longer come for an education, but for an economic payoff—a job.

Third, hegemony is maintained through emulation, a process whereby we adopt the corporation as a status symbol and corporate leadership as role models. For example, we would defer to good management over less bottom-line-oriented leadership. Finally, hegemony is maintained through mystification. In the Middle Ages, mystification was maintained through church ritual—today it is carried out primarily under the auspices of the advertising industry selling us a trendy, corporate, upscale reality. These rituals and symbols are used to enhance social control and perpetuate the dominant perspective.

Ronald Reagan's communication style is an excellent example of successful mystification. His skilled manipulation of symbols central to the American identity—individualism, laissez faire capitalism, and personal initiative—had a hypnotic power. The "great communicator" was the great manipulator, taking his lessons from the advertising industry.

One of the most important tools of mystification is the perpetuation of all the "isms" that separate us: racism, sexism, ageism, classism, heterosexism, and others. Through the manipulation and exploitation of our fears and prejudices, we are kept from appreciating one another or working together collectively. Some corporate or state entity always benefits when these inequalities are perpetuated.

For change to occur we need to begin by challenging the processes that maintain the corporate hegemony. To counter corporate power and its ethical bankruptcy, we need to reintroduce democratic processes into our culture, nourish diversity and pluralism, continue reaffirming moral and ethic guidelines, and reintroduce value questions into politics. To resist contamination, we can revitalize a sense of honor and respect for our own communities and our own experiences, and build a new culture based on cooperative principles. To avoid emulation, we can discard the star-system mentality and hierarchical organizations and replace them with relationships based on mutual respect and noncompetitive economic and political structures. Finally, we should resist the mechanism that mystify us, and at the same time create new symbols.

We must also be aware that an unexamined deference to the power of a system can disempower. We must be very careful not to make an abstract hegemony or system the enemy. If oppression remains only a word, an idea, or an abstraction, it cannot easily be countered. The oppressor has a human face. The system as oppressor is other people—people who have vested interests in maintaining structures of power. As painful as it may be, we must understand and accept the personal nature of oppression. Some person or persons are responsible, and hence accountable.

Change Will Come from Within

Change does not come out of the blue. The seeds of change lie all about us in plain view as part of the problem we are trying to fix. In a society based on linear, progressive, evolutional (and hence predictable) thinking patterns, we have come to see major change only as dramatic revolution, as a spontaneous combustion of human energies coming from outside the rather gentle change within the system. However, revolutionary change is not a sudden break with the past, taking us off in entirely new and foreign directions. What we call revolution is really the realization—by the majority of society—of past accretions of the new hegemony in the process of becoming. According to Lewis Mumford, "The repressed components of our old culture will become the dominants of the new one; and similarly the present megatechnic institutions and structures will be reduced to human proportions and brought under direct human control."[5] Change, then, is a twofold process: It is a freeing up of what has been repressed and denied in our culture and a regaining of control over the institutions where power is concentrated.

From his analysis of the roots of the National Cooperative League, historian Clarke Chambers developed a similar theory of social change to account for the success of the cooperative movement. Cooperatives did not just happen—they emerged as a realignment of preexisting cultural values:

What could be more typically American than to believe that through voluntary association, through plain neighborliness and mutual assistance, the individual could be set free to realize his best inner potentiality for the greater good of society and the progress of the race? What social principle was more central to the traditional American ethos than the notion that a wide distribution of property would make unnecessary the enlargement of state activity to regulate concentrated private economic power? What values were preached more passionately than self-reliance, equality of opportunity, social harmony, brotherhood, love of neighbor, service?[6]

Change Is Intentional and Political

A critical factor in any progressive theory of change is the principle that change can occur because people will it. Too often we succumb to developmental or evolutionary models of change that leave us with the feeling of powerlessness. Just because change comes out of the current situation does not mean that outcomes are predictable. We are not victims of historical forces beyond our control.

We can, and do, choose to take a particular direction—both individually and collectively. Politics is the art of creating intentional action and change, and, according to Marc Tool, the essence of freedom is discretionary choice:

Economic and social change is in large part discretionary. Men and women, in the main, make their own history. . . . Social and economic change *consists* of a revamping of habits of mind and habits of behavior, of institutional forms, of prescriptions and proscriptions, of working rules, all of which organize activity.[7]

If we want to clean up the environment, we will. If we wish to house the homeless, we will find the way. It is this sense of intentionality that we must reclaim.

Further, it is collective action that is central to change. Change has to take place by all of us, for all of us working together. Social change cannot occur through one-by-one personal transformation. The structures of power cannot be changed by individual efforts: Power can only be reappropriated through the creation of new cooperative social structures such as collectives. Political action is best undertaken by decentralized collective groups with highly developed, unique political identities, rather than by a centrally organized mass movement or consciousness. In a future society, these collectives will vary greatly in composition: They may be organized by gender, race, class, ideology, or any other ideological ties that bind. They will have internal coherence, commitment, and structure.

Intentional groups (Gramsci called them "historic blocs") provide another way of organizing for social change that seem to broaden the possibilities for multiple alignments of people. These groups recognize that we are part of many worlds, many perspectives, and that we can easily shift our political energies to address many issues and form many coalitions.

The ideal of historical bloc departs significantly from notions of class embedded in the Marxist tradition: it promotes analysis of social formulations that cut across categories of ownership and nonownership and that are bound by religious or other ideological ties as well as those of economic interest. A historic bloc may or may not become hegemonic, depending on how successfully it forms alliances with other groups or classes.[8]

For example, I might define myself as a feminist, an environmentalist, and a pacifist, and form blocs with other individuals of like mind in order to effect change. Change also comes about through confronting our own personal internal contradictions. As we cultivate our own diversity and see all the intentional groups we have a stake in, we can also see the internal conflicts. It is through connection and ownership that responsibility is born, and it is through responsibility that political action is generated. The hunter and people who fish sooner or later must address environmental pollution, for example. Awareness of how the goals of the structures of power differ from our own is the beginning of transformation. We must also remember that we have the ability to change this reality.

Change is also rooted in the small, the local, the personal. While change can have global impact, it always begins here, and now. Historically, according to T. J. Jackson Lears, self-conscious, well-developed communities were the real source of change, not abstract mass movements with generic agendas. People act politically, he seems to suggest, from their deepest sense of human connectedness. When our community is threatened, we mobilize, and much political activity is undertaken to guarantee basic family/community survival needs. In his analysis of the emergence of the Populist movement, Lears reminds us that "Private needs had public consequences: they helped accelerate the rise of a new hegemonic culture."[9] We cannot remain at the local level, however. Analysis and political action must address the totality of the oppression by the corporate, capitalist hegemony. If we only address the local, we run the risk of impotent separatism.

Finally, change is not linear. The possibility of many inspirations for change is important to nourish. The all-pervasiveness of a hegemony can be overwhelming, but it does not take a force of equal magnitude to transform it. We need not wait for only a single large-scale action such as the rising up of the proletariat en masse. Change can come from many different directions, can emerge from many contexts. Whatever the inspiration for change, we must honor each unique flame as it burns.

SOCIAL ECONOMICS: A BLUEPRINT FOR CHANGE

In his theory of social economics, J. Ron Stanfield places the question of change squarely into its social/political context. Based on an integration of John Kenneth Galbraith's test of anxiety combined with John Dewey's theory of Instrumentalism, social economics is an experientially driven theory—flexible and responsive to contemporary concerns. Social economics allows us to determine the "shape of the coming paradigm battle" in the economy. The task of the social economist, Stanfield begins, is to take a reading of what is creating anxiety in contemporary culture and propose economic solutions in light of that bellweather. According to Stanfield, the most critical anxieties in contemporary culture revolve around politics, economics, the environment, and community.

In politics, the unequal distribution of political power, and especially the problem of corporate power and "its enormous influence over matters of ecology, work routine, political decision making, and cultural attitudes in general," is a central locus for potential change.[10] In economics, the inequitable distribution of income and wealth is our primary concern. There is also the need for a new definition of efficiency in production that is committed to decision making based on cooperative ethics rather than profits, and that addresses the needs of the workers and the community: "An efficient economy abets the cultural process of producing people who are good, and who can do good; justice cannot be read out of the formula for efficiency."[11]

Stanfield identifies the state of the environment as our most pressing concern.

Classical economic theory, he argues, cannot adequately address environmental concerns because it does not have an understanding of the principle of interdependence. Further, interdependence with the environment invites the question of setting limits, and of self-restraint—the idea of quality as reciprocity. "The problem is less one of limits *to* growth than of limits *of* growth. . . . The question is not 'can we grow on like this?' but 'should we?' "[12] Clearly capitalism with its commitment to continued expanding production cannot offer solutions.

Finally, Stanfield identifies "the universal and deepest problem: the general concern for the quality of human life and the institutional configuration that best suits its pursuit."[13] The corporation, he argues, with its emphasis on meeting individual needs through individualized consumption, has no mechanisms to address this larger anxiety about the nature of community and how the economy contributes to both individual and collective well-being.

For the balance of our discussion on social change, I will explore each of these arenas—politics, economics, the environment, and a fourth area, the workplace—and suggest changes that need to occur. The "deepest problem," the problem of community, will be examined in greater depth in the last chapter.

Change and Politics

Political change must occur simultaneously in two directions: The power of the corporation must be diminished, and the redefinition of democracy and the revamping of the political process must be undertaken. Change of this magnitude will take a people more inured to activism, more empowered to action. To generate this new society we will need to nourish a new person, a new kind of individual. According to Lawrence Goodwyn, to enhance the development of political community and democratic principles we must revitalize and empower the real individual, not the faceless member of the mass society. People must believe, he avers, "in the possibility of reclaiming political control or that their vote (or more importantly their ideas and their activism) will produce improvements which will benefit them," without having their individual integrity subsumed under a collective monolith.[14]

"Individual self-respect" and "collective self-confidence" constitute, then, the cultural building blocks of mass democratic politics. Their development permits people to conceive of the idea of acting in a self-generated democratic way—as distinct from passively participating in various hierarchical modes bequeathed by the received culture.[15]

Breaking new ground in both psychology and politics, Michael Lerner's *Surplus Powerlessness* provides important insights into the psychological dynamic that perpetuates the corporate hegemony. We are powerless, he argues, because of the following deeply entrenched belief systems: We believe that we deserve our situation because we are evil; we have been brainwashed to believe that capitalism is the only way to organize our societies (what he calls failed socialism); we have given over our power to the scientific experts and technocrats who control us, thus legitimating their control; and there has been a paralysis of ethical relativism—a "lack of clarity generates powerlessness."[16] Mass political change will come, he argues, when we learn to empower ourselves, and an important part of that empowerment process is becoming politically active with other people. In such a "liberatory community,"

one of the most important ways that people get to actualize their capacities is through politics itself—through the mutual fashioning of a social world together. In this very process of creating our joint reality, we begin to become the embodiments of our potential, because we are actually doing what we have the creative potential to do.[17]

The involvement itself, a process he calls "politics as empowerment," generates change:

Politics is a kind of community production—and the product that is being produced is the future. No longer accepting the passivizing and pacifying theories about how things work, people begin to act as though what is going to happen in history is not independent of what they do. They can play a decisive role in outcomes.[18]

Lerner outlines other steps we must take to create a context for change. We must begin by educating ourselves about how surplus powerlessness manifests itself. Our tendency, for example, toward either discounting or overstating real achievements, feelings of despair about the possibilities for change, demanding that people be "politically correct," and "setting ourselves up" for failure are all disabling behaviors.

Second, our political goal should be to build a compassionate society—a society made up of a variety of small groups that will empower people on a day-to-day basis in their communities and families. In the past, politics has concentrated on economic and organizational issues and excluded these "softer" issues of community and family. We need now to deepen our understanding and expand the scope of politics to include our more profound psychological human needs for love and caring. Capitalism, Lerner argues, has destroyed these traditional "communities of meaning," and our task is to rebuild them.[19]

The Problem of the Corporation.   The capitalist corporation wields vast powers of control over our economic and political lives, and this "Corporate Leviathan" is a major threat to democracy.[20] The Stalinist Soviet bloc societies are not better, according to Robert A. Dahl: We would be hard-pressed to make a distinction between corporate and state-run bureaucratic centralization. We passively accept the power of these corporations, he believes, because we still cling to the belief in the sanctity of private enterprise. Our change agenda should have as a major objective bringing the transnational corporations under public control. To achieve this objective we must determine that economics is indeed a public matter, and that private ownership of the means of production is counter to the common good.

We could begin by reappropriating private property to community use on a local, not a national basis. Nothing is truly national, let alone transnational. There is only the factory or the office where you and I work. Staughton Lynd raises the provocative question of the validity of community property rights over private property rights in a recent article on plant closings: "In Youngstown and Pittsburgh, advocates of eminent domain have argued that *if* a private owner refuses to operate a socially needed enterprise, *then* the community may properly step in, acquire the facility, and ensure its continued operation under alternative management."[21] It is important to note here that I am not talking about nationalizing private property, I am talking about localizing it.

Redefining Democracy. We do not have democracy in the United States today, and in fact, we have not had anything resembling democracy in this country for some time—probably since the end of the nineteenth century. As we begin the task of building true democratic structures, it will help to refresh our memories about those internal factors and conditions that characterize true participatory democracy: (1) a flexible, transitory orientation that resists organizational institutionalization; (2) a process of mutual and self-criticism, especially of leadership; (3) a limit to organizational size—growth by replication rather than expansion; (4) economic marginality to build community and enhance commitment; (5) economic self-sufficiency which encourages a sense of interdependence for existence on members; and (6) diffusion of work knowledge through the rotation of tasks, no division of labor, and the return to simpler technologies so that everyone will know how to use the tool.[22]

The centerpiece of democracy is the necessity for the decentralization of power. There is a direct correlation between the distribution of power and effective use of democratic rights. The exercise of democracy requires intimacy. Further, when size is contained, power is automatically both diminished and decentralized. According to Robert A. Nisbet, "We have tended to overlook the fact that freedom thrives in cultural diversity, in local and regional differentiation, in associative pluralism, and, above all, in the *diversification of power*."[23] Decentralization also enhances participation, and participation is key to democracy: "There must be *many* authorities in society, and . . . that authority must be closely united to objectives and functions which command the response and talents of members."[24]

Change and the Economy

As we discussed in Chapters 6 and 7, all discussions of economics begin with survival economic issues. Our first task will be the establishment of an economy based on a participatory ethic. A participatory survival economy is our economy. We become involved, we create the wealth, we make the decisions. It is important to stress this idea of economics as participation. Just as we forget that we own our labor, we also forget that we have a collective claim to the resources of the land and the collective work we do.

Access to the means of production begins with access to the land. The cry of "save the family farm" is only a code for "save the right to have a place to call home," which should be a basic right for all members of every society. Whether this is translated into owning our factories or our homes, ownership and access to the means of production is a basic human right.

Land and home ownership has declined dramatically in the United States in just the past two decades. According to Nisbet, our contemporary economy is characterized by the "evaporation of property" and the "substitution of 'soft' property of shares of stock and bonds for the 'hard' property of land, buildings, and machines that the property-holder had once managed as well as owned." This loss has also had an impact on the ethical stake that we have in the economy: owners of "hard" property have "a distinct stake in society, a role of social responsibility . . . [but] an atmosphere of not only impersonality but irresponsibility is created by evaporated property."[25]

Several additional principles should guide the development of our survival economy: The economy should be controlled and growth should be limited, economic wealth ought to be distributed equitably, and the economy should be subject to the collective, not individual, will.

A Controlled Economy.   How much is enough? This is a question capitalism never asks, since it assumes that endless growth is not only possible, but also desirable. According to Jonathon Porritt: "The opposite of wealth is not poverty, but sufficiency," and sufficiency should be the guidepost for a sane economy.[26] Our alternative economy must be based on both controlling and limiting growth.

In addition, limits to growth must be determined collectively, and the economy must be subordinated to the political process. No longer will the economy be "out there," external to our collective will. In order to control the economy, we must give up our so-called free market capitalism and lay to rest the myth of competition: Competition does not make things better, it simply eliminates most of us from the game. Climbing the ladder of capitalism means that we must step on the faces of others.

The transition will not be an easy one. We are asking an entire culture to give up its addiction to endless growth and to production and consumption. As a mechanism to ease the transition, I propose the establishment of two separate economies: a survival economy that would meet the basic needs of people, and an affluent economy, where modest wealth, only in a ratio of 3 to 1 between the richest and the poorest individuals, could be accumulated. The idea of a two-tier economy is not a new one. Paul Goodman developed such a system, calling the survival economy a Guaranteed National Income.[27] This survival economy could be implemented fairly quickly. Basic needs could be administered initially through mechanisms similar to our current entitlement programs.

Meeting survival needs would take priority over all other economic activities. Defining need is an incredibly difficult and complex political task—a task most economists avoid. Need, they say, is relative. How much is enough depends on what you already have. Despite the challenge it presents, minimum standards of need can be determined. It is easy, for example, to establish nutritional guidelines. What will be more difficult is defining what things we need. A simple principle should guide us: Individual human greed must be subordinated to collective need.

Need must also be weighed against environmental preservation issues. The tragedy of the commons must not be repeated. Instead of expanding the nuclear power industry, for example, we could close down all the plants and limit consumption of energy. Each household could be "entitled" to 400 KWH of electrical energy each month as their share of the public utility. When the 400 KWH were used up, we could either shut off the power or enact some other disincentive such as heavy taxation. Human beings are infinitely adaptable, and we would soon learn to live within the limits we ourselves have established.

Distributive Justice. The principle underlying the survival economy is, of course, that everyone ought to share in the wealth that is produced by our collective efforts. In addition, everyone ought to participate in distribution decisions. In a recent letter on the U.S. economy, the American bishops expanded the concept of justice to include economics. According to Phillip Berrigan: "The bishops' understanding of justice as participation is richer than that of liberals, such as John Rawls. The opposite of participation is marginalization, whether political or economic. Thus the bishops expand the liberal concern for political rights to the economic sphere."[28] In the tradition of St. Thomas Aquinas, the American bishops argue that when private greed is destructive of society's well-being, society's collective rights supersede individual rights.

Democracies cannot succeed in an environment of economic inequality, and, according to Porritt, to achieve equity, we have only two real choices: "either raising the material living standard of every single person on the planet to the standard we in the West now enjoy, or progressively narrowing the gap to reduce the differential between the wealthiest and the poorest."[29] Since the first is not really an option considering the strains this would place on the environment, and considering that without controls on consumption, there would be no limits to demand, we must choose instead to scale down the world's wasteful economies, bring those below the new survival standard up to equal participation, and redistribute future production in an equitable manner.

Socially Responsible Economics. Finally, economics must be subordinate to new standards and values inherent in a collectivist society. We should have absolute control over the "ends" of our work. What is the purpose of work in a purposeful community? In the Mondragon collectives in Spain—a highly successful network of worker-owned cooperatives—the purpose of work is to link "the economic and technological objectives of the firm with the social concerns of the members."[30] Why would we wish to produce items that we know are destructive of people and the environment? Part of the reason, as I explored in Chapter 9, is that there is no mechanism in our society for making the necessary value judgments about our technology and hence about our levels and kinds of production. When we do set standards, they are generally so flexible so as not to inhibit capitalist economic growth. We set allowable radiation levels, for example, rather than outlaw nuclear energy, and the radiation multiplies in our environment. We seem to do things simply because they can be done, or, more probably, because somebody can make money doing it. We test plastics for toxicity, but do not question the production of plastics generally. If we commit to a socially responsible economics, we will be forced to reevaluate impacts on other people and the physical world.

Change and the Environment

Despite a growing awareness by the average citizen of the ever-increasing pollution of the environment, we still lack the collective will to make real change. We continue to seek reforms rather than real change—as evidenced in our new-found belief in a so-called biodegradable plastic—an oxymoron if there ever was one. Plastic never reverts to organic matter, it merely degrades to tiny bits of plastic. This tendency to seek easy solutions to difficult environmental problems is what Porritt calls green consumerism. Green consumerism assumes that if we change what we consume, we need never question that we consume. In the long run, this strategy won't work.[31]

True change will address the deeper question of the ethical relationship of economics to the environment. We must come to understand the place of our work in what Wendell Berry calls "The household of life": "Judgment could then begin to articulate what is already obvious: that some work preserves the household of life, and some work destroys it."[32] One of the basic assumptions of capitalism is the right to the unlimited exploitation of natural resources in the service of human need and greed. The idea that human beings run the universe must be forever laid to rest. Instead of mastery, we must develop an economic order based on what Marc Tool calls "compatibility":

People are dependent upon and interdependent with other life forms. . . . The environmental ethical principle, then, is the criterion of compatibility—compatibility between the social and biotic communities. The social community, through its political judgments, must assure that it continues to function within constraints of the biotic community.[33]

Finally, there is the question of responsibility to the future. As a popular poster proclaims, "We do not inherit the earth from our forefathers [and foremothers], we borrow it from our children." The bishops' letter on the economy comes to the same conclusion: ecological health must be maintained so that the economy's "ability to meet the essential human needs of this generation and future generations in an equitable fashion" is ensured.[34]

Change and Work

Any significant change in the work environment must come from its major restructuring. Enhancing the quality of work life (QWL) has been a hot topic in business management circles for the past decade. Unfortunately, most of these programs deal only in a cosmetic way with the contradictions inherent in the capitalistic way of getting work done. While they have made some work more interesting and pleasurable, these QWL programs have not made the workplace more democratic and have not significantly redirected profits to the workers. Unions have an additional concern: "QWL undermines union consciousness by replacing labor/management confrontation with a facade of common interest."[35]

The worker-owned Mondragon collectives have recently turned to examining quality of work issues and reorganizing their work environment. The reorganization of the work was based on two principles: (1) work should be organized so as to give the worker more control of the process of production, and (2) work should enhance our social needs to be together rather than making efficient production the standard that drives economic decision making. The division of labor, which is so central to capitalism, really did not make work more efficient. Work was broken down into its simplest components to enhance control over the worker. When work was reorganized at Mondragon, wherever possible the assembly line was reconfigured to integrate more steps in the task. Tasks were also rotated between members of a work team. There were several interesting results: "Because all group members were now performing the same tasks, they all had to receive the same pay. Furthermore, the mastery of a number of different tasks justified a higher pay classification."[36] Under the work reorganization plan, even supervisors had new, more democratic roles, as authority over the work process was decentralized: "Instead of concentrating on the details of operations and giving orders and imposing discipline, the supervisor will be expected to guide workers to build self-managing work groups, to coordinate activities, and to offer advice but not intervene in work operations unless help is needed."[37]

The more we can return control of work to the worker, the more we will enhance not only democratic tendencies but aesthetic ones as well. The dynamic between creativity and control lies at the heart of good work. The more control we have of work, the more creative we are, and vice versa. One of the easiest ways of regaining this aesthetic sense is through a gradual return to simpler technologies.

A return to simpler, more aesthetically pleasing work may have additional benefits—a more efficient use of materials and a higher quality product as a result of greater care in the process of making. While it is true that machines produce more products faster, it has yet to be proven that they produce more efficiently. Whereas in a consumer society, quantity is more important than either the context in which a product is produced or the quality of it, we could instead reward a new aesthetic based on quality and uniqueness, and penalize those products that are standardized and mass-produced.

To encourage a return to more meaningful forms of hand work, people could be awarded time off to do more person-intensive labor. In fact, a major restructuring of the economy could take place simply by paying wages for housework or other work designated as survival economics. Housework could return to its nineteenth-century roots of gardening, scratch cooking, and homemade clothing. This would, in turn, result in reduced demand on the production economy. Goods produced by the production economy could be heavily taxed in some cases, and entirely outlawed in others.

We must also relearn the value of work, and take positive steps to infuse work with a high-minded intentionality. To begin with, we could start by valuing our own work or by changing it until we do value it. One of the ways we determine that value is by comparing it with the work of others; if the work we do is undervalued by others, we won't like it either. What we are paid also determines how we value our work. Value should be collectively determined and should not be based on the principle of how to get the most work done for the lowest wage in order to ensure a profit, but on mutual appreciation of others' work, regard for the effort that went into it, and its contribution to the community. When all work that is done in a society is valued, work itself takes on new value.

Motivation also determines how highly we value our work and the work of others. In his in-depth study of the Israeli kibbutzim collectives, Melford E. Spiro identified several reasons why people were motivated to work: (1) for their own personal economic improvement because they understand that their "own standard of living is dependent upon that of the group which, in turn, depends upon the productive capacity of its members;"[38] (2) for the workers' sense of personal satisfaction; (3) as a source of competitive pride between various work crews on the kibbutz; and (4) for the prestige of work alone:

Labor is one of the paramount values in the culture of Kiryat Yedidim, and . . . hard, efficient labor is a necessary, if not sufficient, determinant of prestige. . . . The respect of one's fellows has become an important motive in this society. . . . Given the importance of labor in the kibbutz hierarchy of values, public opinion—or *daat haka-hal*, as it is known—is a highly important factor in work motivation.[39]

Work, as Marx and so many thinkers before and after him have reminded us, is the source of all value. Through our work we create value—and it is the only way that value is created. It is easy for us to lose sight of this fact, or dismiss it simply as a truism. We have come to denigrate this value, giving up control to the machines, to the corporate decision-makers, to the government. Our task is to reclaim work, and its value, and in that process, come to revalue it.

CONCLUSION

Change—and the potential for change—lie all about us. As we have seen, there is no one way, no true path to a society which honors and celebrates good work. It can come in many shapes, take many forms. It will take place in our economics, our politics, the physical environment, our work environment. It is a process grounded in individual and community empowerment and the will to create a new moral and ethical order.

Making change is work. It is hard work. It is the good work of making a future in which our dreams become reality. Fortunately, change is something we can all make. We all have the skills of knowing how to work with others in a meaningful way, how to speak out on behalf of our children, how to "make do," how to care about the world around us. There are no superhuman talents or skills we need; we have our good hands and good hearts.

Change is just a gesture, an action. It is a decision. It is a movement. We need only begin.

NOTES

1. U.S. Catholic Conference, *Economic Justice for All: Catholic Social Teaching and the U.S. Economy* (Washington, DC, 1986), para. 1.

2. Robert A. Dahl, *After the Revolution? Authority in a Good Society* (New Haven and London, 1970), 110.

3. William M. Dugger, "Power: An Institutional Framework of Analysis," *Journal of Economic Issues* 14 (December 1980): 904.

4. Steven R. Hickerson, "Legal Counsel, Power, and Institutional Hegemony," *Journal of Economic Issues* 16 (March 1982): 191.

5. Lewis Mumford, *The Myth of the Machine: The Pentagon of Power* (New York, 1970), 429.

6. Clarke A. Chambers, "The Cooperative League of the United States of America, 1916–1961: A Study of Social Theory and Social Action," *Agricultural History* 36 (1962): 80.

7. Marc Tool, *The Discretionary Economy: A Normative Theory of Political Economy* (Santa Monica, CA, 1979), 164.

8. T. J. Jackson Lears, "The Concept of Cultural Hegemony: Problems and Possibilities," *American Historical Review* 90 (1985): 571.

9. Ibid., 588.

10. J. Ron Stanfield, *Economic Thought and Social Change* (Carbondale and Edwardsville, IL, 1979), 162.

11. Ibid., 164.

12. Ibid., 165.

13. Ibid., 165–66.

14. Lawrence Goodwyn, *The Populist Moment: A Short History of the Agrarian Revolt in America* (Oxford, 1978), xiv.

15. Ibid., xix.

16. Michael Lerner, *Surplus Powerlessness: The Psychodynamics of Everyday Life . . . and the Psychology of Individual and Social Transformation* (Oakland, CA, 1986), 211.

17. Ibid., 181.

18. Ibid.

19. Ibid., 88.

20. See Dahl, *After the Revolution*, 115.

21. Staughton Lynd, "The Genesis of the Idea of a Community Right to Industrial Property in Youngstown and Pittsburgh, 1977–1987," *Changing Work* 9 (Spring 1989): 17.

22. Joyce Rothschild-Whitt, "Conditions for Democracy: Making Participatory Organizations Work," in *Co-ops, Communes and Collectives: Experiments in Social Change in the 1960s and 1970s*, Eds. John Case and Rosemary C. R. Taylor (New York, 1979), 219–221.

23. Robert A. Nisbet, *The Quest for Community* (London, 1970), 265.

24. Ibid., xiii.

25. Robert Nisbet, *The Present Age: Progress and Anarchy in Modern America* (New York, 1988), 87.

26. Jonathon Porritt, "Sustainability," *One Earth* 18, no. 4 (Winter 1988), 15.

27. Paul Goodman, *People or Personnel* and *Like a Conquered Province* (New York, 1968), 167.

28. Phillip Berrigan, *Our Unfinished Business: The U.S. Catholic Bishops' Letters on Peace and the Economy* (New York, 1989), 134.

29. Porritt, "Sustainability," 14.

30. William Foote Whyte and Kathleen King Whyte, *Making Mondragon: The Growth and Dynamics of the Worker Cooperative Complex* (Ithaca, NY, 1988), 113.

31. Porritt, "Sustainability," 14.

32. Wendell Berry, *Standing by Words* (San Francisco, 1983), 50.

33. Tool, *Discretionary Economy*, 310, 311.

34. U.S. Catholic Conference, *Economic Justice for All*, para. 281.

35. Jeremy Brecher and Tim Costello, "Whose Quality of Work Life?" *Zeta Magazine* 2 (May 1988): 92.

36. Whyte and Whyte, *Making Mondragon*, 113–14.

37. Ibid., 120.

38. Melford E. Spiro, *Kibbutz: Venture in Utopia* (New York, 1970), 84.

39. Ibid., 85.

Chapter 11

Making the Future: Purposeful Community

When actions are performed without unnecessary speech, people say "We did it!"

—Lao Tsu, *Tao Te Ching*

Communities are the primary agents of change, but before a community can act it must come to awareness of itself. One of our tasks, then, will be to rediscover the latent expression of community buried beneath out capitalist culture that celebrates individualism. For capitalism to succeed, it had to destroy traditional community. To move beyond capitalism we need to reinvent community and create our collective reality anew.

To begin with, our revitalized community will be a moral and purposeful community, conscious of itself as a community, and conscious of the responsibility that community brings. Implicit in all social organization is the idea that community—whether it be a small utopian society, a small city state, or a neighborhood in a large urbanized area—is infused with intentionality. If we are to ask people to commit their work to the community, that community must have some collective objective, some communal goal.

On the heels of the activist 1960s, the 1970s spawned a loosely organized, decentralized national movement committed to local organizing and development of community-based groups committed to social change. The mass activism of the streets was abandoned in favor of nourishing the small, the local, the regional. All across the nation, people took up the task of creating purposeful communities. Decentralized, alternative institutions developed to meet a variety of community needs: economic development, cultural awareness, greater involvement in state and city politics, and in general the development of alternative economic activities such as food co-ops, credit unions, bakeries, child-care facilities, and so on.

Despite modest successes, however, these efforts at developing an alternative hegemony remained marginal activities. The decentralist movement suffered two shortcomings, one political and one economic: It never developed satisfactory ways of determining (1) how the dominant "institutions of wealth and state power would be dismantled or (2) how the benefits that can derive from large-scale or even complex trade would be coordinated."[1] Clearly, for major social restructuring to take place, we need communities to take up these challenges. This can best be achieved through a conscious, gradual withdrawal from the dominant hegemony into alternative economic and political structures.

The development of purposeful alternative communities must begin with education. At the Highlander Center, which has a long history of commitment to social change, an educational model has been developed that attempts to address this problem of rebuilding political and economic community. The goal is the revitalization of poverty-stricken communities in Appalachia, through rebuilding what John Gaventa and Helen Lewis call community "infrastructure." Traditional economical development, they argue, is " 'technical' in nature—business plans, feasibility studies, and market research. As important as these may be, case studies and experience suggest a broader view, especially if one is interested in participatory development."[2] Their model addresses the revitalization of deeper human connections which lie at the heart of community.

The development of "infrastructure" includes human development, an education for creativity, regaining an understanding of popular knowledge and history, democratic decision-making, and consciousness of religious and political symbols. With this investment, people can become better equipped to rebuild their own communities and economies.[3]

An important goal of Highlander's model is to involve people in wrestling with real issues that are unique to their own communities. There is no standard community, no simple solution to economic or political problems. There is only the deep commitment to defining our own communities. What works in one, may not work in another. It is important, therefore, that communities explore as many alternatives as they can find. In the sections that follow, I will explore a variety of practical suggestions for building community in three areas: enhancing the sense of community; redeveloping our own culture; and organizing our communities.

THE TIES THAT BIND: COMMUNITY AND COMMITMENT

Belonging is central to community. There are so many faces to human organization, so many dreams of solidarity, brotherhood and sisterhood, association, and communion that speak to the deep human need for connection and the companionship of one another. In the many utopian societies throughout history, where community building was a conscious undertaking, community was enhanced through sharing—sharing work, sharing power, sharing property. The feeling of community was further fostered through such organizational structures as group rituals, alternative marital relationships, and the establishment of various subgroups within the culture. Rosabeth Kanter, in her in-depth analysis of utopian communities, also found an element of self-denial and sacrifice in the successful communities—what we choose to refer to more positively as restraint. Whether it was the Shakers giving up sexual pleasures, other groups denying material comforts, or simply hard work, all served to reinforce the communal bond.[4]

If we are looking for models of social change, however, the utopian tradition will disappoint us. In fact, utopias were, and are, characteristically indifferent to political activism. Utopia is by definition a static, separatist community. Engels was critical of the nineteenth-century utopian socialists for just that reason—they isolated themselves from the revolutionary imperative. Utopias are useful, however, for studying the make-up of successful communities. All communities must struggle with the same problematic issues: homogeneity versus diversity, the nature of commitment, and an authoritarian versus a participatory political philosophy.

Homogeneity is a hallmark of utopian thought. Sameness breeds and reinforces community. Sameness is also the hallmark of an intolerant, fascist society. Mumford was convinced, for example, that the purpose of utopian writing was to manipulate our minds to accept the megamachine hegemony—utopian models were, he believed, the "ideological preparation" for acclimating us to our own oppression.[5]

Uniformity and sameness are reinforced in utopian communities by an emphasis on doing rather than thinking. Thinking people, especially those who might disagree, are a serious threat in many utopian formulations. Plato, we recall, was extremely hostile to the poets because they stir the passions, and he banned them from his utopia, *The Republic*. Dissension and disagreement of any sort are threatening to utopia, where the survival of the community is predicated on a uniformity of commitment and interpretation of the community goals.[6]

Leadership in most utopian communities was authoritarian and paternalistic. According to Kanter, "The most enduring communes were also the most centralized and the most tightly controlled."[7] Centralization aggravated the leadership styles, and Elise Boulding traces the tendency toward paternalism to the liberal tradition, which placed its faith in a small elite that would lead us wisely into the future. Boulding suggests we look instead to the libertarian radical futurists for a model of participatory democracy, and learn to trust the people rather than individual leaders to envision and create the new society.[8]

Maintaining commitment is always problematic, but it is clear that a deeply held belief in something seems to lie at the heart of all successful community. On the plus side, the emphasis on uniformity reflects the value of group coherence and a strong sense of community as community—especially in relation to the outside world. A shared vision of the common good—and working to achieve it—are critical to the development of purposeful collective goals and reinforcing political/social bonds. Part of the joy of sharing in the common good is being part of making something happen. Through the process of participation, we experience the common good and work to perpetuate it.

Shared social experiences also enhance group commitment and are a more positive way of developing and maintaining it. Ana Johnson and William Whyte attribute part of the success of the Mondragon collectives to a characteristic of the Basque culture that they call the "associative spirit." People like to get together in social groups which seem to emerge from friendships that are made at work, that cut across classes, and that carry over into their social lives. These groups undertake many different activities—one example is the gustatory societies, collective eating groups.[9]

Communities also succeed because they give people a sense of security. While security alone cannot maintain community, our highly mobile society reinforces the opposite belief—that happiness lies in moving elsewhere. There is a deeper meaning of social security that we must develop—one that sees the purpose of community to provide economic and social security for its members. It was only after small communities, neighborhoods, and extended family cooperative economic networks were destroyed that capitalism was able to overpower us completely. One continuing appeal of the kibbutzim lifestyle, for example, is the security of having a place to live and a job for life, a sense of belonging, and "freedom from that psychological insecurity which stems from economic competitiveness."[10]

Utopian communities are also characterized by the unity of moral values and political action: "Underlying most utopian formulations is the belief that belief is important and that one's actions can be shaped by deeply held faiths," and further, that those beliefs should be wedded to action.[11] According to Mulford Sibley, utopian belief systems fall into two groups. In classical utopias, the belief system had spiritual roots; and in modern utopias, the belief system has materialistic roots in the scientific method, progress, technology, or development. Many of these intentional communities are motivated by a deep messianic impulse, a sense of self-importance and mission.[12] Whether the driving ideology was Joseph Smith's Mormonism, the "scientific socialism" of Marx, or the behavioralism of B. F. Skinner at Twin Oaks, the burning desire to change the world and strong belief in one's own destiny are profoundly inspirational.

As we say in Chapter 8, the cultivation of aesthetics can also have a powerful impact on creating collective meaning. In many ways, aesthetics bridges the gap between politics and religion. We must keep in mind, however, that rebuilding our communities will be primarily a political act, not a religious one, although politics, aesthetics, and religion all address questions of purpose, meaning, and intention. As I discussed in Chapter 9, religions tend to take us out of the real world whereas community is based in the social and the material reality. We should continue to reinforce the good judgment our founders showed in striking a clear separation between church and state. While a kind of spirituality that celebrates unity can breathe through all political life, what we call religion should remain subordinate.

DEVELOPING CULTURAL ROOTS

Change must take place at all levels of society; it must penetrate to every theater, every classroom, every form of cultural expression. There are many models for developing and maintaining alternative cultures, but one of the earliest and most comprehensive cultural policies in the United States was developed by the Chautauqua Institution.[13] Chautauqua originated in the nineteenth-century Sunday School Movement—a working-class educational movement committed to mass, secular education. From its beginnings, Chautauqua was committed to building cultural communities in which people would study together and educate themselves to the issues of the day in religion, the arts, education, and recreation. One of the most successful of Chautauqua's programs was the Chautauqua Literary and Scientific Circles. They were forerunners of today's continuing education and home extension programs, and were based on the principle of community-based small-group learning via correspondence and discussion.

In the early cooperative movement we have another excellent model of large-scale programs dedicated to cultural change. True to its anarchist roots, the cooperative movement reached out to educate its many members to the fuller concept of a revolutionary alternative society. James Peter Warbasse, an early cooperative leader, believed, like Peter Kropotkin, that cooperation was a "natural human instinct."[14] His utopian vision called for, among other things:

the restoration of craftsmanship and the joy of creative work, which the machine, under capitalism had weakened; the flowering of all the arts, both fine and practical; social security and an end to anxiety, in co-operation there need be no thought for the morrow; the triumph of beauty everywhere in life.[15]

Education also served to reinforce commitment and continually remind co-operative members of the purpose that united them. One of the great successes of the cooperative movement was its commitment to this internal education process. The cooperative lifestyle was continually renewed through small, experientially based group activities.

The need to promote togetherness through group dynamics, was seen most clearly by Carl Hutchinson. . . . "We as a minority group may easily lose our identity in a time of sweeping social change," he warned, "unless we have cultural roots deep enough to unite us and reinforce the cooperative pattern of life."[16]

Cooperative recreation and play was also encouraged:

"To call out the non-competitive, non self-centered impulses; to induce people to experience their pleasures together instead of too exclusively in private." . . . Through playing and singing and dancing together, participants learned to "express their social natures
in the freedom of joyous and wholesome activity."[17]

There are many ways to reclaim our own cultural life. We can begin by research-
ing our own home towns and city neighborhoods. Where do people sing together,
dance together? Where do we read and learn together, especially about ourselves?
What kinds of cooperative experiences do we have in our town or our neighborhood? Does the local chamber of commerce support indigenous culture?

Cultural roots also extend beyond the social to the political and geographic.
The alternative literature is replete with models emphasizing localism, region-
alism, or bioregionalism as the backdrop for true community. Much of this
literature owes its inspiration to Kropotkin and to the ideal societies he described
in *Fields, Factories and Workshops of Tomorrow* and *Mutual Aid*. These models
promote decentralized, regionally grounded economic structures built around a
commitment to simple technologies, self-sufficiency, and participatory democracy. In varying degrees, these new communities are driven by three basic
principles: "prevention rather than treatment, . . . integration rather than separation, and . . . subsidiarity, . . . [the concept] 'that you should never assign to a
large entity what can be done by a smaller one.' "[18] In *The Vermont Papers*, a
contemporary in-depth proposal to decentralize the whole state of Vermont, the
authors suggest the following guideline for determining the boundaries of community: "The question, is a locality *big* enough to provide a welfare *system*,
must read, is the unit *small* enough to provide the human *context* without which
attempts to care for the needy shrivel and die on the bureaucratic vine of depersonalization."[19]

Bioregionalism is a geographically determined concept of decentralization that
brings together politics and environmentalism. It is a strong theme of the emerging worldwide Green movement. Emphasis is on building and preserving local
economics, local politics, and the local environment. In a Green economy,
"success is measured not in import-export surpluses but in how much we can
shorten the distance between the producer, the consumer and the waste disposal
site. The key to achieving a Green future is miniaturizing and localizing the
world economy."[20]

What drives all these models of localism, neighborhood-based economics,
and self-sufficient communities is one simple rule: Live simply. Living simply
is living richly. Again, paradox confronts us, because the more we work to
simplify our lives, the more rich and textured they will become.

There are many characteristics of simple living that could be implemented
immediately. We could encourage people to take time during the work day to
have real, face-to-face cultural exchanges with one another. In a consumer society
such as ours, most of our so-called culture is packaged for purchase. We never
stop to question anymore, for example, why live music isn't written and per-

formed by our neighbors. Instead, we buy music that is sold to us as records, tapes, compact discs, or even live concerts. In other cultures there is no price attached to the music that is experienced in the context of family or neighborhood or community. In the English Folk Club movement, we find an excellent example of community-supported music. It is participatory rather than passive, it is live rather than packaged and marketed. People sing with one another.

We could also begin to choose activities that give us intensive as opposed to extensive experiences. By this I mean that we could cultivate the sense of taking time to smell the flowers. We would no longer be interested in getting ahead but rather would enjoy where we are right now. One of my new pleasures is learning to identify all the plants and grasses I pass on my daily walks. A whole new world has opened to me and I find I'm more interested in my immediate environment generally.

People who are adept at simple living know the difference between their needs and their wants. They have unplugged themselves from things and are more interested in the world and in people. They delight in finding things that can be done in their communities without spending money. They have discovered the secret of simple living—if you don't have a lot of things to take care of, you have more time to spend in meaningful leisure.

THE ORGANIZATION OF COMMUNITY

Rebuilding community organizationally can begin with the development of a wide variety of cooperatives. The cooperative movement was initially founded in the nineteenth century as a reaction to the more blatant abuses of market capitalism, and concentrated on establishing nonprofit cooperative efforts in both the production and consumption arenas. Cooperatives are potentially revolutionary in two ways: They create new economic and social networks, and they redirect economic resources from the corporate hegemony.

Despite their enlightened ideology, historically most cooperatives concentrated their efforts in the economic arena and were content, by and large, with coexisting with capitalism rather than replacing it. Some of the more radical cooperatives, however, did not limit themselves to softening the abuses of capitalism or making themselves major players in the game with private corporations. They were committed to alternative community building across a whole range of issues: economic, cultural, political, educational.

In his study of the cooperative movement in the northern Midwest, Leonard Kercher found that there were two important qualities that contributed to the cooperatives' success: the homogeneity of the Finnish community, with its strong social and ethnic ties and its cooperative tradition, and the fact that most co-operatives were located in small, rural communities where their economy was more isolated from the market economy. Urban areas generated "socially detached urban consumers," and a major weakness of the cooperative movement was its inability to spread the cooperative idea to the urban setting.[21]

For all their strengths, however, cooperatives are basically a holding action. Collectives, on the other hand, are characterized by autonomy and independence, a clearer political commitment to change, and a more revolutionary agenda. Collectives are more political because they are committed to social change; more comprehensive, because they offer a model of transformation at all levels of society, not just the economic. Collectives reach out at the same time as they embrace; they create change at the same time as they build new stable communities.

The concept of the collective is a relatively modern one, although it shares some similarity to small tribal and village life throughout human history. In our own time, the collective is characterized by a quality of purposefulness and commitment to action. If the essence of democracy is action, the collective is the ideal structure for political action. Collective organization is purposeful, practical, and task-oriented—it sees itself as acting, and it defines itself in terms of clearly articulated objectives. It wants to do work. It is a free association that acts to perform a function for the society, and in which the members of that society determine the action together. Decision making is generally achieved through a process of reaching democratic consensus.

The idea of a collective as a self-conscious political unit was explored in detail by Kropotkin in his book *Mutual Aid*. As he looked back to the medieval era, Kropotkin identified the village commune or *obschina* as the predominant, and in his mind, ideal political structure. It was integrated into a larger decentralized federation that met many human needs.[22] The great power of the collective lay in its small size, its decentralized power structure, and its supportive network for self-actualization for the individual. Its other great strength, according to Kropotkin, was that it was a social organization—it met human needs for cooperation and intimacy.

As paradoxical as it may seem, the collective is also the best environment for the development of free individuals. The essence of collective structures is their ability to nourish both individual expression and group solidarity to ensure the freedom of all. Bakunin used the term *reciprocity* to describe this interactive, dialectical cooperative experience:

To be personally free means for every man living in a social milieu not to surrender his thought or will to any authority but his own reason and his own understanding of justice. ... *To be free collectively* means to live among free people and to be free by virtue of their freedom.... Man cannot become a rational being, possessing a rational will, (and consequently he could not achieve individual freedom) apart from society and without its aid.[23]

For Bakunin, this cooperative quality was grounded in work, because work is the source of all value, and it was only through working together that a good society could be maintained.

Ralph Waldo Emerson, in his philosophy of Transcendentalism, articulated a similar understanding of reciprocity: the recognition between people of one another's good work. When I do my best work and you do yours, and we share our mutual delight in that process, and then "behold we are communists, brothers, members one of another."[24] Through sharing our work we create the feelings of community, and the collective provides the individual the ideal opportunity to reintegrate work, self, and community:

Self-activity is the reconstruction of the consciousness (wholeness) of one's individual life activity. The collective is what makes the reconstruction possible because it defines individuality not as a private experience but as a social relation. What is important to see is that work is the creating of conscious activity within the structure of the collective.[25]

It is the social nature of the group that creates the space for good work, and reciprocally, good work that creates society.

Bakunin's ideas about collective work and collective life inspired a whole society to change. In the Spanish collectives of the 1930s we find one of the best examples of a successful, collective-based society. Like the cooperative movement in the United States, the success of the Spanish collectives lay in the fact that they combined production and distribution efforts, that they were run as participatory democracies, and that they developed in rural areas isolated from the market economy, thus encouraging economic self-sufficiency.

The Spanish collectives operated as small, participatory economic and social units. Over time, they evolved into a federated, decentralized network of collectives that, at their height in the 1930s, involved hundreds of thousands of individuals across Spain. The collectives were destroyed by the Franco government in the civil war, but a detailed record exists outlining their achievements.[26] Although they only existed for a short time, their success was remarkable for its extensive diversification.

There are many other examples of successful collectives, but only two models have persisted over time—the Israeli kibbutzim and the Hutterite communities. The Hutterite communities, in continued existence for over 450 years, are intensely religious and authoritarian, and cannot serve as a democratic model.[27] It is important to note, however, that both the Hutterite communities and the kibbutzim owe part of their success to their large population base. Most utopian experimental communities were small, isolated groups, and were extremely marginalized. Because they failed, we tend to generalize their experience to all alternative communities, which reinforces the belief that things will never change because alternative models fail. The successful replication and maintenance of the Hutterite communities and the Israeli kibbutzim involving large numbers of people, force us to take a second, and serious, look at the collective as a model of community.

The kibbutzim emerged from turn-of-the-century utopian socialism with its emphasis on fellowship and reciprocity. From the beginning, the development of the kibbutzim was tied to the Israeli state, and this is clearly a factor in their persistence over time. However, this ongoing relationship is the source of the primary contradictions of the kibbutzim: (1) economic and ideological ties to the state call into question their freedom and real commitment to building a participatory society; (2) their economic success was built on an infrastructure largely underwritten by the Israeli government; and (3) their survival and maintenance requires continued armed vigilance, and their community ethos may be colored by a military mindset. While the kibbutzim are internally democratic, their ties to the state make their true objectives problematic. Nevertheless, it is important to understand these contradictions. Self-sufficient collectives in the United States will confront similar issues. The Hutterites, for example, have remained far more isolated and independent of governments, and have been just as economically successful. In Minnesota they have even been accused of destroying local economies in areas where their numbers are a significant portion of the population because their own economies are so self-sufficient.

The success of the kibbutzim can be traced to several factors. According to Buber, the kibbutzim have succeeded because the collective ideal remained "loose and pliable."[28] Most utopian communities failed, he believed, because of rigidity (the Hutterites being an obvious and glaring exception, partly through their continuing commitment to asceticism). Successful community is based on continually recreating and re-visioning the future, and commitment to the kibbutzim is renewed through change and new ideas rather than rigid conformity to fixed principles.

Second, like many collectives, the kibbutzim were committed to meeting as many of their own needs as possible. However, unlike other collectives where self-sufficiency is a principle applied throughout all aspects of economic life, much of the macroeconomic success of the kibbutzim can be traced to economic support from the Israeli government. While the kibbutzim have been praised for their internal ethics of self-denial and a mutually determined low standard of living (at least initially), the massive irrigation projects that allow the cultivation of the desert and provide the agricultural base of the kibbutzim economy were underwritten and built by the government. Massive loan programs—both private and governmental, as well as government subsidies for farm commodities, have always been available to the kibbutzim in varying degrees. In addition, the internal accounting system of the kibbutzim, which is based on the concept of work-days, does not include costs of running the kibbutz itself "on the theory that this is analogous to the work which the housewife would do in her private home."[29]

In more recent times the kibbutzim have drifted from their original objectives in important ways. One of the most significant changes has been the abandonment of the austerity of early kibbutz life-styles. Private possessions have replaced collectively owned goods, and, to enhance recruitment efforts, the general standard of living has been raised to provide an attractive alternative to the larger economy.

In a recent article in the *Wall Street Journal*, Geraldine Brooks documented the kibbutzim's continuing drift toward the values of capitalism and consumerism. To meet the demands of residents for increased amenities, she wrote, the kibbutzim have accumulated a debt of four billion dollars. In addition, major shifts in the organization of work are underway, although socialist principles have not been entirely abandoned:

"Capitalism has proved itself the best way to solve the problems of production," says Mr. Harel. What capitalism hasn't done, he believes, is solve the problems of society. "So we want to take the capitalist way in our businesses but continue to keep the socialist way—our kibbutz—in our community."[30]

Attitudes toward work have also changed significantly. Work has been demythologized, and is no longer perceived as a calling. The nature of work on the kibbutz has changed dramatically as some of the cooperative economies diversify and shift from agriculture to industrial production. Distasteful jobs are still rotated ("black work"), however, and work assignments are still carried out in an egalitarian manner.[31]

The Mondragon federation of cooperatives in the Basque region of Spain is another example of a successful, expanding, work-based system of cooperatives. At one point in time, up to eighteen thousand workers were involved in a broad network of cooperatives, including a credit union, worker cooperatives, educational cooperatives, social service cooperatives, women's cooperatives, industrial cooperatives, consumer cooperatives, cooperatives in the areas of housing, agriculture, and construction and so on. The whole system is based on worker control at the lowest level.

In their in-depth study, *Making Mondragon*, William Whyte and Kathleen Whyte identified several principles that contributed to the success of Mondragon. As in other communities, the homogeneity of culture contributed immensely to stability. In addition, there were other preexisting factors in the Basque culture: a commitment to principles of equality and democratic governmental forms; a guild tradition with its deep respect for craft; a commitment to education as a core collective institution from the very beginning; and the internal workers' organizations called social councils, which functions like unions within the cooperative.[32]

According to Alfred Andersen, however, the Mondragon cooperatives are basically flawed because they are not political. Even in the economic sphere there are serious shortcomings: "the Capital from which the workers get income must all first be earned by them through their own labor. These producer cooperatives make no provision for, nor can they enforce, Fair Sharing of income from our Common Heritage of Capital."[33] C. George Benello feels that, despite the ideological neutrality of the current Mondragon organization, it has the potential for creating an alternative hegemony and making revolutionary change:

Its structure of democratic governance, with worker ownership and control, challenges the capitalist system at its very heart. . . . Mondragon awards profit and control to labor

and, in the process, has developed a worker-centered culture which, rather than infan-
tilizing, empowers. Mondragon members are citizens of a worker commonwealth, with
the full rights that such citizenship confers.[34]

Through its organizational structure, the potential exists in the Mondragon
model for workers to relearn the skills necessary for functioning in a democratic
society. When people are skilled at functioning in a collective organization, that
sense of empowerment has a ripple effect in all aspects of their lives.

On a small scale, efforts are underway to replicate the Mondragon idea in the
United States. In an interview with Christopher Mackin, policy director of the
Industrial Cooperative Association of Somerville, Massachusetts, Robert Gilman
explored the policies guiding that Association. The co-op's activities are based
on structure that "emphasize values of solidarity between people," and there
are various ways to encourage that solidarity: (1) As people work together, they
emphasize geographic or political solidarity: "one substitute form of solidarity
is the sense of local ownership and control over your economic destiny, or your
economic future . . . in order to prevent future plant closings and so forth''; (2)
union membership is encouraged; (3) where ethnic differences exist, members
work to encourage solidarity of cultural similarities; and (4) they encourage
chosen-life-style solidarity (e.g., nonsmokers, vegetarians, and other life-style
choices).[35] They have achieved success in adapting the Mondragon work style
with its emphasis on worker control and solidarity, Gilman reports, despite a
climate of skepticism.[36]

All these examples of collectives—Spain in the 1930s, American cooperatives,
the kibbutzim, the Hutterites, the Mondragon group—share one additional institution in common: a membership in a federated organization. There are certain
tasks that surpass the capabilities of a single collective and need to be organized
at a broader level. This network is further characterized by its celebration of
diversity. Indeed, the principle of federation is based on sound political and
ecological principles. A healthy political environment involves collectives rep-
resenting a broad range of human activity. As the Whytes learned in Mondragon,
"The integration of mutually supporting organizations—from education to bak-
ing to research and development to manufacturing—has clearly been important
to the success of the Mondragon firms."[37]

It is difficult for us to comprehend that a society could function as a loosely
knit group of collectives. We should be heartened, however, by the knowledge
that the principle on which a collective society is built is that economic and
political decision making is decentralized. A collective-based society does not
preclude activities that have a broad impact. It does necessarily require broad
affirmation and endorsement down to the level of the individual.

Can we establish a democratic, cooperative society in the United States? Can
we make massive changes in our economy, our life-styles, our politics? To assess
the possibilities for such massive change, we need only appreciate the prairie
fire of democracy sweeping across Eastern Europe. I don't know, at this writing,

whether the rebellions against what Mikhail Gorbachev calls the "Command and Administer" systems in those countries will continue to be smooth and peaceful, but indeed, the whole world is watching revolution on a scale we have never seen before, or, for that matter, seen in such close profile. While our news accounts of events are still hampered by being filtered through a cold war mindset, we can easily read between the lines. We share with the Eastern Europeans a broad range of similar concerns: the demand for greater participation in government and greater control over the economy; concern for the environment; distrust of centralization and bureaucracy; a return to celebrating local community.

CONCLUSION

We have come to the end, and we are once again reminded that it is indeed only another beginning. We are called to our greatest work now. The work of creating the purposeful community of the future beckons us; the task of rebuilding the networks of self, community, environment; the task of revitalizing democracy; the task of creating what Wendell Berry calls a loving economy, based on "the love of neighbors, of creatures, and of places."[38] The transition necessarily will be broad-ranging and intense: It must move from the self to the collective, from elitism to community, from capitalism to social economics, from exploitation to stewardship, from consumption to self-restraint, from hierarchy to decentralization, and from high-tech to simple technologies.

We must move along many planes, picking our way carefully through the debris of the crumbling hegemony of industrial capitalism, making our step firm and confident as we negotiate the maze of possibility. We are at a profound moment of historical emergence. We are nearly ready: The dawn of economic justice is about to break, the flower of democracy is about to bloom. Words and images fail us. We are, however, on the verge of turning a corner into a new reality, a new world. About us we will have those experiences most dear and familiar: the joy of creating, the fellowship of our friends and family, a healing earth, children no longer starving. We will have our self-respect, our good work, and a renewed community.

NOTES

1. David Moberg, "Experimenting with the Future: Alternative Institutions and American Socialism," in *Co-ops, Communes and Collectives: Experiments in Social Change in the 1960s and 1970s*, Eds. John Case and Rosemary C. R. Taylor (New York, 1979), 297.

2. John Gaventa and Helen Lewis, "The Highlander Economic Education Project," *Rural Adult Education Forum* 1 (August/September 1989): 3.

3. Ibid.

4. Rosabeth Moss Kanter, *Commitment and Community: Communes and Utopias in Sociological Perspective* (Cambridge, MA, 1972).

5. Lewis Mumford, *The Myth of the Machine: The Pentagon of Power* (New York, 1970), 229.

6. Ursula LeGuin, *The Dispossessed* (New York, 1975) for an excellent treatise on how dissidents are treated in utopia.

7. Kanter, *Commitment and Community*, 129.

8. Elise Boulding, "Futurism as Galvanizer of Education," in *Educational Reconstruction*, edited by N. Shimhara (Columbus, OH, 1972).

9. Ana Gutierrez Johnson and William Foote Whyte, "The Mondragon System of Worker Production Cooperatives," *Industrial and Labor Relations Review* 31 (October 1977): 22–23.

10. Melford E. Spiro, *Kibbutz: Venture in Utopia* (New York, 1970), 87.

11. Mulford Q. Sibley, "Religion and Belief Systems in Utopian and Dystopian Thought," paper presented at the 1974 Annual Meeting of the American Political Science Association (Chicago, IL): 3.

12. Norman Cohn, *The Pursuit of the Millenium: Revolutionary Messianism in Medieval and Reformation Europe and Its Bearing on Modern Totalitarian Movements* (New York, 1961).

13. Theodore Morrison, *Chautauqua: A Center for Education, Religion, and the Arts in America* (Chicago and London, 1974).

14. Clarke A. Chambers, "The National Cooperative League of the United States of America, 1916–1961: A Study of Social Theory and Social Action," *Agricultural History* 36 (1962): 64.

15. Ibid., 66.

16. Ibid., 72.

17. Ibid.

18. David Morris, *The New City-States* (Washington, DC, 1982), 19.

19. Frank Bryan and John McClaughry, *The Vermont Papers: Recreating Democracy on a Human Scale* (Chelsea, VT, 1989), 83.

20. David Morris, "The Materials We Need to Create a Sustainable Society Lie Close to Home," *Utne Reader* 36 (November/December 1989): 85.

21. Leonard C. Kercher, Vant W. Kebker, and Wilfred C. Leland, Jr., *Consumers' Cooperatives in the North Central States* (Minneapolis, MN, 1941), 40, 134–35.

22. Peter Kropotkin, "The State: Its Historic Role," *Selected Writings on Anarchism and Revolution* (Cambridge, MA, and London, 1970), 227.

23. Michael Bakunin, *The Political Philosophy of Bakunin: Scientific Anarchism*, compiled and edited by G. P. Maximoff (Glencoe, IL, 1953), 340–41.

24. Ralph Waldo Emerson, "From the *Journals*," Vol. 7 (December, 1845), 139–40, in *Selections of Ralph Waldo Emerson*, edited by Stephen B. Whichev (Boston, 1957), 283.

25. *The Anti-Mass: Methods of Organizing for Collectives*, anon., circa 1970.

26. A wide range of literature is available in many languages. Of special interest are the following: Augustin Souchy Bauer, "With the Peasants of Aragon: Libertarian Communism in the Liberated Areas," (Minneapolis: Soil of Liberty, 1982); Murray Bookchin, *The Spanish Anarchists: The Heroic Years 1868–1936* (New York: Harper and Row, 1977); Juan Gomes Casas, *Anarchist Organization: The History of the F.A.I.*, Translated by Abe Bluestein (Montreal-Buffalo: Black Rose Books, 1986); Sam Dolgoff, Ed., *The Anarchist Collectives: Workers' Self-Management in the Spanish Revolution 1936–1939* (Montreal: Black Rose Books, 1974); Hans Magnus Enzenberger, *Der kurze Sommer der*

Anarchie: Buenaventura Duruttis Leben und Tod Roman (The Hague, Netherlands: Dutch Editing Co., 1971); Temma Kaplan, *Anarchists of Andalusia 1868–1903* (Princeton, NJ: Princeton University Press, 1977); Robert W. Kern, *Red Years, Black Years: A Political History of Spanish Anarchism, 1911–1937* (Philadelphia, PA: Institute for the Study of Human Issues, 1978); Gaston Leval, *Collectives in the Spanish Revolution*, Translated from the French by Vernon Richards (London: Freedom Press, 1975); Jerome R. Mintz, *The Anarchists of Casas Viejas* (Chicago and London: University of Chicago Press, 1982); Abel Paz, *Durruti: The People Armed* (Montreal: Black Rose Books, 1976); Jose Peirats, *Anarchists in the Spanish Revolution* (Toronto, Canada: Solidarity Books, 1977); David Porter, Ed. and Introduction, *Vision on Fire: Emma Goldman on the Spanish Revolution* (New Paltz, NY: Commonground Press, 1983); and Vernon Richards, *Lessons of the Spanish Revolution, 1936–1939* (Montreal: Black Rose Books, 1972).

27. Lawrence C. Anderson and Michael Engelhart, "Prudent Plain People: The Hutterite Brethren," *Heritage of the Great Plains* 17 (Fall 1984): 12.

28. Martin Buber, *Paths in Utopia* (Boston, 1958), 142.

29. Eliyahu Kanovsky, *The Economy of the Israeli Kibbutz* (Cambridge, MA, 1966), 45.

30. Geraldine Brooks, "The Israeli Kibbutz Takes a Capitalist Tack to Keep Socialist Ideals," *The Wall Street Journal*, September 21, 1989, 1.

31. Spiro, *Kibbutz*, 265.

32. William Foote Whyte and Kathleen King Whyte, *Making Mondragon: The Growth and Dynamics of the Worker Cooperative Complex* (Ithaca, NY, 1988).

33. Alfred F. Andersen, *Liberating the Early American Dream* (New Brunswick, NJ, and Oxford, England, 1983), 148.

34. C. George Benello, "The Challenge of Mondragon," *Black Rose* (Winter 1986/1987): 28.

35. Robert Gilman, "Enabling Employee Ownership," *In Context*, Autumn 1985, 51.

36. Ibid., 33.

37. Johnson and Whyte, "The Mondragon System," 29.

38. Wendell Berry, *Home Economics* (San Francisco, 1987), 188.

Bibliography

Adams, Frank, with Myles Horton. *Unearthing Seeds of Fire: The Idea of Highlander*, Winston-Salem, NC: John F. Blair, 1975.

Adams, Henry. *The Education of Henry Adams*. New York: Modern Library, 1931.

Agnew, Jean-Christopher. "A Touch of Class." *Democracy* 3, no. 2 (Spring 1983): 52–79.

Alperovitz, Gar. "Toward A Decentralist Commonwealth." In *Reinventing Anarchy: What Are Anarchists Thinking These Days?* edited by Howard J. Ehrlich, Carol Ehrlich, David DeLeon, and Glenda Morris. London: Routledge and Kegan Paul, 1979.

Andersen, Alfred F. *Liberating the Early American Dream*. New Brunswick, NJ, and Oxford, England: Transaction Books, 1983.

Anderson, Lawrence C., and Michael Engelhart. "Prudent Plain People: The Hutterian Brethren." *Heritage of the Great Plains* 17, no. 4 (Fall 1984): 11–16.

Ansara, Michael. "Practical Politics." *Zeta Magazine* 1, no. 5 (May 1988): 37–38.

The Anti-Mass: Methods of Organization for Collectives. Mimeograph. Anon., circa 1970.

Arendt, Hannah. *The Human Condition*. Chicago: University of Chicago Press, 1958.

Aronson, Ronald. "Historical Materialism, Answer to Marxism's Crisis." *New Left Review* 152 (July/August 1985): 74–94.

Astin, H. "The Meaning of Work in Women's Lives: A Sociological Model of Career Choice and Work Behavior." *The Counseling Psychologist* 12, no. 4 (1984): 117–26.

Bakunin, Michael. *The Political Philosophy of Bakunin: Scientific Anarchist*, compiled and edited by G. P. Maximoff. Glencoe, IL: The Free Press, 1953.

————. *Bakunin on Anarchy*, edited by Sam Dolgoff. New York: Vintage, 1971.

Baldelli, Giovanni. *Social Anarchism*. Chicago and New York: Aldine Atherton, 1971.

Baldwin, James. "The Forging of the Sampo." *The Junior Classics*. Vol. 4. *Hero Tales*. USA: P. F. Collier and Son, 1938.

Baneigem, Raoul. *The Book of Pleasures*. London: Pending, 1983.

Barkin, David, and John W. Bennett. "Kibbutz and Colony: Collective Economies and the Outside World." *Comparative Studies in Society and History* 14 (January 1974): 456–83.

Bateson, Gregory. "Form, Substance and Difference." *General Semantics Bulletin* 37 (1970): 5–13.

———. *Steps to an Ecology of Mind*. London: Paladin, 1973.

———. *Mind and Nature: A Necessary Unity*. New York: Dutton, 1979.

Bell, Daniel. *Work and Its Discontents: The Cult of Efficiency in America*. New York: League for Industrial Democracy, 1970.

———. *The Cultural Contradictions of Capitalism*. New York: Basic Books, 1976.

Bellamy, Edward. *Looking Backward 2000–1887*. Boston: Houghton Mifflin Co., 1966.

Benello, George C. "The Challenge of Mondragon." *Black Rose* 12 (Winter 1986/1987): 24–34.

Benello, George C. "Putting the Reins on Technology." *Changing Work* 7 (winter 1988): 21–25.

Beneria, Lourdes. "Women's Participation in Paid Production under Capitalism: The Spanish Experience." *Women and the Economy* (Spring 1976): 18–33.

Beneria, Lourdes, and Gita Sen. "Accumulation, Reproduction, and Women's Role in Economic Development: Boserup Revisited." *Signs: Journal of Women in Culture and Society* 4 (1981): 775–81.

———. "Class and Gender Inequalities and Women's Role in Economic Development." *Feminist Studies* 8, no. 1 (Spring 1982): 157–76.

Bensman, Joseph. *Dollars and Sense: Ideology, Ethics, and the Meaning of Work in Profit and Non-Profit Organizations*. New York: Macmillan Co., 1967.

Benson, Susan P. "Advertising America." *Socialist Review* 43 (January/February 1979): 143–55.

Ben-Yosef, Avraham C. *The Purest Democracy in the World*. New York and London: Herzl Press and Thomas Yoseloff, 1963.

Berger, Peter, Brigitte Berger, and Hansfried Kellner. *The Homeless Mind: Modernization and Consciousness*. New York: Vintage, 1974.

Berman, Morris. *The Reenchantment of the World*. Ithaca and London: Cornell University Press, 1981.

Berneri, Marie Louise. *Journey through Utopia*. London: Routledge and Kegan Paul, 1950.

Berrigan, Phillip. *Our Unfinished Business: The U.S. Catholic Bishops' Letters on Peace and the Economy*. New York: Pantheon Books, 1989.

Berry, Wendell. *The Unsettling of America: Culture and Agriculture*. New York: Avon Books, 1977.

———. *The Gift of Good Land: Further Essays Cultural and Agricultural*. San Francisco: North Point Press, 1981.

———. *Standing by Words*. San Francisco: North Point Press, 1983.

———. *Home Economics*. San Francisco: North Point Press, 1987.

Birnbaum, Norman. *The Crisis of Industrial Society*. London, Oxford, and New York: Oxford University Press, 1969.

Black, Bob. *The Abolition of Work*. San Francisco: Out-of-Control Data Corp., 1986.

Blake, Casey. "Lewis Mumford: "Values over Techniques." *Democracy: A Journal of Political Renewal and Radical Change* 3, no. 2 (Spring 1983): 125–37.

Bloom, Allan. *The Closing of the American Mind: How Higher Education Has Failed*

Democracy and Impoverished the Souls of Today's Students. New York: Simon and Schuster, 1987.

Boggs, Grace Lee, and James Boggs. *Revolution and Evolution in the Twentieth Century*. New York: Monthly Review Press, 1974.

Boggs, James, Grace Lee Boggs, Freddy Paine, and Lyman Paine. *Conversations in Maine: Exploring Our Nation's Future*. Boston: South End Press, 1978.

Bookchin, Murray. *Post Scarcity Anarchism*. Berkeley, CA: Ramparts Press, 1971.

———. *The Limits of the City*. New York: Harper and Row, 1974.

———. *Toward an Ecological Society*. Montreal: Black Rose Books, 1980.

Borgmann, Albert. *Technology and the Character of Contemporary Life: A Philosophical Inquiry*. Chicago: University of Chicago Press, 1987.

Boulding, Elise. "Futurism as Galvanizer of Education." In *Educational Reconstruction*, edited by N. Shimhara. Columbus, OH: Charles Merrill Publishing Co., 1972.

Bourque, Susan C., and Kay B. Warren. "Technology, Gender and Development." *Daedalus* 116, no. 4 (Fall 1987): 173–97.

Bradford, George. "Marxism, Anarchism and the Roots of the New Totalitarianism." *Fifth Estate* 15, no. 5 (July 1981): 9.

———. "How Deep Is Deep Ecology?" *Fifth Estate* 22, no. 3 (Fall 1987): 3–30.

Bradley, Wendell S. "Power, Aesthetics and Community." Unpublished paper.

Braverman, Harry. "The Degradation of Work in the 20th Century." *Monthly Review* 34 (May 1982): 1–13.

Brecher, Jeremy. "American Labor: The Promise of Decline." *Zeta Magazine* 1, no. 5 (May 1988): 75–80.

Brecher, Jeremy, and Tim Costello. "Whose Quality of Worklife?" *Zeta Magazine* 2, no. 5 (May 1989): 89–94.

Bridenthal, Renate. "The Dialectics of Production and Reproduction in History." *Radical America* 10 (March-April 1976): 3–11.

Brod, Craig. *Technostress*. Reading, MA: Addison Wesley, 1984.

Brooks, Geraldine. "The Israeli Kibbutz Takes a Capitalist Tack to Keep Socialist Ideals." *The Wall Street Journal*, 21 September 1989, 1.

Brower, Kenneth. "The Naked Vulture and the Thinking Ape." *The Atlantic Monthly*, October 1983, 70–88.

Bryan, Frank, and John McClaughry. *The Vermont Papers: Recreating Democracy on a Human Scale*. Chelsea, VT: Chelsea Green Publishing Co., 1989.

Buber, Martin. *Paths in Utopia*. Boston: Beacon Press, 1958.

Burrows, Edwin G. "The Transition Question in Early American History: A Checklist of Recent Books, Articles, and Dissertations." *Radical History Review* 18 (Fall 1978): 173–90.

Butler, Samuel. *Erewhon and Erewhon Revisited*. New York: Dutton–Everyman's Library, 1965.

C. George Benello on the Liberation of Work. Special issue of *Changing Work* 7 (Winter 1988).

Caffentzis, George, and Silvia Federici. "Mormons in Space." In *Semiotext[E]USA*, edited by Jim Fleming and Peter Lamborn Wilson, 55–61. New York: Autonomedia Inc., 1987.

Callicott, J. Baird. "Traditional American Indian and Western European Attitudes toward Nature: An Overview." *Environmental Ethics* 4 (winter 1982): 293–318.

Camatte, Jacques. *Against Domestication*. London: Black Thumb Press, 1981.

Carroll, Peter N. *It Seemed Like Nothing Happened: The Tragedy and Promise of American in the 1970s*. New York: Holt, Rinehart and Winston, 1982.

Case, John, and Rosemary C. R. Taylor, eds. *Co-ops, Communes and Collectives: Experiments in Social Change in the 1960s and 1970s*. New York: Pantheon Books, 1979.

Caudwell, Christopher. *Illusion and Reality*. New York: International Publishers, 1977.

Chambers, Clarke A. "The National Cooperative League of the United States of America, 1916–1961: A Study of Social Theory and Social Action." *Agricultural History* 36 (1962): 59–81.

Chernyi, Lev. "The Cult of the Sacred." *Anarchy: A Journal of Desire Armed* 24 (March–April 1990): 20.

Chianese, Robert L., ed. *Peaceable Kingdoms: An Anthology of Utopian Writings*. New York: Harcourt Brace Jovanovich, Inc., 1971.

Chomsky, Noam. *Noam Chomsky: Radical Priorities*, edited by C. P. Otero. Montreal: Black Rose Books, 1981.

Clark, Christopher. "The Household Mode of Production." *Radical History Review* 18 (Fall 1978): 166–72.

Clark, John. *The Anarchist Moment: Reflections on Culture, Nature and Power*. Montreal and Buffalo: Black Rose Books, 1984 (See especially "Marxism and Technology," 101–15.)

Clecak, Peter. *Radical Paradoxes: Dilemmas of the American Left: 1945–1970*. New York: Harper Torchbooks, 1933.

Coates, Vary T. "The Potential Impact of Robotics." *The Futurist* 17 (February 1983): 28–32.

Cohn, Norman. *The Pursuit of the Millenium: Revolutionary Messianism in Medieval and Reformation Europe and Its Bearing on Modern Totalitarian Movements*. New York: Harper Torchbooks, 1961.

Cole, G. D. H. *The Meaning of Marxism*. Ann Arbor: University of Michigan Press, 1966.

———. *Marxism and Anarchism, 1850–1890*. London: Macmillan, 1969.

Cooley, Mike. *Architect or Bee? The Human/Technology Relationship*. Boston: South End Press, 1983.

Cotter, John J. "Ethics and Justice in the World of Work: Improving the Quality of Working Life." *Review of Social Economy* 40 (December 1982): 393–406.

Cotton, John. "A Christian Calling." In *The American Puritans: Their Prose and Poetry*, edited by Perry Miller, Garden City, NY: Anchor Doubleday, 1956.

Cowan, Ruth Schwartz. "The Industrial Revolution in the Home: Household Technology and Social Change in the 20th Century." *Culture and Technology* 17, no. 1 (January 1976): 1–23.

Dahl, Robert A. *After the Revolution? Authority in a Good Society*. New Haven and London: Yale University Press, 1970.

Daly, Herman E., ed. *Toward a Steady-State Economy*. San Francisco: W. H. Freeman, 1973.

———. *Economics, Ecology, Ethics: Essays toward A Steady-State Economy*. San Francisco: W. H. Freeman, 1980.

Davis, Angela Y. *Women, Culture, and Politics*. New York: Random House, 1989.

Davis, Natalie Zemon. "Women in the Crafts in Sixteenth-Century Lyon." *Feminist Studies* 8, no. 1 (Spring 1982): 47–80.

Debord, Guy. *Society of the Spectacle*. Detroit: Black and Red, 1977.

deGrazia, Sebastian. *Of Time, Work and Leisure*. Garden City, NY: Anchor Books, 1962.

DeLeon, David. "For Democracy Where We Work: A Rationale for Social Self-Management." In *Reinventing Anarchy: What Are Anarchists Thinking These Days?*, edited by Howard J. Ehrlich, Carol Ehrlich, David DeLeon, and Glenda Morris, 304–23. London: Routledge and Kegan Paul, 1979.

de Tocqueville, Alexis. *Democracy in America*, edited and abridged by Richard D. Heffner. New York: New American Library, 1956.

Dewey, John. *Art as Experience*. New York: Capricorn Books, 1958.

Dey, Jennie. *Women in Food Production and Food Security in Africa*. Rome: Food and Agriculture Organization of the United Nations, 1984.

Diacou, Zoe. "An Interview with Anne Kanten: 'I'm a Farmer, I'm a Woman, and I'm Angry.' " *World Women News* 1, no. 2 (Winter 1989): 1.

Didsbury, Howard F., Jr., ed. *The World of Work: Careers and the Future*. Bethesda, MD: World Future Society, 1983.

Disch, Robert, ed. *The Ecological Conscience: Values for Survival*. Englewood Cliffs, NJ: Prentice-Hall, Inc., 1970.

Dooling, D. M., ed. *A Way of Working: The Spiritual Dimension of Craft*. New York: Parabola Books, 1986.

Drago, Robert. "Capitalism and Efficiency: A Review and Appraisal of the Recent Discussion." *Review of Radical Political Economics* 18, no. 4 (1986): 71–92.

Dugger, William M. "Power: An Institutional Framework of Analysis." *Journal of Economic Issues* 14 (December 1980): 897–907.

DuPlessis, Robert S. "From Demesne to World-System: A Critical Review of the Literature on the Transition from Feudalism to Capitalism." *Radical History Review* 3, no. 4 (1976): 3–41.

Ehrlich, Carol. "The Unhappy Marriage of Marxism and Feminism: Can It Be Saved?" In *Women and Revolution*, edited by Lydia Sargent, 109–33. Boston: South End Press, 1981.

Ehrlich, Howard J., Carol Ehrlich, David DeLeon, and Glenda Morris, eds. *Reinventing Anarchy: What Are Anarchists Thinking These Days?* London: Routledge and Kegan Paul, 1979.

Ellul, Jacques. *The Technological Society*. New York: Vintage Books, 1964.

Emerson, Ralph Waldo. "Man the Reformer." *Dial*, April 1841, 523–38.

———. *Selections from Ralph Waldo Emerson*, edited by Stephen B. Whicher. Boston: Houghton Mifflin Co., 1957.

Faragher, John Mack. "History from the Inside-Out: Writing the History of Women in Rural America." *American Quarterly* 33, no. 5 (Winter 1981): 537–57.

Faux, Jeff. "Does Worker Ownership Work?" *Utne Reader* 15 (April/May 1986): 24–33.

"Fifth of New Jobs in Early '80s Low-Wage." *The Free Press* (Mankato, MN), 10 December 1986.

Fink, Deborah. *Open Country, Iowa: Rural Women, Tradition and Change*. Albany: State University of New York Press, 1986.

Fisher, Marvin. "The Iconography of Industrialism, 1830–1860." In *The American Culture*, edited by Hennig Cohen. New York: Houghton Mifflin, 1968.

Fleming, Marie. *The Anarchist Way to Socialism: Elisee Reclus and Nineteenth-Century European Anarchism*. Totowa, NJ: Rowman and Littlefield, 1979.

Folbre, Nancy. "Families of the World Unite." *Zeta Magazine* 1, no. 12 (December 1988): 31–36.

Foster, Lawrence. *Religion and Sexuality: Three American Communal Experiments of the Nineteenth Century*. New York and Oxford: Oxford University Press, 1981.

Freeman, Jo. "The Tyranny of Structurelessness." *Ms* 11, no. 1 (July 1973): 76.

Fried, Albert, and Ronald Sanders, eds. *Socialist Thought: A Documentary History*. Garden City, NY: Anchor Books, 1964.

Fromm, Erich. *The Sane Society*. Greenwich, CT: Fawcett, 1955.

Fuentes, Annette, and Barbara Ehrenreich. *Women in the Global Factory*. Institute for New Communications Pamphlet No. 2, Boston: South End Press, 1983.

Fulano, T. "Against the Megamachine." *Fifth Estate* 15, no. 5 (306 July 1981): 4–8.

———. "Uncovering a Corpse: A Reply to the Defenders of Technology." *Fifth Estate* 15, no. 6 (30 November 1981): 5.

Fuller, R. Buckminster. "Technology and the Human Environment." In *The Ecological Conscience: Values for Survival*, edited by Robert Disch, 174–80. Englewood Cliffs, NJ: Prentice-Hall, 1970.

Fulmer, Robert M. "Nine Paradoxes for the 1990s." In *The World of Work*, edited by Howard F. Didsbury, Jr., 39–48. Bethesda, MD: World Future Society, 1983.

Gardell, Bertil. "Reactions at Work and Their Influence on Nonwork Activities: An Analysis of a Sociopolitical Problem in Affluent Societies." *Human Relations* 29, no. 9 (1976): 885–904.

Gaventa, John, and Helen Lewis. "The Highlander Economic Educational Project." *Rural Adult Education Forum* 1, no. 6 (August/September 1988): 1.

Gehlen, Arnold. *Man in the Age of Technology*. New York: Columbia University Press, 1980.

George, Henry. *Progress and Poverty*. New York: Robert Schalkenbach Foundation, 1966.

Giese, Paula. "How the 'Political' Co-ops Were Destroyed." *North Country Anvil* 13 (October/November 1974): 26–30.

Gilbert, Lucia Albino. "Comments on the Meaning of Work in Women's Lives." *The Counseling Psychologist* 12, no. 4 (1984): 129–30.

Gilk, Paul. "Nature's Unruly Mob: Farming and the Crisis in Rural Culture." *North Country Anvil* 53 (Fall 1986).

Gill, Eric. *The Necessity of Belief: An Enquiry Into the Nature of Human Certainty, the Causes of Skepticism and the Grounds of Morality, and a Justification of the Doctrine that the End is the Beginning*. London: Faber and Faber, Ltd., 1936.

———. "The End of the Fine Arts." In *Work and Property*. London: J. M. Dent and Sons, Ltd., 1937.

———. "The Value of the Creative Faculty in Man." In *Work and Property*. London: J. M. Dent and Sons, Ltd., 1937.

———. *Autobiography*. London: Jonathan Cape, 1940.

———. *Christianity and the Machine Age*. London: The Sheldon Press, and New York: The Macmillan Co., 1940.

———. "Ownership and Industrialism." In *Sacred and Secular Sc*. London: J. M. Dent and Sons, Ltd., 1940.

———. *A Holy Tradition of Working: Passages from the Writing of Eric Gill*. West Stockbridge, MA: The Lindisfarne Press, 1983.

Gilligan, Carol. *In a Different Voice: Psychological Theory and Women's Development*. Cambridge, MA: Harvard University Press, 1982.

Gilman, Robert. "Enabling Employee Ownership." *In Context*, Autumn 1985, 49–54.

Glacken, Clarence J. *Traces on the Rhodian Shore: Nature and Culture in Western Thought from Ancient Times to the End of the Eighteenth Century*. Berkeley: University of California Press, 1976.

Glenn, Evelyn, and Roslyn Feldberg."Degraded and Deskilled: The Proletarianization of Clerical Work." *Social Problems* 25 (October 1977): 52–64.

Golod, Fluffy. "Power: What *Should* Women Want?" *Soil of Liberty* 6, no. 3 (1980): 2.

Goodman, Ellen. "Learning a Lot By Doing Nothing." Minneapolis *Tribune*, 30 August 1988, 8A.

Paul Goodman. *People or Personnel* and *Like A Conquered Province*. New York: Vintage Books, 1968.

———. "Can Technology Be Humane?" In *The Ecological Conscience: Values for Survival*, edited by Robert Disch, 103–17. Englewood Cliffs, NJ: Prentice-Hall, Inc., 1970.

———. *Drawing the Line: The Political Essays of Paul Goodman*, edited by Taylor Stoehr. New York: Free Life Editions, Inc., 1977.

Goodman, Paul, and Percival Goodman. *Communitias: Means of Livelihood and Ways of Life*. New York: Vintage Books, 1960.

Goodwyn, Lawrence. *The Populist Moment: A Short History of the Agrarian Revolt in America*. Oxford: Oxford University Press, 1978.

Gorny, Yosef. "Open Utopism in Tabenkin's 'Weltanschauung.' " *Kibbutz Studies* 21 (November 1986): 7–13.

Gramsci, Antonio. *The Open Marxism of Antonio Gramsci*. New York: Cameron Associates, 1957.

———. *The Modern Prince and Other Writings*. New York: International, 1959.

———. *Selections from the Prison Notebooks of Antonio Gramsci*, edited and translated by Quintin Hoare and Geoffrey Nowell Smith. New York: International, 1971.

Grant, George. *Technology and Justice*. Toronto: Anansi, 1986.

Graves, Clare W. "Human Nature Prepares for a Momentous Leap." *The Futurist*, April 1974, 72–85.

Griffin-Pierson, Sharon. "Achievement and Competitiveness in Women." *Journal of College Student Development* 2 (November 1988): 491–95.

Haavio-Mannila, Elina. "Satisfaction with Family, Work, Leisure and Life Among Men and Women." *Human Relations* 24, no. 6 (December 1971): 585–601.

Hall, David L. "The Advance to Nature from Technique to 'Techne.' " Paper presented to the Association of American Studies meeting in Minneapolis, MN, September 27–30, 1979.

Halstead, Fred. *The 1985–86 Hormel Meat-Packers Strike*. New York: Pathfinder Press, 1986.

Handy, Charles. "The Changing Shape of Work." *Organizational Dynamics* 9, 2 (Autumn 1980): 26–34.

Hardin, Garrett. "The Tragedy of the Commons." *Science* 162 (13 December 1968): 1243–48.

Harel, Yehuda. "Tabenkin and Anarcho-Communism." *Kibbutz Studies* 24 (October 1987): 19–21.

Hargrove, Eugene C. "The Historical Foundations of American Environmental Attitudes." *Environmental Ethics* 1 (Fall 1979): 209–40.

Harmon, Lenore W. "What's New? A Response to Astin." *The Counseling Psychologist* 12, no. 4 (1984): 127–29.

Harper, Douglas. *Working Knowledge: Skill and Community in a Small Shop*. Chicago and London: University of Chicago Press, 1987.

Harrison, Bennett, and Barry Bluestone. "Changes in the Nature of Work." Minneapolis *Star and Tribune*, 15 July 1984, 11A.

Hartmann, Heidi. "The Unhappy Marriage of Marxism and Feminism: Towards a More Progressive Union." In *Women and Revolution*, edited by Lydia Sargent, 1–41. Boston: South End, 1981.

Hartshorne, Charles. *Creative Synthesis and Philosophical Method*. LaSalle, IL: Open Court, 1970.

————. "The Environment Results of Technology." In *Philosophy and Environmental Crisis*, edited by William T. Blackstone. Athens: University of Georgia Press, 1974: 69–78.

Haug, Marie R. "The Deprofessionalization of Everyone?" *Sociological Focus* 8, no. 3 (August 1975): 197–213.

Heresies Editorial Collective. "Editorial." *Heresies* 2, no. 3 (Spring 1979): 3.

————. "True Confessions." *Heresies* 2, no. 3 (Spring 1979): 93–96.

Hickerson, Steven R. "Legal Counsel, Power, and Institutional Hegemony." *Journal of Economic Issues* 16, no. 1 (March 1981): 191–210.

Hightower, Jim. *Hard Tomatoes, Hard Times: A Report of the Agribusiness Accountability Project on the Failure of America's Land Grant College Complex*. Cambridge, MA: Schenkman Publishing Co., 1973.

Hirschhorn, Larry. "The Soul of a New Worker." *Working Papers Magazine* 9, no. 1 (January/February 1982): 42–47.

Hobsbawm, E. J. *Primitive Rebels: Studies in Archaic Forms of Social Movements in the Nineteenth and Twentieth Centuries*. New York: Norton, 1965.

Hobsbawm, Eric. "Man and Woman in Socialist Iconography." *History Workshop Journal* 6 (Autumn 1978): 121–38.

Hofstadter, Albert. *Truth and Art*. New York: Columbia University Press, 1965.

————. "On the Consciousness and Language of Art." *Philosophy East and West* 19, no. 1 (January 1969): 3–15.

————. *Agony and Epitaph: Man, His Art, and His Poetry*. New York: George Braziller, 1970.

————. "On Artistic Knowledge: A Study in Hegel's Philosophy of Art." In *Beyond Epistemology: New Studies in the Philosophy of Hegel*, edited by Frederick G. Weiss. The Hague: Martinus Nijhoff, 1974.

Hofstadter, Douglas R. *Godel, Escher, Bach: An Eternal Golden Braid*. New York: Vintage, 1980.

Hofstadter, Douglas R., and Daniel C. Dennett, "composers and arrangers." *The Mind's I: Fantasies and Reflections on Self and Soul*. New York: Bantam, 1982.

Holloway, Mark. *Heavens on Earth: Utopian Communities in America 1680–1880*. New York: Library Publishers, 1951.

Hook, Sidney. *From Hegel to Marx: Studies in the Intellectual Development of Karl Marx*. Ann Arbor: University of Michigan Press, 1971.

Hooks, Bell. *Feminist Theory: From Margin to Center*. Boston: South End, 1984.

Horowitz, Irving L., ed. *The Anarchists*. New York: Dell, 1964.

Hughes, J. Donald. "GAIA: Environmental Problems in Chthonic Perspective." *Environmental Review* 6, no. 2 (Fall 1982): 92–104.

Hull, Frank M., Nathalie S. Friedman, and Theresa F. Rogers. "The Effect of Technology on Alienation from Work." *Work and Occupations* 9 (1982): 31–57.

Hyams, Edward. *Soil and Civilization*. New York: Harper and Row, 1976.

Illich, Ivan. *Shadow Work*. Boston and London: Marion Boyars, 1981.

International Wages for Housework Campaign. *Wages for Housework*. Pamphlet, 1985.

James, Selma. *The Global Kitchen*. London: Housewives in Dialogue, 1985.

Jenkins, Iredell. *Art and the Human Enterprise*. Cambridge: University Press, 1958.

Jensen, Joan M. *With These Hands: Women Working on the Land*. Old Westburg, NY: Feminist Press, 1981.

John XXIII. *Encyclical Mater et Magistra* (Christianity and social progress), 15 May 1961. Washington, DC: National Catholic Welfare Conference, 1961.

John Paul II. *Encyclical Laborem Exercens* (On human work). Washington, DC: U.S. Catholic Conference, September 14, 1981.

Johnson, Ana Gutierrez, and William Foote Whyte. "The Mondragon System of Worker Production Cooperatives." *Industrial and Labor Relations Review* 31, no. 1 (October 1977): 18–30.

Johnson, Warren. *Muddling toward Frugality: A Blueprint for Survival in the 1980s*. Boulder, CO: Shambhala, 1979.

Judd, Richard W. "Grass-Roots Conservation in Eastern Coastal Maine: Monopoly and the Moral Economy of Weir Fishing, 1893–1911." *Environmental Review* 12, no. 2 (Summer 1988): 80–104.

Juster, Norton. *So Sweet to Labor: Rural Women in America 1865–95*. New York: Viking Press, 1979.

Kamerman, Sheila B. "Work and Family in Industrialized Societies." *Signs: Journal of Women in Culture and Society* 4, no. 4 (Summer 1979): 632–50.

Kanovsky, Eliyahu. *The Economy of the Israeli Kibbutz*. Cambridge, MA: Harvard University Press, 1966.

Kanter, Rosabeth Moss. *Commitment and Community: Communes and Utopias in Sociological Perspective*. Cambridge, MA: Harvard University Press, 1972.

Kelly, Marjorie. "Revolution In the Marketplace." *Utne Reader*, January/February 1989, 54–62.

Kephart, William M. *Extraordinary Groups: The Sociology of Unconventional Life-Styles*. New York: St. Martins, 1982.

Kerber, Linda K. "Separate Spheres, Female Worlds, Woman's Place: The Rhetoric of Women's History." *The Journal of American History* 75, no. 1 (June 1988): 9–39.

Kercher, Leonard C., Vant W. Kebker, and Wilfred C. Leland, Jr. *Consumers' Cooperatives in the North Central States*. Minneapolis: The University of Minnesota Press, 1941.

Kessler-Harris, Alice. *Out To Work: A History of Wage-Earning Women in the United States*. New York: Oxford University Press, 1982.

Khan, Salma. *The Fifty Percent: Women in Development and Policy in Bangladesh*. Dhaka, Bangladesh: University Press Ltd., 1988.

Klingner, Kate. "Elvia Alvarado, Honduran Peasant Activist." *World Women News* 1, no. 2 (Winter 1989): 3.

Krimerman, Leonard. "Anarchism Reconsidered: Past Fallacies and Unorthodox Remedies." *Social Anarchism* 1, no. 2 (October 1980): 1–18.

Kropotkin, Peter. *Mutual Aid: A Factor in Evolution*. Montreal: Black Rose Books, n.d.

———. "The State: Its Historic Role." In *Selected Writings on Anarchism and Revolution: P. A. Kropotkin*, edited by Martin A. Miller, 211–64. Cambridge, MA, and London: The MIT Press, 1970.

———. *Fields, Factories and Workshops Tomorrow*. New York: Harper and Row, 1974.

Kuhn, Thomas S. *The Structure of Scientific Revolutions*. Chicago and London: University of Chicago Press, 1970.

Kuic, Vukan. "Work, Leisure, and Culture." In *The World of Work*, edited by Howard F. Didsbury, Jr., 310–17. Bethesda, MD: World Future Society, 1983.

LaFargue, Paul. *The Right to Be Lazy*. Chicago: Charles H. Kerr Publishing Co., 1975.

Laslett, Peter. *The World We Have Lost: England before the Industrial Age*. New York: Charles Scribner's Sons, 1965.

Lazerow, Jama. "Religion and Labor Reform in Antebellum America: The World of William Field Young." *American Quarterly* 38, no. 2 (Summer 1986): 265–86.

Leach, Dirk. "Against Nihilism: Technik." *Fifth Estate* 21, no. 2 (Summer 1987): 18–19.

Leacock, Eleanor. "History, Development, and the Division of Labor by Sex: Implications for Organizations." *Signs: Journal of Women in Culture and Society* 7 (1981): 474–91.

Lears, T. J. Jackson. "The Concept of Cultural Hegemony: Problems and Possibilities." *American Historical Review* 90 (June 1985): 567–97.

Leff, Walli F., and Marilyn G. Haft. *Time without Work*. Boston: South End Press, 1983.

LeGoff, Jacques. *Time, Work and Culture in the Middle Ages*. Chicago: University of Chicago Press, 1982.

LeGuin, Ursula K. *The Dispossessed*. New York: Avon, 1975.

Lehmann, Scott. "Do Wildernesses Have Rights?" *Environmental Ethics* 3 (Summer 1981): 129–46.

Leo XIII. "Encyclical Rerum Novarum" (The condition of labor), May 1981. In *Five Great Encyclicals*, 1–30. New York: The Paulist Press, 1953.

Lerner, Max. "Big Technology and Neutral Technicians." In *The American Culture*, edited by Hennig Cohen, 180–90. New York: Houghton Mifflin, 1968.

Lerner, Michael. *Surplus Powerlessness: The Psychodynamics of Everyday Life . . . and the Psychology of Individual and Social Transformation*. Oakland, CA: The Institute for Labor and Mental Health, 1986.

Leval, Gaston. *Collectives in the Spanish Revolution*. London: Freedom Press, 1975.

Lewin, Ellen. "Feminist Ideology and the Meaning of Work: The Case of Nursing." *Catalyst* 10 and 11 (Summer 1977): 78–103.

Lewis, Helen Matthews, Linda Johnson, and Donald Askins. *Colonialism in Modern America: The Appalachian Case*. Boone, NC: The Appalachian Consortium Press, 1978.

Lewis, Helen, and John Gaventa. *The Jellico Handbook: A Teacher's Guide to Community-Based Economics*. New Market, TN: The Highlander Center, 1988.

Lonnrot, Elias. *The Kalevala: Or Poems of the Kaleva District*. Cambridge, MA: Harvard University Press, 1963.

Lord, Miles W. "A Deadly Depth Charge in their Wombs," Minneapolis *Star and Tribune*, May 18, 1984: 15A.

Lovins, Amory B. *Soft Energy Paths*. New York: Harper and Row, 1979.

Lynd, Staughton. "Solidarity Unionism." *Zeta Magazine* 1, no. 3 (March 1988): 85–91.

———. "The Genesis of the Idea of a Community Right to Industrial Property in Youngstown and Pittsburgh, 1977–1987." *Changing Work* 9 (Spring 1989): 14–19.

Macarov, David. "Reciprocity between Self-Actualization and Hard Work." *International Journal of Social Economics* 3 (1976): 39–44.

———. "Pursuing Leisure as a Moral Imperative." *Leisure Information Newsletter* 9 (1983): 6–7.

———. "Changes in the World of Work: Some Implications for the Future." In *The World of Work*, edited by Howard F. Didsbury, Jr., 3–24. Bethesda, MD: World Future Society, 1984.

Maglin, Nan Bauer. "Visions of Defiance: Work, Politics, Commitment and Sisterhood in Twenty-One Works of Fiction, 1895–1925." *Praxis* 1, no. 3 (1976): 98–112.

Mallon, Florencia E. "Patriarchy in the Transition to Capitalism: Central Peru, 1830–1950." *Feminist Studies* 13, no. 2 (Summer 1987): 379–407.

Maly, Kenneth. "Work is Reality." *North Country Anvil*, 45 (Fall 1983): 12–14.

Mander, Jerry. *Four Arguments for the Elimination of Television*. New York: William Morrow, 1978.

Mankin, Don. "Autonomy, Control, and the Office of the Future: Personal and Social Implications." In *The World of Work*, edited by Howard F. Didsbury, Jr., 165–70. Bethesda, MD: World Future Society, 1983.

Marcuse, Herbert. *One Dimensional Man*. Boston: Beacon, 1964.

Marx, Karl. *Capital, the Communist Manifesto and Other Writings*, edited by Max Eastman. New York: The Modern Library, 1959.

———. *Capital: A Critical Analysis of Capitalist Production*, Vol. 1, edited by Frederick Engels and translated by Samuel Moore and Edward Aveling. Moscow: Progress Publishers, 1965.

———. "Economic and Philosophic Manuscripts (1844)," in *Writings of the Young Marx on Philosophy and Society*, translated and edited by Loyd D. Easton and Kurt H. Guddat, 283–337. Garden City, NY: Doubleday, 1967.

Marx, Karl, and Frederick Engels. *The German Ideology*, Parts I and III, translated and edited by Roy Pascal. New York: International, 1939.

Marx, Leo. *The Machine in the Garden: Technology and the Pastoral Ideal in America*. New York: Oxford University Press, 1964.

May, Martha. "The Historical Problem of the Family Wage: The Ford Motor Company and the Five Dollar Day." *Feminist Studies* 8, no. 2 (Summer 1982): 399–424.

McGlynn, Bob. "What Is to Be Undone?" In *Semiotext[E]USA*, edited by Jim Fleming and Peter Lamborn Wilson, 142–47. New York: Autonomedia Inc., 1987.

McKinley, Blaine. " 'The Quagmires of Necessity': American Anarchists and Dilemmas of Vocation." *American Quarterly* 34, no. 5 (Winter 1982): 503–23.

Melville, Herman. "The Paradise of Bachelors and the Tartarus of Maids." In *American Issues I*, edited by Merle Curti, Willard Thorp, Carlos Baker, and Joseph M. Dowling. Philadelphia, PA: J. B. Lippencott Co., 1971.

Merchant, Carolyn. "The Theoretical Structure of Ecological Revolutions." *Environmental Review* 11, no. 4 (Winter 1987): 265–74.

Merrill, Michael. "Cash Is Good to Eat: Self-Sufficiency in the Rural Economy." *Radical History Review* 14 (Winter 1977): 42–71.

———. "So What's Wrong with the 'Household Mode of Production?' " *Radical History Review* 22 (Winter 1978–80): 141–46.

Merrill, Richard, ed. *Radical Agriculture*. New York: Harper and Row, 1976.

Miller, Jack. "Technology as Possession." *North Country Anvil* 48 (Summer/Fall 1984): 1.

———. "The Problem of a Job: Parts I–II." *North Country Anvil* 50 (September 1985): 1; and 51 (Fall/Winter 1985–86): 1.

Miller, Perry. "The Responsibility of Mind in a Civilization of Machines." *American Scholar* 31 (Winter 1961–1962): 51–69.

———. *The Life of the Mind in America: From the Revolution to the Civil War*. New York: Harvest Books, 1965.

———. *Nature's Nation*. Cambridge, MA: Harvard University Press, 1967.

———, ed. *The American Puritans: Their Prose and Poetry*. Garden City, NY: Anchor Doubleday, 1956.

Minnesota Commission on the Economic Status of Women. *Women in Minnesota*. St. Paul: Minnesota Commission on the Economic Status of Women and the Hubert Humphrey Institute of Public Affairs, August 1984.

Moberg, David. "Experimenting with the Future: Alternative Institutions and American Socialism." In *Co-ops, Communes and Collectives: Experiments in Social Change in the 1960s and 1970s*, edited by John Case and Rosemary C. R. Taylor, 274–311. New York: Pantheon Books, 1979.

Morgan, Edmund S. "The Puritan Ethic and the American Revolution." *William and Mary Quarterly* 24 (1967): 3–43.

Morris, David. *The New City-States*. Washington, DC: Institute for Local Self-Reliance, 1982.

———. "Free Trade: The Great Destroyer." *Clinton Street Quarterly* 10, no. 1 (Spring 1988): 28–33.

———. "The Materials We Need to Create a Sustainable Society Lie Close to Home." *Utne Reader* 36 (November/December 1989): 84–90.

Morris, David, and Karl Hess. *Neighborhood Power: The New Localism*. Boston: Beacon, 1975.

Morris, William. *Political Writings of William Morris*, edited by A. L. Morton. New York: International Publishers, 1973.

Morrison, Theodore. *Chautauqua: A Center for Education, Religion, and the Arts in America*. Chicago and London: The University of Chicago Press, 1974.

Mowoshowitz, Abbe. "The Conquest of Will: Information Processing in Human Affairs." In *Questioning Technology: A Critical Anthology*, edited by John Zerzan and Alice Carnes, 99–101. London: Freedom Press, 1988.

Mumford, Lewis. *The Golden Day: A Study in American Experience and Culture*. New York: Boni and Liveright, 1926.

———. *Faith for Living*. London: Readers Union, 1942.

———. *Art and Technics*. New York: Columbia University Press, 1952.

———. *In the Name of Sanity*. New York: Harcourt, Brace and Company, 1954.

———. "Apology to Henry Adams." *The Virginia Quarterly Review* 38 (September 1962): 196–217.

———. *The Story of Utopias*. New York: Viking, 1962.

————. *The Myth of the Machine: The Pentagon of Power*. New York: Harcourt Brace Jovanovich, Inc., 1970.

————. *The Future of Technics and Civilization*. London: Freedom Press, 1986, with an Introduction by Colin Ward.

Murdoch, Iris. *The Sovereignty of Good*. New York: Shocken, 1971.

Nevill, Dorothy D. "The Meaning of Work in Women's Lives: Role Conflict, Preparation, and Change." *The Counseling Psychologist* 12, no. 4 (1984): 131–33.

Newland, Kathleen. *Women, Men, and the Division of Labor*. Worldwatch Paper 37. USA: Worldwatch, May 1980.

Newman, William. "Technology and Alchemical Debate in the Late Middle Ages." *Isis*, 80 (1989): 423–45.

Nisbet, Robert A. *Social Change and History: Aspects of the Western Theory of Development*. London: Oxford University Press, 1969.

————. *The Quest for Community*. London: Oxford University Press, 1970.

————. *The Present Age: Progress and Anarchy in Modern America*. New York: Harper and Row, 1988.

Noble, David F. "Present Tense Technology: Parts I–III." *Democracy: A Journal of Political Renewal and Radical Change* 3, no. 2 (Spring 1983): 8–23; 3, no. 3 (Summer 1983): 70–82; and 3, no. 4 (Fall 1983): 71–93.

Nomad, Max. *White Collars and Horny Hands*. Edmonton, Canada: Black Cat Press, 1983.

Noy, Danny. "The Kibbutz as an Open Social System." *Kibbutz Studies* 14 (August 1984): 13–29.

O'Connor, Francis V., ed. *Art for the Millions: Essays from the 1930s by Artists and Administrators of the WPA Federal Art Project*. Boston: New York Graphic Society, 1975.

Olds, Larry. *Essays on Freedom*. Education Exploration Center Newsletter, February 1972, n.p.

O'Neill, Gerard K. *2081: A Hopeful View of the Human Future*. New York: Simon and Schuster, 1981.

Ophuls, William. *Ecology and the Politics of Scarcity: Prologue to a Political Theory of the Steady State*. San Francisco: W. H. Freeman, 1977.

Ord-Hume, Arthur W. J. G. *Perpetual Motion: The History of an Obsession*. New York: St. Martin's Press, 1980.

Ostreicher, Richard. "From Artisan to Consumer: Images of Workers 1840–1920." *Journal of American Culture* 4 (Spring 1984): 47–64.

Paddock, Joe, Nancy Paddock, and Carol Bly. *Soil and Survival: Land Stewardship and the Future of Agriculture*. San Francisco: Sierra Club Books, 1986.

Papanek, Hanna. "Family Status Production: The 'Work' and 'Non-Work' of Women." *Signs: Journal of Women in Culture and Society* 4 (1979): 775–81.

Paterson, R. W. K. *The Nihilistic Egoist: Max Stirner*. Oxford: Oxford University Press, 1971.

Pellis, Richard H. *Radical Visions and American Dreams*. New York: Harper and Row, 1973.

Perlman, Fredy. *The Reproduction of Daily Life*. Detroit: Black and Red, 1972.

Piercy, Marge. *Circles on the Water: Selected Poems of Marge Piercy*. New York: A. A. Knopf, 1973.

Pirsig, Robert M. *Zen and the Art of Motorcycle Maintenance: An Inquiry Into Values*. Toronto: Bantam Books, 1975.

Pius XI. "Encyclical Quadragesimo Anno" (Reconstructing the social order), 15 May 1931. In *Five Great Encyclicals*, 125–68. New York: The Paulist Press, 1953.

Porritt, Jonathon. "Let the Green Spirit Live!" *Resurgence*, 127, March/April 1988, 4–12.

———. "Sustainability." *One Earth*, 18, no. 4 (Winter 1988): 13–15.

Preston, Yvonne. "What's A Woman Worth?" *Ms* 18, nos. 1–2 (July-August 1989): 78.

Proudhon, Pierre Joseph. "Property and Revolution." In *The Anarchists*, edited by Irving L. Horowitz. New York: Dell, 1964.

Pym, Denis. "The Other Economy as a Social System." In *Why Work: Arguments for the Leisure Society*, edited by Vernon Richards, 137–49. London: Freedom Press, 1983.

Quarter, Jack, and George Melnyk, eds. *Partners in Enterprise: The Worker Ownership Phenomenon*. Montreal and New York: Black Rose Books, 1989.

Ralph, Diana. *Work and Madness: The Rise of Community Psychiatry*. Montreal: Black Rose Books, 1983.

Rapp, Rayna. "Family and Class in Contemporary America: Notes Toward an Understanding of Ideology." In *Rethinking the Family: Some Feminist Questions*, edited by B. Thorne and M. Yalom, 168–87. White Plains, NY: Longman, Inc., 1982.

Read, Herbert. *The Philosophy of Anarchism*. London: Freedom Press, 1940.

———. *Education through Art*. New York: Pantheon, 1956.

———. *To Hell with Culture and Other Essays*. New York: Schocken Books, 1963.

———. *Anarchy and Order: Essays in Politics*. New York: Beacon, 1971.

Regan, Tom. "The Nature and Possibility of an Environmental Ethic." *Environmental Ethics* 3 (Spring 1981): 19–34.

Rescher, Nicholas. *Unpopular Essays on Technological Progress*. Pittsburgh: University of Pittsburgh Press, 1980.

Richard, Vernon, ed. *Why Work? Arguments for the Leisure Society*. London: Freedom Press, 1983.

Rocker, Rudolf. *Nationalism and Culture*. St. Paul: Michael E. Coughlin, 1978.

Rorabaugh, W. J. *The Craft Apprentice: From Franklin to the Machine Age in America*. New York and Oxford: Oxford University Press, 1986.

Rose, Sonya O. "Gender Segregation in the Transition to the Factory: The English Hosiery Industry, 1850–1910." *Feminist Studies* 13, no. 1 (Spring 1987): 163–84.

Rosenfeld, Morris. *The Teardrop Millionaire and Other Poems by Morris Rosenfeld*. Selected and trans. by Aaron Kramer. New York: Manhattan Emma Lazarus Clubs, 1955.

Roszak, Theodore. *The Making of the Counterculture: Reflections on the Technocratic Society and Its Youthful Opposition*. Garden City, NY: Anchor Doubleday, 1969.

Rothschild-Whitt, Joyce. "Conditions for Democracy: Making Participatory Organizations Work." In *Co-ops, Communes, and Collectives: Experiments in Social Change in the 1960s and 1970s*, edited by John Case and Rosemary C. R. Taylor. New York: Pantheon Books, 1979.

Roussopoulos, Dimitrious I., ed. *The Radical Papers*. Montreal: Black Rose Books, 1987.

Rowbotham, Sheila. "Stress at Work." *Zeta Magazine* 1, no. 5 (May 1988): 32–36.

———. "Casualization." *Zeta Magazine* 2, no. 7–8 (August 1989): 62–68.

Ruddick, Sara, and Pamela Daniels, eds. *Working It Out*. New York: Pantheon, 1977.

Ryan, John Julian. *The Humanization of Man*. New York, NY, and Paramus, NJ: Newman Press, 1972.

Sargent, Lydia, ed. *Women and Revolution: A Discussion of the Unhappy Marriage of Marxism and Feminism*. Boston: South End Press, 1981.

Sayres, Sohnya, Anders Stephanson, Stanley Aronowitz, and Frederic Jameson, eds. *The 60s without Apology*. Minneapolis, MN: University of Minnesota Press in Cooperation with *Social Text*, 1984.

Schleuning, Neala J. *America: Song We Sang without Knowing—The Life and Ideas of Meridel Le Sueur*. Mankato, MN: Little Red Hen Press, 1983.

———. "A Look Back: The U.S. Cultural Policy Debate." *Theaterwork* 3, no. 4 (May/ June 1983): 53–58.

———. "We Have No Art, We Do Everything the Best We Can: The Aesthetics of Work." *Human Economy Newsletter* 7, no. 2 (June 1986): 3–8.

Schofield, Ann. "Rebel Girls and Union Maids: The Woman Question in the Journals of the AFL and IWW." *Feminist Studies* 9, no. 2 (Summer 1983): 335–58.

Schor, Juliet B. "Manufacturing Crisis?" *Zeta Magazine* 1, no. 11 (1988): 40–44.

Schrank, Robert. *Ten Thousand Working Days*. Cambridge, MA, and London: The MIT Press, 1978.

Schumacher, E. F. *Small Is Beautiful*. New York: Harper and Row, 1973.

———. *Good Work*. New York: Harper and Row, 1979.

Schwalbe, Michael L. *The Psychosocial Consequences of Natural and Alienated Labor*. Albany, NY: State University of New York Press, 1986.

Schwartz, Adina. "Meaningful Work." *Ethics* 92 (July 1982): 634–46.

Schwartz, Tony. "Acceleration Syndrome: Does Everyone Live in the Fast Lane Nowadays?" *Utne Reader* 31 (January/February 1989): 36–43.

Scrivener, Michael. "The Anarchist Aesthetic." *Black Rose* 1, no. 1 (Spring 1979): 7–21.

Seeger, Peter, and Bob Reiser. *Carry It On: A History in Song, and Picture of America's Working Men and Women*. New York: Simon and Schuster, 1985.

Segal, Howard P. *Technological Utopianism in American Culture*. Chicago and London: University of Chicago Press, 1985.

Sen, Gita. "The Sexual Division of Labor and the Working Class Family: Toward a Conceptual Synthesis of Class Relations and the Subordination of Women." *Review of Radical Political Economics* 12 (Summer 1980): 76–86.

Service Employees International Union, AFL-CIO, CLC. *Americans Deserve a Living Wage: Minimum Wage*. Washington, DC: SEIU, 1988.

Shallis, Michael. *The Silicone Idol*. New York: Schocken, 1984.

Shi, David E. *The Simple Life: Plain Living and High Thinking in American Culture*. New York: Oxford University Press, 1985.

Shimony, Uzi. "Patterns of Industrialization in the Kibbutz." *Kibbutz Studies* 13 (April 1984): 8–19.

Sibley, Mulford Q. *Political Ideas and Ideologies: A History of Political Thought*. New York: Harper and Row, 1970.

———. *Technology and Utopian Thought*. Minneapolis: Burgess, 1971.

———. "The Relevance of Classical Political Theory for Economy, Technology and

Ecology." *Alternatives: Perspectives on Society and Environment* 2, no. 2 (1973): 14–35.

———. "Religion and Belief Systems in Utopian and Dystopian Thought." Paper presented at the 1974 Annual Meeting of the American Political Science Association, Chicago, IL.

———. *Nature and Civilization: Some Implications for Politics*. Itasca, IL: F. E. Peacock Publishers, 1977.

Sircello, Guy. *Mind and Art: An Essay on the Varieties of Expression*. Princeton, NJ: Princeton University Press, 1972.

Sklar, Martin J. "On the Proletarian Revolution and the End of Political-Economic Society." *Radical America* 3, no. 3 (May/June 1969): 1–39.

Snow, C. P. *The Two Cultures: And a Second Look*. New York: Cambridge University Press, 1964.

Spiro, Melford E. *Kibbutz: Venture in Utopia*. New York: Schocken, 1970.

Stanfield, J. Ron. *Economic Thought and Social Change*. Carbondale and Edwardsville, IL: Southern Illinois University Press, 1979.

Stanley, Manfred. *The Technological Conscience: Survival and Dignity in an Age of Expertise*. Chicago: University of Chicago Press, 1978.

Steinberg, Theodore L. "An Ecological Perspective on the Origins of Industrialization." *Environmental Review* 10, no. 4 (Winter 1986): 261–76.

Stephenson, Charles, and Robert Asher, eds. *Life and Labor: Dimensions of American Working-Class History*. Albany: State University of New York Press, 1986.

Stirner, Max. *The Ego and His Own*, edited by John Carroll. London: Cape, 1971.

Terkel, Studs. *Working: People Talk about What They Do All Day and How They Feel about What They Do*. New York: Pantheon, 1974.

Thomas, Paul. *Karl Marx and the Anarchists*. London: Routledge and Kegan Paul, 1980.

Thompson, E. P. *The Making of the English Working Class*. New York: Vintage, 1966.

Thompson, John. "The Right to Scab." Oklahoma *Observer* 18, no. 16 (10 September 1986): 1.

Thompson, W. R. " 'The Paradise of Bachelors and Tartarus of Maids': A Reinterpretation." *American Quarterly* 9 (Spring 1957): 34–45.

Thoreson, Elliot H. "The Meaning of Work: A Hutterian Perspective." Paper presented at the 18th Annual South Dakota History Conference, Madison, SD, April 1988.

Thurow, Lester C. *The Zero-Sum Society: Distribution and the Possibilities for Economic Change*. New York: Penguin, 1981.

Tolstoy, Leo N. *The Kingdom of God Is within You*. London: Oxford University Press, 1935.

———. *What is Art?* 1896, rpt. New York: Bobs-Merrill Co., Inc., 1960.

———. *Resurrection*. New York: Washington Square Press, 1963.

Tool, Marc R. *The Discretionary Economy: A Normative Theory of Political Economy*. Santa Monica, CA: Goodyear Publishing Co., Inc., 1979.

Tuan, Yi-Fu. "The Significance of the Artifact." *Geographical Review* 70, no. 4 (October 1980): 462–72.

Turkle, Sherry. *The Second Self: Computers and the Human Spirit*. New York: Simon and Schuster, Inc., 1984.

Twelve Southerners. "I'll Take My Stand." In *American Issues 2*, edited by Merle Curti, Willard Thorp, Carlos Baker and Joseph A. Dowling. Philadelphia: J. B. Lippincott Co., 1971.

U.S. Agency for International Development. *Women in Development: The First Decade, 1975–1984.* Washington, DC: Office of Women in Development, 1984.

U.S. Catholic Conference. *Economic Justice for All: Catholic Social Teaching and the U.S. Economy.* Washington, DC: U.S. Catholic Conference, 1986.

U.S. Women's Bureau. *The United Nations Decade for Women, 1976–1985: Employment in the United States.* Washington, DC: U.S. Dept. of Labor, 1985.

Vanek, Jaroslav. *The Participatory Economy: An Evolutionary Hypothesis and a Strategy for Development.* Ithaca and London: Cornell University Press, 1971.

Vazquez, Adolpho Sanchez. *Art and Society: Essays in Marxist Aesthetics.* New York and London: Monthly Review, 1973.

Veblen, Thorstein. *The Theory of Business Enterprise.* New York: Charles Scribner, 1904.

———. *The Portable Veblen*, edited by Max Lerner. New York: Viking Press, 1972.

Veysey, Laurence. *The Communal Experience: Anarchist and Mystical Communities in Twentieth-Century America.* Chicago and London: University of Chicago Press, 1978.

Vonnegut, Kurt, Jr. *Player Piano.* New York: Avon Books, 1970.

Wallace, Anthony F. C. *Rockdale: The Growth of an American Village in the Early Industrial Revolution.* New York: Knopf, 1980.

Ward, Colin. *Anarchy in Action.* New York: Harper and Row, 1973.

Ward, C. Osborne. *The Ancient Lowly: A History of the Ancient Working People from the Earliest Known Periods to the Adoption of Christianity by Constantine.* Vols. 1 and 2. Chicago: Charles H. Kerr and Co., 1907.

Waxman, Chaim I., ed. *The End of Ideology Debate.* New York: Simon and Schuster, 1968.

Weil, Simone. *The Need for Roots: Prelude to a Declaration of Duties toward Mankind.* New York: G. P. Putnam's Sons, 1952.

———. *Waiting for God.* New York: Harper and Row, 1973.

———. *Lectures on Philosophy.* Cambridge: Cambridge University Press, 1979.

Wessman, James W. "A Household Mode of Production—Another Comment." *Radical History Review* 22 (Winter 1979–1980): 129–39.

Wetzel, Tom. "On Organization." *Ideas & Action* (Spring 1988): 6–8.

———. "Origins of the Spanish Collectives." *Ideas & Action* (Spring 1988): 16–17.

Wheelis, Alan. *The End of the Modern Age.* New York: Harper and Row, 1973.

White, Lynn Jr. "The Historical Roots of Our Ecological Crisis." *Science* 155 (10 March 1967): 1203–7.

Whyte, William Foote, and Kathleen King Whyte. *Making Mondragon: The Growth and Dynamics of the Worker Cooperative Complex.* Ithaca, NY: ILR Press, 1988.

Williamson, Judith. *Consuming Passions: The Dynamics of Popular Culture.* London and New York: Marion Boyars, 1986.

Wind, Edgar. *Art and Anarchy.* New York: Vintage Books, 1969.

Winner, Langdon. "Mythinformation." *Whole Earth Review*, January 1985, 22–28.

Wirth, Arthur G. "New Work and Education: Socio-Technical Work Theory and School Learning." In *The World of Work*, edited by Howard F. Didsbury, Jr., 219–31. Bethesda, MD: World Future Society, 1983.

Women and Technology: Deciding What's Appropriate. Conference Proceedings. Missoula, MT: Women's Resource Center, 1979.

Women in Agricultural Production and Rural Development Service. *Women in Developing*

Agriculture. Rome: Food and Agriculture Organization of the United Nations, 1985.

Women Working Together. Special Issue of *Heresies* 2, no. 3 (Spring 1979).

"Women's Time Is Not Money." Special issue on Women and Work, *Connexions* 30 (1989): 2–3.

Women's Work Study Group. "Loom, Broom and Womb: Producers, Maintainers and Reproducers." *Radical America* 10 (March/April 1976): 29–45.

Woodcock, George. *Anarchism: A History of Libertarian Ideas and Movements*. Cleveland and New York: World Publishing Co., 1970.

Woolf, Virginia. *A Room of One's Own*. New York and London: Harcourt Brace Jovanovich, 1957.

Youngdale, James M. *Populism: A Psychohistorical Perspective*. Port Washington, NY: Kennikat Press, 1975.

Zerzan, John. *Elements of Refusal: Essays by John Zerzan*. Seattle: Left Bank Books, 1988.

Zerzan, John, and Paula Zerzan. *Industrialism and Domestication*. Detroit: Black Eye Press, 1979.

Zerzan, John, and Alice Carnes. *Questioning Technology: A Critical Anthology*. London: Freedom Press, 1988.

Index

About the Author

NEALA SCHLEUNING is on the faculty of the anthropology and women's studies departments at Mankato State University in Minnesota, where she is also director of the Women's Center. She is the author of *America, Song We Sang Without Knowing: The Life and Ideas of Meridel Le Sueur*, as well as many journal articles.